THE PROCESS OF POLITICAL SUCCESSION

Also by Peter Calvert

THE MEXICAN REVOLUTION, 1910–1914: The Diplomacy of Anglo-American Conflict

LATIN AMERICA: Internal Conflict and International Peace

REVOLUTION (Key Concepts in Political Science)

A STUDY OF REVOLUTION

MEXICO

THE MEXICANS: How They Live and Work

EMILIANO ZAPATA

THE CONCEPT OF CLASS

THE FALKLANDS CRISIS: The Rights and the Wrongs

POLITICS, POWER AND REVOLUTION: An Introduction to Comparative Politics

REVOLUTION AND INTERNATIONAL POLITICS
GUATEMALA: A Nation in Turmoil

THE FOREIGN POLICY OF NEW STATES

The Process of Political Succession

Edited by
Peter Calvert
Professor of Comparative and International Politics
University of Southampton

St. Martin's Press   New York

Chapter 6 is reproduced by kind permission
of the Regents of the University of California.

First published in the United States of America in 1987

Printed in Hong Kong

ISBN 0-312-00771-X

Library of Congress Cataloging-in-Publication Data
The Process of political succession.
Bibliography: p.
Includes index.
1. Heads of state—Succession. I. Calvert, Peter
JF285.P76   1987   351.003'6   87-4845
ISBN 0-312-00771-X

SSH

Contents

DISCARD

$37.50

List of Tables

Notes on the Contributors

Peter Calvert is Professor of Comparative and International Politics at the University of Southampton. Many of his published works deal with the politics and international relations of the western hemisphere countries. His keen interest in extending the theory of comparative politics and in Europe is, however, reflected in his *Revolution* (1970) and *A Study of Revolution* (1970), *The Concept of Class* (1982) and *Politics, Power and Revolution* (1983).

Alan Brier is Lecturer in Politics at the University of Southampton. He has specialised in quantitative approaches to the study of politics and political sociology, and is the joint author of *Computers and the Social Sciences* (1975).

John Coakley is Lecturer in Politics in the Department of European Studies, National Institute for Higher Education, Limerick. Among his recent articles are 'Nationalist movements and national minorities', *European Journal of Political Research*, 1980, and 'National territories and cultural frontiers', *West European Politics*, 1982; his planning session paper, 'Selecting a prime minister – the Irish experience', was published in *Parliamentary Affairs* in 1984.

C. H. Dodd is Professor of Politics at the University of Hull and Professorial Research Associate in the School of Oriental and African Studies, University of London. He is author of *Political Development* (1974), *Democracy and Development in Turkey* (1979), *The Crisis of Turkish Democracy* (1983), and other books and articles mainly on Middle Eastern subjects.

Peter Frank is Senior Lecturer in Soviet Government and Politics at the University of Essex. He is co-author (with R. J. Hill) of *The Soviet Communist Party* (3rd edition, 1987) and of articles on Soviet government and politics.

Susan Milbank is Head of Sociology at Corfe Hills School, Wimborne, Dorset. A research student in politics at the University of Southampton, working on 'Political culture and political instability in Argentina', she is the author of 'An Argentinian security perspective', in Caroline Thomas (ed.), *Third World Perceptions of Security*.

Hannu Nurmi is Associate Professor of the Methodology of the Social Sciences in the Department of Philosophy, University of Turku, Finland. He is the author of *Rationality and Public Goods* and *Comparing Voting Systems*, and his Planning Session paper, 'On Riker's theory of political succession', was published in *Scandinavian Political Studies* in 1983.

A. M. Potter, formerly James Bryce Professor of Politics at the University of Glasgow, was previously Professor of Government at the University of Essex and Director of the SSRC Data Bank. He is the author of works on the government and politics of the United States and the United Kingdom.

Eberhard Sandschneider is a research associate working under Professor Jürgen Domes in the Research Unit on Chinese and East Asian Politics of the University of the Saarland, Saarbrücken, German Federal Republic.

WORKSHOP PARTICIPANTS

Susan Baker (Istituto Universitario Europeo, Firenze)*
Dr A. P. Brier (University of Southampton)
Professor P. A. R. Calvert (University of Southampton)
John Coakley (NIHE, Limerick)
Professor C. H. Dodd (University of Hull)*
Professor W. Dewachter (University of Leuven)†
Peter Frank (University of Essex)
Ken Gladdish (University of Reading)†
Susan Milbank (University of Southampton)*
Professor H. Nurmi (University of Turku)
Professor A. M. Potter (University of Glasgow)†
Professor Uriel Rosenthal (Erasmus University of Rotterdam)*
Eberhard Sandschneider (University of Saarbrücken)*

* In Workshop only
† In Planning Session only

Preface

The European Consortium for Political Research (ECPR) generously allowed me to organise a Planning Session on Political Succession at their Joint Sessions of Workshops at Freiburg on 20–5 March 1983, in preparation for a Workshop which was held under the same auspices at Salzburg on 13–18 April 1984. This book is the product both of the hard work of the individuals who wrote the papers that were presented and the intensive discussions among the group which the format of the Joint Sessions made possible.

To the European Consortium, to our colleagues who attended the two sessions, and to all others who assisted in the venture, the thanks of the group is gratefully accorded. I personally should particularly like to thank Uriel Rosenthal, who encouraged me to organise the Workshop but unfortunately was only briefly able to attend it; Jean Blondel and Maurice Vile, who gave it their encouragement; and Joanne Fluck, who typed much of the final text as it appears here. Chapter 6 has been reproduced by kind permission of the Regents of the University of California, and our thanks are also due to them and to the editors of *Asian Studies*.

PETER CALVERT

1 Political Succession and Political Change

Peter Calvert

Political succession is, in the broad sense of the phrase, the way in which political power passes, or is transferred, from one individual, government or regime to another. In a narrower sense, it refers to the way in which orderly arrangements are made for the transfer of power such that the momentary crisis of legitimacy which inevitably arises is reduced to manageable proportions. The ability to make transitions of this kind consistently over a period of time is often taken as one of the indicators of political stability. But so too is the total avoidance of change by the monopoly of power over a period by a single individual or group, and it is the ability to discriminate between these two solutions to the problem of political stability that makes the concept of political succession particularly useful.

Succession is a fundamental feature of politics, since the biological nature of mankind makes it inevitable that it will occur. However long change is put off it must come in the end. Equally clearly, many power-holders are very reluctant to face this fact. They identify the stability of the system with their own continuance in office. Yet that continuance, as in the case of Ferdinand Marcos in the Philippines or Jean-Claude Duvalier in Haiti, may actually be a significant factor in the destabilisation of the incumbent political order. The expectation of reward from a failing leader rapidly declines to the point at which the leader eventually loses the power effectively to regulate the succession. But it does not follow that anyone else gains that ability; hence the attempt to secure continuity ends up defeating the purpose for which it is publicly justified.

Succession, therefore, implies not only the acceptance or act of choice of a successor, but a series of decisions to implement that choice. These in turn involve not only a competition among possible power-holders but an interaction between government and governed. The fact of succession, whether those who are involved in it are aware of it or not, involves a renewal of the 'contract' between ruler and ruled. The transactions which take place at this time

1

become a point of departure for the maintenance or otherwise of the continuity of the political system. Their formal ratification is embodied in the oath of office which accompanies the induction of a new political leader in many societies. By the formal act of the assumption of office, the statement of the authority of the power-holder, power is renewed in the person of the new office-holder.

Succession, then, is to an office. But to what office, and how is that office designated? Offices are themselves the product of constitutional evolution, and the question is not always as easy to answer as it seems. In the case of a written constitution the situation looks quite clear. The 1787 Constitution of the United States established the office of President of the United States with certain enumerated powers and duties. To hold this office is therefore to have the right to exercise those powers; it is equally clear that anyone who is not given these powers by the Constitution, such as the Speaker of the House or the Chief Justice of the Supreme Court, may not exercise them. But what of the position of Vice President Tyler on the death of William Henry Harrison in 1841? Tyler believed that by Harrison's death he had become President. His opponents believed he was merely Vice President exercising the powers of the office. The Constitution says (Article 2, Section 1):

> In the case of the removal of the President from office, or of his death, resignation, or inability to discharge the powers and duties of the said office, the same shall devolve upon the Vice President, and the Congress may by law provide for the case of removal, death, resignation, or inability, both of the President and Vice President, declaring what officer shall then act as President, and such officer shall act accordingly, until the disability be removed, or a President shall be elected.[1]

What is 'the same'? Does it refer to 'powers and duties' or to 'the said office'? Tyler behaved as if it were the latter, and he got away with it. It was not until the ratification of the Twenty-Fifth Amendment, on 23 February 1967, that the question was placed beyond doubt by the plain statement: 'In the case of the removal of the President from office or of his death or resignation the Vice President shall become President.'[2]

By contrast the office of prime minister in Great Britain (subsequently the United Kingdom) had no legal standing until 1904, when it was first officially recognised by being assigned a place in the Order of Precedence. Its first mention in an enactment came in 1917 (the Chequers Estates Act, 1917). The term had been used in a critical or derisive fashion much earlier, but it was Sir Robert Walpole (1721–42) who as First Lord of the Treasury first achieved the ascendancy over his colleagues of the Cabinet which caused him thereafter to be regarded as the first Prime Minister. To this day it is this, now secondary, office of First Lord of the Treasury which gives the modern British prime minister the ability to direct affairs that goes with responsibility for finance. Not all prime ministers have been First Lords of the Treasury: the elder Pitt, Earl of Chatham, led the Cabinet instead from the Secretaryship of State, though the Ministerial Salaries Act, 1937, provides for only one salary for the two offices conjointly.[3] (The First Lord of the Treasury does not actually exercise these financial responsibilities directly except during the brief interval in which a government is being formed.[4]) The British finance minister, confusingly, is called the Chancellor of the Exchequer, although in virtually every other country in the world the term 'chancellor' (*chancelier, Kanzler, cancelliere, canciller*) is associated not with finance but with diplomacy, and the Exchequer was abolished in the mid-nineteenth century. Since 1916 the role of the Cabinet Office has been formalised, the experience of two world wars has strengthened the prime ministerial office against those of other ministers and in the age of peripatetic diplomacy the British prime ministers have sought from time to time to mould foreign policy as well, aspire to the role of world leaders and mix with presidents on equal terms. Fortunately, most of them have had some previous experience at the Foreign Office, though not all authors (or all prime ministers) have regarded that as an advantage.[5] The British case, therefore, admirably illustrates the slow evolution of offices possible under a flexible constitution.

By the nature of the parliamentary system, however, the British system is in other ways very different from that of the United States. The two systems have derived from common roots, certainly, but they have evolved in very different ways. In consequence, although English-language writers (especially in the United States) tend to write of and to distinguish 'Anglo-American democracy' from its equivalent on the mainland of Europe, as far as political succession is concerned European systems, including that of the United Kingdom, in practice have far more in common with one another than any of them has with the United States. This is particularly the case with prime ministerial succession, as can be seen from Wilson's summary:

> There have been twenty-one changes of prime minister this century, involving fifteen men. Of these, nine have, owing to death or retirement, been the replacement of the outgoing prime minister by a colleague, who was a member of his own party; nine more have kissed hands as the result of a shift in the control of Parliament, through a general election, or a shift in parliamentary power. In addition, in 1905 Balfour resigned and let in the Liberals, who promptly called an election and gained a substantial majority.[6]

As we shall see later, in the case of states such as the Soviet Union and China,[7] the question of what constitutes the highest office has itself been disputed, and it may be the possession of different offices at different times (like eighteenth-century Britain), or more than one office at any one time, that marks out the successful aspirant for power. What ultimately decides the question is the way in which the individual concerned is treated by his or her colleagues, and presented to the outside world in the leadership role. Yet long before this moment of acceptance there will have been a much more complex system of transactions and bargains, often stretching back for many years. Some of these relate to the political system. As we have just seen there must, naturally, first be an office to which to aspire, there must be lesser offices in which to show merit and there must also be a degree of consensus about what constitutes an acceptable set of qualifications. Second, there has to be a consensus on timing. When and how is the office vacated? What special arrangements are needed, if any, in the event of the death, disability or resignation of the incumbent? And do others have to await the inexorable processes of time or mortality, or have they the right under certain circumstances to force a change in incumbency through constitutionally agreed processes? Other questions relate to the aspirants who then become eligible for the highest office; how do they show that they merit it, and who decides whether or not they have done so?

It is with this last question that we reach the most difficult problem any practicable political order has to solve; that of providing an orderly succession to an office where by definition there is no superior power to ensure that the rules are obeyed. The problem is not necessarily solved by the existence of a well-recognised number of lesser offices from which the highest office can be filled. Availability in the case of top offices is open at any one time only to a very limited number of aspirants, and competition is as keen as the rewards are high. This is the case whether or not the formal structure of the state opens recruitment regardless of limiting criteria, or the ruling ideology requires that offices in theory be open to all. For the requirement of candidature to the highest office is almost invariably the previous fact of holding a lesser office, and even among lesser offices some will be associated with a greater likelihood of being selected than others. In European states such offices are termed 'ministries' and their incumbents 'ministers', and they work constantly under the watchful eye of their leader, the incumbent prime minister:

> The aspirant is then doubly tested, both as an administrator and as a politician. He may get a department that has few problems and creates few problems; but even here, a subordinate may commit some intolerable blunder or some unforeseen accident may make the job suddenly politically dangerous. In alloting jobs, the prime minister is alloting the good and bad tickets in the political lottery.[8]

Though these offices will in all probability be those that give their incumbents training in areas of special importance, it is clear that the advantage of any particular office or type of specialisation varies not only from country to country, but also from time to time in any given country, according to the salience of national policy issues. Leadership is not just a question of the qualities of the individual, it is also determined by the nature of the ruling group, of the task and of the situation.[9] Yet appointment to such qualifying posts will not necessarily in the first instance have been made with the needs of the succession in mind. It is in the prime minister's own interests to appoint the best colleagues to key offices. As Brogan and Verney put it, 'since the prime minister is interested in the success of his administration, he may genuinely welcome support and be glad of it. He may think that A, in addition to being the runner-up in the race, is admirably fitted in every way for every office in the state – except, of course, the top office.'[10] Hence while aspirants may by their performance in office be able to enhance their chances of ultimate succession only slightly, they will stand a considerable risk of destroying these chances, either by inadequate performance, or by a performance seen as threatening to their own hopes of ultimate success by other aspirants.

The Western European states, with which we begin, are parliamentary democracies, and the highest offices are grouped within a Cabinet responsible to the legislature. In the case of succession within a Cabinet, competition for higher office is a continuous function of their operation. All acts of appointment within the Cabinet or group necessarily have implications for the succession, even if they are not necessarily designed to facilitate it, since they alter the balance of votes in a context in which very small changes of opinion count for a lot. In the event of appointment to the office of prime minister or chief executive becoming necessary or desirable, the balance of support is to some extent already known to the members of the group, and candidates 'emerge' from within the group with their capacity and views already well known. In this process a special role is played by certain individuals who have had long service within the group and know the contending parties, but who are not themselves aspirants for the job. It is they who act as the 'power-brokers' in the management of the succession between competing factions and/or individuals. If they have done their work properly, their choice will meet with ratification by the legislature; though, unlike British prime ministers, Irish and other European prime ministers designate may have first formally to be voted out of office by failing to achieve that ratification.[11]

In the case of a presidential succession, the holding of Cabinet office, on the other hand, is only one of a number of possible qualifications for presidential candidature. Holding an important position in the armed services, the legislature, state or provincial government, may be as important , or more important as immediate qualifications. However, since this means that there is not just one route to political power but several, it means also that the possible pre-qualifications are correspondingly multiplied.

Pre-qualification here means those biographical characteristics that commonly recur in individuals selected for office, which we are therefore justified in taking as necessary conditions of canditature. Clinton Rossiter, in his detailed analysis of the qualifications of candidates for the American presidency, noted that besides the formal constitutional requirements of being over 35, a natural-born citizen of the United States and 14 years resident in the United States, there were additional requirements which were not formally necessary, but which the practice of American politics seemed to confirm had almost equal force. All American presidents have been male, professed Christians and of North European ancestry. None has been an only child and all but one have been married. Virtually all have been politically experienced in elective office, have come from a state larger than Kentucky and all, since parties formed, have been the choice of a major political party. Most have had a legal training, undergone military service, served as a State Governor, and belonged to Rotary or similar organisations. Rossiter estimated that whatever the population of the United States might be, not more than 200 people at any one time had any chance of becoming president, at most five or six might be seriously considered and only two actually be nominated with the slightest chance of success.[12]

The key to this situation, of course, lies in the mechanism of nomination, which is firmly under the control of the political parties. These have in turn developed their own institutional structures for dealing with the problem of selection from among contending candidates. It will help us understand this process better and also relate it to the, at first sight very different, process of selection within parliamentary systems, if we regard all processes of selection as being modifications of the principle of cooptation. Cooptation means in general American usage what is termed in England 'cooption', or filling vacancies by appointment. In political science usage it means more specifically the process of disarming competitive elements by appointing them to offices within the political structure and so harnessing their talents to the maintenance of the incumbent government and/or regime.

Cooptation is such a normal and indeed essential feature of politics that its fundamental significance is often overlooked. Usually it is treated as an afterthought, as if it were in fact ancillary to other mechanisms: election, for example. Yet the history of political systems suggests just the reverse: that it is cooptation that is the fundamental mechanism, on which in the course of long constitutional struggles other mechanisms of selection have been imposed in order to try to modify if not to eliminate the effects of power being retained for too long within a self-replacing group with control over its own succession. Furthermore, when systems are modified in order to reduce the importance of cooptation in the choice of successor, new mechanisms are rapidly developed by those in power to attempt to restore their regulation of choice.

Seen in this light, the growth of political parties appears as the development of new means of control for the nomination of candidates for the Assembly, following the introduction of Assemblies or their opening-up to wider forms of suffrage. The wider the suffrage, the greater the incentive to restrain its exercise by restricting the choice of candidates to those given the prior approval of the party's central organisation. Thus in Britain, following the opening-up of the franchise in 1832, political parties became formalised and established central organisations to coordinate the work of their supporters in the constituencies. Such central organisations have an ultimate veto power to this day, even though in the Labour Party it has been hotly disputed. In 1918, the widening of the franchise to include women was accompanied by the introduction of the provision that each candidate must lodge a deposit with the returning officer, and that this deposit is forfeited if the candidate does not secure a sufficent percentage of the poll. This provision, which is totally contrary to the principle of free candidature, is justified on the ground that it ends 'frivolous' candidatures; however, its real effect is to strengthen the power of the party machines over the process of nomination. As the Cabinet has been enlarged, the prime minister's freedom of choice has expanded, and, with more than a hundred members of the governing party holding some kind of office, patronage helps keep backbenchers in line to an extraordinary degree (See Table 1.1).

The United States since 1945 has seen the rise of the 'Imperial Presidency', and it is much too soon to assume that that trend has really ended, still less been reversed.[13] Certainly, as the failure of the honourable and well-meaning attempts of Jimmy Carter to wield a new broom showed, previous experience in Washington, once something to be dismissed as unnecessary, has become much more significant to a presidential hopeful.[14] To be a Senator is more important than holding state office, and to be Vice President (formerly the kiss of death) best of all. At the same time, with changes in the rules about campaign funding, a small-town background is now a disadvantage; the presidency is increasingly an office for which any millionaire may apply (see Table 1.2).[15]

Cooptation is of prime importance to those close to the centre of political power. It enables them to work for a period of time in relative isolation from pressures for particular policy outcomes, to develop medium- and long-term strategies of government, and to form a staff organisation to secure their implementation. It is the basic principle on which all bureaucracies are founded, and the success of bureaucracy is in itself proof of the value of cooptative mechanisms in providing for continuity in administration.[16] Significantly all governments

Table 1.1   United Kingdom: political succession since 1940

Date	Prime Minister	Cause
(1937)	Chamberlain (C.)	National
11.5.40	Churchill (C.)	War cabinet
23.5.45	Churchill II	End of wartime truce
26.6.45	Attlee (Lab.)	Election
23.2.50	Attlee II	Election
26.10.51	Churchill III	Election
6.4.55	Eden (C.)	Resignation of Churchill
26.5.55	Eden II	Election
13.1.57	Macmillan (C.)	Resignation of Eden
15.10.59	Macmillan II	Election
19.10.63	Douglas-Home (C.)	Resignation of Macmillan
16.10.64	Wilson (Lab.)	Election
31.3.66	Wilson II	Election
19.6.70	Heath (C.)	Election
4.3.74	Wilson III	Election
10.10.74	Wilson IV	Election
5.4.76	Callaghan (Lab.)	Resignation
4.5.79	Thatcher (C).	Election
9.6.83	Thatcher II	Election

Table 1.2   United States: presidential succession since 1940

Date	President	Cause
(1933)	F. D. Roosevelt (D.)	
20.1.41	F. D. Roosevelt III	Election
20.1.45	F. D. Roosevelt IV	Election
12.4.45	Truman (D.)	Death of Roosevelt
20.1.49	Truman II	Election
20.1.53	Eisenhower (R.)	Election
20.1.57	Eisenhower II	Election
20.1.61	Kennedy (D.)	Election
22.11.63	L. B. Johnson (D.)	Assassination of Kennedy
20.1.65	L. B. Johnson	Election
20.1.69	Nixon (R.)	Election
20.1.73	Nixon II	Election
8.8.74	Ford (R.)	Resignation of Nixon
20.1.77	Carter (D.)	Election
20.1.81	Reagan (R.)	Election
20.1.85	Reagan II	Election

seem to prefer to rely on appointment to fill posts in the personal staff of the head of government, and to exclude as far as possible outsiders who owe their position to any other mechanism of choice.[17] At other levels, appointive office may also form a vital link in the individual aspirant's career structure, enabling him or her to progress towards higher office without awkward, potentially disabling, gaps when electoral offices are already filled or the timetable does not permit of an appropriate vacancy. Thus, for example, Merrilee S. Grindle calls attention to the important bridging role provided by party office in the Mexican political system, where the rule of 'no re-election' creates discontinuities at regular intervals.[18]

Grindle also notes, as do many other writers, the vital significance of a 'patron' in the initial launch of a political career, as well as in its timely refreshment during its earlier stages. Thus the patronage of the young Lyndon Johnson by Sam Rayburn was a decisive importance in his ascent to Senatorial power,[19] and though John F. Kennedy himself is supposed to have said that the full story of Johnson's choice as Vice President would never be known, [20] it is clear that at this critical juncture the influence of the Speaker of the House was a significant factor in his favour. In Britain the patronage of Churchill influenced the succession of Eden, and even more strikingly that of Macmillan the succession of Douglas Home. For patronage can either be direct, or by recommendation by one patron to another, more advantageously placed, patron. In this case a reciprocal obligation is created between patrons to support one another's protégés.

It follows, however, that opportunities for cooptation, like opportunities for election, are limited to a certain time-span at each stage in an aspirant's career and, if not exercised at the appropriate time, will lapse. Moreover they must coincide with the attainment by the aspirant of any necessary qualifications, such as age, residence, completion of legal or military training, party membership or office, or other occupational criteria. Thus Robert F. Kennedy, who had attained the necessary legal age, was unable to secure candidature for a Senate seat from Massachusetts, but was able to establish the necessary minimum residence period to seek election from the State of New York, where family patronage was a significant advantage. By contrast, the aspirations to the presidency of his brother, Edward M. Kennedy, have been constantly frustrated as much by the accidents of bad timing as by the memory of the Chappaquiddick affair.[21]

The importance of cooptation is, moreover, by no means limited to the formative stages of an aspirant's career and the occasional break in it. Even in a relatively unstructured Assembly, appointment to party positions enhances the effectiveness of a representative or deputy, increases their importance in the eyes of those who voted and so improves both their chances of re-election and their prospects of a continued smooth ascent. In both Italy and West Germany, with their party list systems of election, the advantage to an aspirant of the role of Secretary General is very marked, as witness the success of the uninspiring Helmut Kohl. At this point, therefore, it can be said that selection and appointment processes are necessary to the actual implementation of the decision of the electorate. The representative has in any case to engage in dialogue with the appointive officials of the permanent bureaucracy if he or she is to make an effective contribution to the decision-making process. If they are prepared to answer the representative's questions and feed out information, they contribute to that person's improved effectiveness as well as to his or her standing in the party, whether they intend to or not. Hence the choice of these officials will in the end have contributed in some small degree to the process of political succession, by placing bounds on or extending the range of the freedom of action of the elected representative.

In analysing the ultimate succession to the highest office, therefore, the effect of all these elements in the career structures of the aspirants ought ideally to be taken into account. Individual personal qualities, the existing structure of the ruling group and the situation of the government at the moment of succession will each act in part to determine the final outcome.

THE TRANSITION

However far these factors may act to reinforce one another, it is inevitable even in the most orderly political structures that at the actual moment of transition there will be a momentary crisis of legitimacy. Characteristically at such moments the continuity of the ruling group is demonstrated by acts of collective solidarity, and reinforced by traditional ceremonials designed to recreate the pattern of authority and speeches in which patriotic and religious invocations play a large part. Once the new leader 'acts the part' with reasonable proficiency, force of habit reasserts the custom of obedience, and the state machinery resumes its normal pattern of operation.

Succession to the highest office or offices differs from succession to lesser offices in three respects. First, the absence of a superior makes cooptation technically impossible. Presentation to a higher office by those surrounding or subordinate to it is fundamentally different from the act of choice by a superior. Specifically, even where there are well-established rules of succession – and few sets of rules can provide effectively for all possible contingencies – the option of varying these rules in itself forms part of the strategic pattern in which the choice has to be made. An example is the change in the rules of the British Conservative party for the selection of leaders between the choice of Lord (subsequently Sir Alec Douglas-)Home in 1963 and that of Mr Edward Heath in 1965. The decision to abandon the customary processes of consultation in favour of an electoral system not only facilitated choice, but determined the selection of a specific individual. Rules are seldom changed so as to exclude a candidate favoured by the incumbents, unless they have made a mistake in calculating the probable effect of the proposed changes. In this connection it is interesting to note that on each occasion in which the franchise was extended in the United Kingdom, from 1867 onwards, the party carrying out the change lost the subsequent election. Peter Campbell has noted a similar phenomenon in France under the Third and Fourth Republics, and the legislative elections of 1986 to some extent have seemed to confirm that it is still true at least in part.[22]

Since the rules themselves are open to question at times of transition, the ritual reaffirmation of those rules, and of their validity, forms part of the ceremonial, broadly construed, that surrounds and follows the act of choice. The process of choice of the next leader begins not later than this moment, the moment of the act of installation of his predecessor. At this time it will be a prime aim of the principal office-holder to ensure that no effective challenge to his or her primacy has the opportunity to manifest itself. Later the leader can afford to relax, making all possible use of rivals to build support for his or her own government.

Much will depend on timing. A sudden, unexpected failure in the succession introduces random factors which are particularly hard to calculate. Parliamentary systems both in Europe and the Common-wealth involve the constant competition for power which the possibility, however remote, that the government may fall makes central. This ensures that they have come to cope with the eventuality of an unexpected succession (as by death or incapacity) in an orderly and effective way. Ruling parties in such a situation operate under the temporary leadership of the ranking member of the Cabinet until bargaining and consultation over a choice of permanent leader can take place and a constitutional election be held. Before the election takes place, however, the candidate has already been in effect selected, and in this process of choice the key factors can be distinguished as being interest group support, patronage and recommendation, ideology and personal qualities.

Even in Western Europe the importance of non-associational group membership, and in particular that of family relationships, remains strong. The hereditary principle is formally maintained in the succession of the head of state in Belgium, Denmark, Liechtenstein, Luxembourg, Monaco, the Netherlands, Norway, Spain, Sweden and the United Kingdom. The formal rules governing the succession are highly elaborated and precise, but the office itself is now largely symbolic in function, its principal function being to act as a flywheel to the machinery of government. But the value of heredity and familial connections is much greater than that. Even in republics, family connections have great weight within the elite groups, factions and political parties that enjoy disproportionate access to political power. The continuity of political interest and political power-holding in families in the choice of candidates, deputies and ministers can readily be illustrated. In France family connections have been of considerable significance in the choice of ministers (including prime ministers and would-be presidents) under the Fifth Republic. In the selection of deputies in Ireland inter-generational succession has been a marked feature, particularly in factions within the party of the majority tendency, Fianna Fáil (see Table 1.3). Intermarriage between 'presidential' families in the United States has been strikingly common, and the most common way for a woman to achieve political office in the United States is still to succeed her husband.

IRREGULAR SUCCESSION

Among institutional groups that influence political succession a particular role is played by the armed forces. This is so distinctive and so important that it is impossible to ignore. The common interest created by membership of the armed forces as an institution acts to create a uniquely powerful pressure group which is at one and the

Table 1.3   Ireland: nomination of Taoiseach, 1938–82

Date	Candidate	For	Against	Not voting
30.6.38	de Valera (FF)	75(FF)	45(FG)	17(L)
1.7.43	de Valera	67(FF)	37(FG)	33(L,CT)
9.6.44	de Valera	81(FF,NLP)	37(FG,L)	19(CT)
18.2.48	de Valera	70(FF)	75(FG,L,CP,CT,NLP)	1
18.2.48	Costello(FG)	75(FG,L,CP,CT,NLP)	68(FF)	3
13.6.51	Costello	72(FG,L,CP,CT)	74(FF)	–
13.6.51	de Valera	72(FF)	69(FG,L,CP,CT)	5
2.6.54	de Valera	66(FF)	78(FG,L,CP,CT	2
2.6.54	Costello	79(FG,L,CP,CT)	66(FF)	1
20.3.57	de Valera	78(FF)	53(FG,L,CT)	16(SF)*
23.6.59†	Lemass(FF)	75(FF)	51(FG,L,CT)	21(SF)
11.10.61	Lemass	72(FF)	68(FG,L,CT,NPD)	3
21.4.65	Lemass	72(FF)	67(FG,L)	4
10.11.66†	Lynch(FF)	71(FF)	64(FG,L)	8
2.7.69	Lynch	74(FF)	66(FG,L)	3
14.3.73	Lynch	69(FF)	73(FG,L)	1
14.3.73	Cosgrave(FG)	72(FG,L)	70(FF)	1
5.7.77	Lynch	82(FF)	61(FG,L)	4
12.12.79†	Haughey(FF)	82(FF)	62(FG,L)	3

Table 1.3 *continued*

Date	Candidate	For	Against	Not voting
30.6.81	*Haughey*	79(FF)	83(FG,L)	3
30.6.81	FitzGerald(FG)	81(FG,L)	78(FF)	6
9.3.82	Haughey	86(FF,SFWP)	79(FG,L)	–
14.12.82	*Haughey*	77(FF)	88(FG,L,WP)	–
14.12.82	FitzGerald	85(FG,L)	79(FF,WP)	1

* The four Sinn Féin deputies refused to attend the Dáil.
† Denotes change of leader within ruling party.

Key:
CP	=	Clann na Poblachta
CT	=	Clann na Talmhan
FF	=	Fianna Fáil
FG	=	Fine Gael
L	=	Labour Party
NLP	=	National Labour Party
NPD	=	National Progressive Democrats
SF	=	Sinn Féin
SFWP	=	Sinn Féin The Workers Party
WP	=	The Workers Party

Names of candidates failing to gain a majority are printed in italics.
Source: John Coakley, 'Prime-ministerial succession: the Irish experience', paper presented to Planning Session on Political Succession, ECPR Joint Sessions of Workshops, Freiburg, March, 1983.

same time an official branch of government, armed, and with the special privilege of operating in secrecy under the cloak of national security. It is for the purpose of regulating the political succession, moreover, that the majority of armed military interventions in politics take place, either with a view to excluding someone who is regarded as particularly dangerous or even undesirable, or with a view to installing a military candidate of known allegiances and predictable views.

Though detailed information on career patterns in armed services tends, for obvious reasons, to be hardest to come by precisely where from the political point of view it would be most interesting, there is more than enough evidence in the public domain to indicate that such interventions, irregular and apparently unpredictable though they are, are the product of a tenacious and long-lasting power structure in which the process of cooptation and appointment that regulate the military hierarchy are consistently exercised over a very long period.

Paradoxically, military intervention tends to be closely linked to the cycle of elections in civilian politics, the majority of armed interventions taking place in a period stretching from six months before to six months after the holding of an election. It has been a consistent feature of new states where the rules of succession to high political office have not had time to consolidate through regular and habitual use. It has become institutionalised in many Latin American states, and (as in the case of Argentina which will be discussed in Chapter 8) originated in the vacuum of legitimacy that followed the failure of the political succession in Spain in the early nineteenth century, was developed during the contests for political authority between local political leaders, and more recently has been revived and extended in the quest for economic development. It has been found even in well-established states when the internal stresses were sufficiently great, as in France in 1958. Once the pattern of armed intervention is established it appears very difficult to re-establish civilian succession, one possible exception, which presents its own problems, being a state like Mexico where one-party dominance with cooptation to pre-candidature replaces the free nomination and election of candidates to the highest offices.[23] Another may be an occasion in which unsuccessful involvement in international war, as in Greece in 1975 or Argentina in 1982, discredits the armed forces by showing up their incapacity to perform their primary role of defending the country.

But as the case of nineteenth-century Peru shows, armed forces may on more than one occasion actually be defeated by their own civilians, and still succeed in reasserting an active role in regulating the political succession.

Cooptation is a regular feature of succession within military regimes. There are even cases in which military coups are used to disguise a planned transfer of power to a new office-holder in order to renew an unpopular or unsuccessful regime without risking the loss of overall military control. In Nigeria in 1975 General Gowon was replaced in this way during his absence from the country, his successor, Brigadier Mohammed, being a relative of a former Minister of Defence who had established a good military reputation during the Civil War and had been a member of the federal executive since the previous year. As Alan Brier notes in Chapter 7, on his assassination the ranking member of the executive, General Obasanjo, succeeeded him (1976). In fact all aspects of military intervention offer strong support for the thesis that cooptation is the fundamental mechanism of political succession. Though military regimes customarily seek to legitimise their actions by holding elections, they seldom fail to ensure that the choice of candidates is very limited and reflects their own conceptions of what orderly succession to office requires.

Despite these significant parallels and linkages, some students of politics will naturally be reluctant to admit that military intervention can be regarded as political succession at all, given that armed intervention is on the face of it the negation of the ideal of orderly constitutional transfer of power. To hold this view is laudable but incorrect. Most constitutions contain all-too-extensive provisions for them to be set aside at the will of the executive, and some, such as the Constitutions of Haiti designating the Duvaliers as Presidents-for-life, clearly sought to legitimise propositions contrary to the spirit of natural justice. When desired changes occur, modern political thought has still not succeeded in freeing itself from the dangerous habit of retroactive validation of actions which *at the time* were in breach of current constitutional provisions. Lawyers and judges have, as we shall see, also all too often stooped to 'lick the iron hand' and accord its actions *de facto* if not *de jure* recognition.

Such actions do not, of course, invalidate the view of succession as a matter of orderly replacement in constitutionally designated offices. Rather it recognises that in many states there are parallel streams of legitimacy, represented by parallel hierarchies of office, and that to understand the politics of these countries we must first understand the ways in which these alternative hierarchies work. For military succession, however important, is still only a special case of a general phenomenon. Even military governments have to take into account the views of established political parties and certain non-governmental institutional or associational groups, among them the financial and commercial establishment, religious leaders, teachers and other opinion-formers, significant provincial leaders or interests, some trade unions (for example, the Bolivian Workers' Central (COB) in Bolivia) and professional groups with needed technical expertise. Each of these has its own hierarchy, and when juntas are formed as an interim measure, expertise in any of these fields may be a qualification for at least token participation in the process of government.

REGIME SUCCESSION

As has already been hinted, opinions differ considerably on whether the substantial disjunctures in the political order that occur when one regime is replaced by another can really properly be regarded as 'succession' at all. But this is only a definitional problem. One regime certainly 'succeeds' another if only because it comes after it in the sequence of time. The more interesting question is *why* it does so.

Before seeking answers, however, we have first to be clear about our other terms. What is a regime? A regime is the name usually given to a government or sequence of governments in which power remains essentially in the hands of the same social group. This in itself raises serious problems of definition, and even more serious problems of research, if only because as we have already seen biology ensures that all social groups are either continuously renewed or they die out. Some cases of regime change are almost universally recognised. The fall of a monarchy and its replacement by a republic (as in Italy in 1946) or the voting of full powers by a parliamentary assembly to one man (as in Germany in 1934 and in France in 1940) are clear examples. Secession, decolonisation or recombination of territories under a new form of independent government – termed here 'complex regime succession' – presents, as we shall see later, many problems of analysis but few of definition.

Military intervention, as in Argentina in 1943, 1966 and 1976, seems equally clear-cut where a civilian regime is replaced by a military one staffed by military personnel and acting according to a design intended to bring about substantial modifications in the social order. Here there are difficulties, however, for while in Europe military intervention has in recent years been very rare and would almost inevitably involve a change of regime, the well-established nature of political institutions enables such a change, as in France in 1958, to be accommodated to the norms of constitutional succession and in Latin America military intervention is so stylised that constitutional forms (if not substance) are often maintained. Consequently identifying a change of regime may well in some cases be a matter for the historian rather than the political scientist; a recognition of the import of changes that have already taken place rather than ones that are in progress.

Rules for political succession, after all, are of the most significance not in the case of routine transitions of power, when there is general agreement on the rules, but in the case of emergency. It is a sad fact that a major cause of political succession in the United States has historically been political assassination, and Marcus Cunliffe argues that the reason is the fear, hatred and suspicion that focuses on the power-holder.[24] Classical democratic theory holds that in a republic any citizen should be equally worthy of political office, but though this is the belief on which the United States was founded, and its experience, like that of the major European democracies since 1944, suggests that at times it has been taken rather too literally, it still leaves the question of who is actually the power-holder at such moments of crisis. The orderly transition on the assassination of John F. Kennedy was not in fact as orderly as it was made to seem to the outside world, but compared with the chaos that followed the attempted assassination of Ronald Reagan in 1981 it was a model. Vice President Bush displayed the usual reluctance of Vice Presidents to be seen to grasp for power too eagerly. Secretary of State Al Haig declared that he was in charge when he plainly was not. And worst of all, in the scramble to get the stricken President to hospital, the man with the 'football' – the black briefcase containing the secret codes that enable the President to launch a nuclear strike – was kicked down the steps, trampled on, and finally left behind. It was only in July 1985, when the President entered Bethesda Naval Hospital for major surgery to the colon, that the United States had its first 'acting President' formally designated in a letter to leaders of both Houses of Congress, and even then the White House staff made the usual claims that he was 'back at work' within hours of the operation.[25] If this was really true, it displayed a degree of irresponsibility for those likely to be affected by presidential decisions which it would be hard to find strong enough words to condemn.

In a parliamentary system failure in the health of the leader does not necessarily raise the question of succession. It can be treated in a much calmer manner; the deputy leader of the government automatically takes over for the necessary period and the government continues to function. But the political effect of a lapse in continuity is still feared by politicians, who make every effort to conceal the facts as long as possible. In Britain Churchill's heart attack in 1953 was entirely concealed from the public, and the bulletin prepared by the doctors was entirely altered in a manner calculated to mislead anyone who took it seriously, as most people did. On the other hand, in West Germany Chancellor Schmidt had a heart pacemaker fitted on 13 October 1981. In the meanwhile, several blackouts had resulted in extensive loss of memory; a major handicap for a politician. Yet he recovered well enough to fight hard and long to avert the fall of his government in 1982, and one biographer argues that if he had had the operation a year earlier the coalition might well have survived.[26]

The leader of a new regime is faced *a fortiori* with a very similar problem of legitimation. Leaders of secessionist or post-colonial regimes inherit both traditional and legal–rational authority, and the only problem is deciding which forms the firmer base for power. Emphasis on the forms of constitutionalism makes it easier to reconcile opposing traditions. Such emphasis can also disguise much more profound changes within an existing state. Both Mussolini and Hitler made full use of the constitutional forms to give legitimacy to their assumption of extraordinary and unlimited powers, yet in doing so they did not disguise their intention of establishing a new order. Rather that new order was brought into being one step at a time, in each case taking opportunistic advantage of favourable circumstances or unexpected lack of resistance among the democratic leaders of the other parties, many of whom, in fact, voted enthusiastically in favour of change. We cannot therefore take formal votes and resolutions as an accurate indicator of regime stability. In consequence there is, it must be said, a 'grey area' between generally acknowledged regime changes (such as those of Hitler and Mussolini) and everyday succession between political leaders.

A good example of this is the dramatic transformation of the French Fifth Republic in 1962 by the institution of the directly elected presidency. As will be seen later, Stanley Hoffman for one regards this change (which was carried out in an unconstitutional manner) as more significant than the succession crisis of 1958.[27] Military interventions to replace one leader by his automatic successor, as in Argentina at the fall of Frondizi, are another area of concern where, as in this instance, the aim was to cut short political changes intended to facilitate incorporation of a major political grouping into the existing order. Seen in this light they mark a major disjuncture in the process of political succession; yet on the other hand military continuity was maintained, and the rival streams of Argentine political culture flowed on, to reappear above the surface as soon as opportunity again allowed.

The chapters presented here, which have been modified, amended and even rewritten in the light of our collective discussions, offer a wide range of views on these and other questions. They have been selected to present first a series of case studies of political succession, ranging from the relatively stable patterns existing in Europe to the uncertainties of the European periphery, the formative patterns of the major Communist states, and the experiences of states brought by past colonial experience within the European tradition. Second, we return to aspects of the theory of political succession, with particular attention to the processes of legitimation, policy formation and the access to power of alternative and parallel hierarchies. Since many readers will be unfamiliar with the intricacies of the succession in most of the countries studied, tables have been included covering the major examples. They make instructive and sometimes surprising reading on their own account.

Notes

1. John D. Lees, *The Political System of the United States* (London: Faber, 1969) p. 342.
2. Ibid., p. 354.
3. Harold Wilson, *The Governance of Britain* (London: Weidenfeld & Nicolson and Michael Joseph, 1976) pp. 14–15.
4. Ibid., p. 107.
5. Joe Haines, *The Politics of Power* (London: Jonathan Cape, 1977) pp. 72–3; Winston Churchill quoted by Selwyn Lloyd, *Suez 1956: A personal account* (London: Hodder & Stoughton/Coronet, 1980) p. 4.

22   *Political Succession and Political Change*

6. Wilson, *The Governance of Britain*, p. 21. This was the situation in 1976. One more change has taken place since, by election in 1979, and the word 'men' is no longer applicable. The phrase 'kissed hands' is misleading. The Prime Minister does not actually kiss the Sovereign's hand; he or she is only deemed to have done so.
7. See Chapters 5 and 6.
8. D. W. Brogan and Douglas V. Verney, *Political Patterns in Today's World* (London: Hamish Hamilton, 1963) p. 79.
9. Peter Calvert, *Politics, Power and Revolution: An introduction to comparative politics* (Brighton: Wheatsheaf, 1983) p. 118.
10. Ibid.
11. John Coakley, 'Prime-ministerial succession; the Irish experience', paper presented to Planning Session on Political Succession, ECPR Joint Sessions of Workshops, Freiburg, March 1983; see also his 'Selecting a prime minister – the Irish experience', *Parliamentary Affairs*, 37 (1984) pp. 403–17.
12. Clinton Rossiter, *The American Presidency* (New York: Time, 1960).
13. Richard E. Neustadt, *Presidential Power* (New York: New American Library, 1964); Vincent Davis (ed.), *The Post-Imperial Presidency* (New York: Praeger, 1980); esp. Thomas E. Cronin, 'An Imperiled Presidency?', in ibid., pp. 137–51.
14. Glenn Abernathy, Dilys M. Hill and Phil Williams, *The Carter Years: The president and policy-making* (London: Frances Pinter, 1984); James Earl (Jimmy) Carter, *Keeping Faith: Memoirs of a President* (New York: Bantam Books, 1982).
15. Stephen J. Wayne, *The Road to the White House; The politics of presidential elections* (London: Macmillan, 1980).
16. Calvert, *Politics, Power and Revolution*, pp. 120–4.
17. For the role of presidential staff in the US see *inter alia* Patrick Anderson, *The President's Men* (Garden City, NY: Doubleday, 1968); Stephen Hess, *Organizing the Presidency* (Washington, DC: The Brookings Institution, 1976); John H. Kessel, 'The structures of the Reagan White House', *American Journal of Political Science*, 28 (1984) pp. 231–58.
18. Merrilee S. Grindle, *Bureaucrats, Politicians and Peasants in Mexico* (Berkeley, Calif.: University of California Press, 1977).
19. Alfred Steinberg, *Sam Johnson's Boy: A close-up of the President from Texas* (New York: Macmillan; London: Collier-Macmillan, 1968).
20. Pierre Salinger, *With Kennedy* (Garden City, NY: Doubleday, 1966) pp. 40–2.
21. Elizabeth Drew, *Portrait of an Election; the 1980 presidential campaign* (London: Routledge & Kegan Paul, 1981).
22. Peter Campbell, *French Electoral Systems and Elections since 1789* (Hamden, Conn.: Archon Books, 1965), pp. 112–23.
23. Pablo González Casanova, *Democracia en México* (Mexico: Ediciones Era, 2nd edn, 1967).
24. Marcus Cunliffe, *American Presidents and the Presidency* (London: Fontana/Collins, 1972) pp. 141–52.
25. *The Guardian*, Monday, 15 July, 1985.

26. Jonathan Carr, *Helmut Schmidt, Helmsman of Germany* (London: Weidenfeld & Nicolson, 1985) p. 170.
27. Stanley H. Hoffman, 'Succession and stability in France', in Arend Lijphart (ed.), *Politics in Europe: Comparisons and interpretations* (Englewood Cliffs, NJ: Prentice-Hall, 1969) pp. 150–64.

Part I
Case-Studies in Political Succession

2 Political Succession in Western Europe

Peter Calvert

The history of state formation in Western Europe is a history of succession struggles. The Thirty Years War, the War of the Spanish Succession, the War of the Polish Succession and the War of the Austrian Succession each originated in dynastic rivalries. Orderly hereditary succession became the very hallmark of the successful imperial state. At the end of the nineteenth century only two states in Europe were republics: France and Switzerland. The dynastic tradition has lasted longer in Europe than most other places: even the Pyrenean principality of Andorra remains under the joint suzerainty of the Bishop of Seo de Urgel and His Most Christian Majesty the President of the French Republic. Nor can we be sure that dynastic succession may not have an unexpected renaissance; the Balkan monarchies that vanished with the unsuccessful counter-coup of Constantine XIII (II) are unlikely to return, but the Spanish monarchy has proved much more successful than anyone expected and its entry into the European Community aligns it clearly with the bulk of its fellows in Europe. Europe after the French Revolution has also a great deal to teach us about other forms of succession, and it is therefore particularly appropriate as a place to begin.

Kings have always had ministers, and among their ministers one has generally stood out, whether for reasons of tradition (Archbishop Laud, Cardinal Richelieu), legal/rational authority (Cavour, Bismarck) or outstanding personal qualities (Cardinal Mazarin). As long as the sovereign power was fully effective, the cooptation of a new chief minister presented few problems. Difficulties did arise under a minority like that of Louis XV or Alfonso XIII when only relative nonentities like the amiable Cardinal Fleury were available to be chosen, but between Pepin II and Napoleon Bonaparte, or Ferdinand and Isabella and General Prim, no overmighty subject dared to aim at the throne itself. In consequence the stability of the throne maintained the stability of political succession. Ministers came and went, their powers varying with their abilities, but there was no question about their authority to act.

FRANCE

France broke with the mediaeval pattern of hereditary succession, and into our own time France has continued to experience not only changes of personnel or government, but also changes of regime. The French Revolution, which ironically put an end to the veteran Republic of Venice, created a republic by default, by deposing the King. Those who supported republicanism believed in a republic in the classical mould of Ancient Rome, a unified state, 'the republic . . . one and indivisible', with all power confided to an elected assembly.[1] The practice of waging war with such a structure presented difficulties. The ultrademocratic Constitution of 1793, presented to the Convention by Condorcet (who was to go to the guillotine during the Terror), was at once superseded by revolutionary government. Within a few months (April 1794) even the structure of ministries that had survived from the days of the monarchy was swept away and replaced by committees responsible for the conduct of the individual departments.[2] The creation of the twin Committees of Public Safety and General Security gave the government the powerful executive that it otherwise lacked, but ultimate power remained with the Convention, and on the fall of Robespierre in 1794 half the members of the Committee of Public Safety were replaced by it, and the once-feared Committee was to survive for a further year before being wound up.[3] In its place the Constitution of the Year Three (1795) was to select the Directory, a collective executive of five members (effectively three after the coup of Fructidor 1797), one retiring each year, who took it in turn to act as President for a three-month term. The Directory regularly resorted to unconstitutional force to gain their way, and were ultimately displaced in 1799 by the coup that established the Consulate which Bonaparte was intended to dominate.[4]

None of these forms collapsed because of their failure to solve the succession problem; indeed it can be argued that the Directory, with all its faults, provided a perfectly adequate model for a plural executive on the lines later to be followed by the Swiss Council of State. It was the growing demand for one-man rule that was to provide the pretext, and as early as September 1797 Bonaparte wrote from Italy to identify himself with what he and like-minded people termed in code 'representative government'. Arguing that once efficiently reorganised 'the government, taken in the wide sense that I [Bonaparte] would give it, ought to be regarded as the real representative of the nation', by implication he argued that government by assembly would then become superfluous.[5] As First Consul Bonaparte was in all but name President-for-life; in 1802 he held the Presidency of the Italian Republic concurrently. By 1848 when the Second Republic was created, it began where the first had left off, with an elected executive presidency. To this there was no regular succession and when in 1875 France again became a republic (by one vote) the royalist majority in the Assembly gave real as well as formal powers to the President, especially the right to dissolve the Chamber of Deputies. This power was almost immediately discredited by its misuse by Marshal MacMahon in 1877, but the office, filled by the Chamber with safe men who would not challenge their authority, retained substantial prerogative powers. The most serious restraint on the office was the character of the men chosen to fill it.[6] As Brogan put it, 'Thiers had been chosen as the greatest living French statesman, MacMahon as the most honourable French soldier: Grévy had been elected in 1879 because of what he had said in 1848, Carnot was elected in 1887 because of what his grandfather had done in 1793.'[7] The new magistracy was not particularly popular and was satirised by Anatole France in memorable terms:

> After a succession of amazing vicissitudes, the memory of which is in great part lost by the wrongs of time and the bad style of historians, the Penguins established the government of the Penguins by themselves. They elected a diet or assembly, and invested it with the privilege of naming the Head of the State. The latter, chosen from among the simple Penguins, wore no formidable monster's crest upon his head and exercised no absolute authority over the people. He was himself subject to the laws of the nation. He was not given the title of king, and no ordinal number followed his name ... These magistrates did not make war. They were not suited for that.[8]

The undistinguished office established almost by mistake was to prove enduring. It survived a world war, two political assassinations and innumerable scandals; it even survived the incumbent who descended from his presidential train in his nightshirt by mistake in the middle of the night and found railway officials understandably reluctant to believe they were in the presence of the President of the Republic. The collapse of France, and the vote of full powers to

Marshal Pétain on 10 July 1940,[9] totally discredited the regime in the eyes of the electorate, and as head of the provisional government of the Liberation General de Gaulle did not revive it, and governed without formal constitutional authority.[10] His foresight was justified when in October 1945 the Third Republic was rejected by referendum by more than 18 million votes to 700,000.[11] Yet the more the Constitutional Convention deliberated the clearer it became that no agreement could be reached on any other form of regime to put in its place. With Pétain in prison, the most obvious heir of the Bonapartist tradition was de Gaulle himself, combining the powers of Head of State and Head of Government under the provisional governments of the Liberation.[12] But the General was almost alone in wanting a strong executive, and in January 1946 resigned and retired to Colombey-les-deux-Églises, leaving the politicians of the Third Republic to run the country. The Left-wing majority in the Constitutional Convention voted for the traditional Jacobin framework, concentrating power in a new National Assembly, but, opposed by both de Gaulle and the Christian Democratic Mouvement Républicain Populaire (MRP), it failed narrowly at a referendum in May 1946.[13] It was only at the third attempt, in October 1946, that the Constitution of what was to be the Fourth Republic was accepted by a small majority of the electorate (see Table 2.1).

Under the new Constitution the president, who was chosen for a fixed term by a secret ballot of the National Assembly, actually gained in power as well as in status. He or she not only retained the prerogative powers of his or her predecessors, but now actually nominated the prime minister, who had to present a policy statement to the Assembly and have it accepted. He or she took the chair in Cabinet, became responsible for keeping its minutes, and gained the right to refer bills back to the National Assembly, full access to all diplomatic documents, and, as nominal Commander-in-Chief with the chairmanship of the national defence council, the effective leadership and continuity in national defence. He or she signed treaties, received ambassadors, granted pardons and so on, and though these actions – as previously – required a ministerial counter-signature, under the Socialist Vincent Auriol (the first holder of the office) it became clear that with an exceptional leader adept in management of the parliamentarians, the office was a very powerful one.[14]

Auriol paid the price of his success. He was not re-elected, and in December 1953 it took 13 ballots to settle the name of his successor.

'The successful candidate was in the Third Republican tradition, unknown to the public but esteemed in Parliament; many of his predecessors had presided over the upper house, of which he was senior vice-president', wrote P.M.Williams.[15] 'He was personally so modest that he brought no tail-coat to Versailles on the day of his election, and politically inoffensive, since he had never been a controversial figure and had been ill during the bitter EDC [European Defence Community] debates. Once again the senators seemed to have swayed the decision in favour of a moderate conservative from their own ranks.'

René Coty began his term with a warm tribute to General de Gaulle, and in the final crisis of the Fourth Republic was at an early stage to establish secret communications with the General and to play a major role in ensuring a smooth transition to the new regime by using the presidential right of message to inform Parliament that he would resign if the deputies rejected his nomination for the premiership. For his part, de Gaulle had given assurances that 'he would adhere to the provision of the 1946 constitution in soliciting investiture and the authority to introduce constitutional reforms'.[16] Ironically it was the premiership, not the presidency, that had proved to be the weak point of the Fourth Republic; the total number of ministers in office was much the same as in Britain during the same period, but the premiership rotated much more frequently, few governments managing to survive much more than six months before being worn down by the impossibility of acting as an effective executive while constantly facing censure in the Assembly. The root cause, as in the Third Republic, was the divided nature of the party system, and it was the reorganisation of the party structure, not the governmental machine, that was to prove essential to the survival of the new order.

Though it was force that dislodged the Fourth Republic; and was to threaten on more than one occasion to dislodge the new before it had time to consolidate its position,[17] the transition to the new regime was managed quite constitutionally, de Gaulle serving as the last premier of the Fourth Republic before being elected, by the electoral college of notables he had always favoured, to the executive Presidency of the Fifth. During this period, however, he enjoyed quite exceptional powers, conferred upon him by the Assembly, comparable only to those given to Pétain in 1940.[18] Although based loosely on the General's Bayeux speech of 1946, it was during this period that the actual constitutional arrangements of the new order were arrived at,

Table 2.1   France: presidential and parliamentary succession since 1940

Date	President	Prime Minister	
1940	Lebrun	Daladier (Rad-Soc)	III Republic
20.3.40		Reynaud (Rep)	
16.6.40		Pétain (NP)	
10.7.40	Pétain* (NP)	Laval (NP)	Vichy
10.9.44	De Gaulle (NP)	–	Liberation
22.11.45	De Gaulle	–‡	Provisional
26.1.46	Gouin (SFIO)	–	Governments
26.3.46	Bidault (SFIO)	–	
16.12.46	Blum (SFIO)	–	
22.1.47	Auriol (SFIO)	Ramadier (SFIO)†	IV Republic
(9.5.47)		Ramadier II	PCF expelled
22.10.47		Ramadier III	
24.11.47		Schuman (MRP)	
26.7.48		Marie (Rad.)	
5.9.48		Schuman II	
11.9.48		Queuille (RI)	
29.10.49		Bidault II	
2.7.50		Queuille II	
12.7.50		Pleven (UDSR)	
10.3.51		Queuille III	
10.8.51		Pleven II	
20.1.52		E. Faure (Rad.)	
8.3.52		Pinay (RI)	
8.1.53		R. Mayer (Rad.)	
28.6.53		Laniel (RI)	
22.1.54	Coty (RI)		
19.6.54		Mendès-France (Rad.)	
23.2.55		Faure II	
1.2.56		Mollet (SFIO)	
12.6.57		Bourgès-Maunoury (Rad.)	
5.11.57		Gaillard (Rad.)	
14.5.58		Pflimlin (MRP)	
1.6.58		De Gaulle	Military coup
8.1.59	De Gaulle	Debré (UNR/UDR)	V Republic
14.4.62		Pompidou (UDR)	
10.7.68		Couve de Murville (UDR)	Dismissal
28.4.69	Poher		Resignation
20.6.69	Pompidou	Chaban-Delmas (UDR)	Election
5.7.72		Messmer (UDR)	
27.2.74		Messmer II	
2.4.74	Poher (UC)		Death
27.5.74	Giscard (PR)	Chirac (UDR)	Election
8.76		Barre (UDR/RPR)	

Table 2.1 *continued*

Date	President	Prime Minister	
21.5.81	Mitterrand (PS)	Mauroy (PS)	Election
17.7.84		Fabius (PS)	
20.3.86		Chirac (RPR)	Legislative elections; 'cohabitation'

* Proclaimed self Chief of State.
† President of the Provisional Government.
‡ President of the Council of Ministers.
Key: PCF   = Parti Communiste Français (Communists)
     PR   = Parti Républicain
     PS   = Socialist Party
     Rad.   = Radicals
     Rad-Soc = Radical Socialist
     Rep   = Republican Alliance
     RI   = Républicains Indépendants
     RPR   = Rally for the Republic
     SFIO   = Section Française de l'Internationale Ouvrière (Socialists)
     UC   = Union Centriste
     UDR   = Union for a Democratic Republic
     UDSR   = Union démocratique et socialiste de la Résistance
     UNR   = Union for the New Republic
     NP   = non-party
Sources: Philip M. Williams, *Crisis and Compromise: Politics in the Fourth Republic* (London: Longman, 1964); *The Annual Register*.

since the General either would not or could not state clearly to the Assembly what he saw the relationship between President and Parliament to be. It was only in the Inter-Ministerial Council (IMC), where leading parliamentarians helped put flesh on the proposals, that he stated his views.

The president should have 'an essential role', but that of an 'arbiter ... not involved in the details of policy.' He would be 'elected by a very broad college,' not by Parliament or universal suffrage and would be responsible for ensuring 'the regular functioning of the political branches of government,' especially by using the power of dissolution and referendum.[19]

De Gaulle, as his comments at a subsequent meeting of the IMC made clear, was obsessed, perhaps naturally, with the ability of the state to respond to an emergency. A President, he believed, could have more easily have been entrusted with the future of France in 1940 than an entire Assembly. It is therefore particularly ironic that having used his favourite device, the referendum, successfully and in defence of the Constitution to obtain a peaceful settlement in Algeria, he was in 1962 to invoke the same procedure unconstitutionally to effect the amendment of the Constitution,[20] and so reintroduce the Bonapartist notion of direct election of the President, whom he now described as 'the essential cornerstone of the constitution of 1958, the keystone . . ., the head of the State, and not the arbiter'.[21] In the same campaign he disclosed that he had concealed his more presiden-tialist views in 1958 since he believed that he personally would have sufficient authority to carry out his programme virtually regardless of the form of his mandate.[22]

His bold, pre-emptive move, prompted by his narrow escape from assassination, was a major change in the constitutional order, and Stanley Hoffman, who takes 1962 as marking the beginning of the 'Fifth-and-a-Half Republic', rates it as more important than 1958 as far as the future of France was concerned.[23] For as later events were to prove, France retained a strong urge towards parliamentarianism, and without the consolidation or political support enforced by the need for direct elections, could well have reverted to the general practice of the Third if not the Fourth Republic. De Gaulle himself was the initial beneficiary, as he intended, and after 1963, when he threw cold water on Britain's candidature for entry to the EEC,[24] assumed a new confidence in his self-chosen role as a world states-man defending France's independence by assuming a third position between East and West. He was re-elected for a second septennial term in 1965, though only after being forced into a run-off election. In the event he himself terminated his own mandate in April 1969 by his abrupt resignation. He had used the threat of this to force through, in the aftermath of the events of 1968,[25] a new referendum on three rather minor issues, and, being defeated, went off on holiday to Parknasilla in the south-west of Ireland while his successor was being chosen.

The 1962 amendment to the Constitution required that Alain Poher, the President of the Senate, serve as acting President while a fresh election was held. He himself was a candidate. But it was Georges Pompidou, who as Premier in 1964 had defended the notion of the supreme and uncircumscribed power of the presidency,[26] who emerged as the second President of the Fifth Republic, and found his conception of the expanded role of the presidency loyally supported by Chaban-Delmas (Premier 1969–72). Pompidou had graduated from the École Normale Supérieure, entered the civil service and had been appointed to the council of state in 1946 as a reward for his services to de Gaulle. De Gaulle's entourage tended to be either aristocratic or wealthy, and Pompidou came from the Rothschild Bank to serve de Gaulle as Premier in 1962. Although subject to a vote of censure on the October referendum de Gaulle kept him because he was able to maintain the Gaullist majority at the November elections, just as Pompidou when President was first to retain Chaban-Delmas despite criticism of his having failed over a period of years to pay income tax, and then dismiss him only six weeks after the Assembly had given him a massive vote of confidence (368 votes to 96).[27] Ironically, by then he himself had been dismissed by de Gaulle in July 1968 for complacency, as a sacrifice to the forces of opposition.

Pompidou's sudden death in office in 1974 broke the Gaullist succession. Again Alain Poher served as acting President until elections were held, but the Gaullist UDR – renamed Rally for the Republic, RPR, in 1976 – failed to unite in time and on the first ballot the socialist François Mitterrand gained a slight lead, with the aid of Communist support. This was the more remarkable since his career under the Fourth Republic, though distinguished enough, had also been marked by a curious if minor political scandal,[28] and his Socialist Party (PS), founded on the wreck in 1969 of the celebrated Section Française de l'Internationale Ouvrière, SFIO (on whose behalf he had contested the presidency in 1965) had only been an effective force since 1971. With support from many of the divided Gaullists, however, it was Valéry Giscard d'Estaing, of the Right-wing RI – from 1977 Parti Républicain, PR – who had served as Finance Minister under Pompidou before distancing himself and his party from the ruling coalition, whom the electorate chose as the new President.

Giscard's family background combined almost every conceivable stream in French public life over the previous one hundred years. 'His great-great-grandfather had been a minister of public instruction in 1877–79 and his maternal grandfather had been a senator in the Third Republic, was appointed to Pétain's National Council, and was a deputy until he bestowed his seat on his grandson in 1955.'[29] His father had been an *Inspecteur des Finances* who was a director of Thompson-Houston, one of the top ten corporations in France, and several others, and he himself had been noted in de Gaulle's Cabinet, not only as the youngest full minister at the age of 35, but for his willingness to argue and the brilliance of his financial presentations.[30] In contrast to his predecessor, whose typically bourgeois style had aroused a considerable affection in his fellow-citizens, Giscard returned to the General's more aristocratic style.[31] Despite the appointment of the non-party Raymond Barre as Prime Minister in 1976 and a strong stress on technical competence, his majority was unstable and proved easily eroded on both sides.[32] The slow erosion of his popularity was evident long before the end of his term in 1981, when he was defeated for re-election by François Mitterrand, who thus became the first President of the Fifth Republic without Gaullist credentials of any kind.

This was the first occasion on which a Fifth Republic President had given way to an elected successor at the end of a normal term of office, and the Constitution did not, it turned out, state exactly when the handover should take place.[33] But transition to a Socialist government was eased by the decision of the electorate to give the Socialists a majority in the Assembly. Until 1986, therefore, when the Socialists lost their majority in the Assembly, France has not had to experience the sort of division between President and Assembly which the American system institutionalises, but which seems likely to create many more difficulties in the French system where there is an essential role for the premier. This role, as it has developed under the Fifth Republic, is not only to decide the price of milk,[34] but to head an orderly series of administrations capable of organising domestic affairs while the President represents the nation abroad in peace and war. The strengthening of the premier's office is most clearly seen in two respects: the long and orderly periods of tenure compared with the Third and Fourth Republics and the fact that the office now has its own staff and is no longer, as used to be the case, combined with the finance or foreign ministries. Mitterrand himself had from 1958 onwards stated his belief in parliamentarianism,and his policies initially emphasised decentralisation and local responsibility. He himself, with his experience as a centre-Left parliamentarian under the Fourth Republic and his strong power base in Burgundy (where he served as President of the Regional Economic Development Council),[35] was in the mainstream of the French parliamentary political tradition. Yet he and his supporters have found the strengthened presidential office too useful to change. Though the evidence is still incomplete it appears that the distinctive French system has now become fully institutionalised, and that the succession to the presidency, having surmounted two changes of party without major changes in substance rather than style, can be expected to follow very similar lines in the immediate future. Though it is still too early to say that France has developed, under the pressures of presidential electoral politics, a two-party system like the traditional British one, the continuing decline of the Communist vote in the early 1980s has so far suggested that such a process of institutionalisation of choice may be well developed.

MULTI-PARTY SYSTEMS

The contrast between the French system and those of its immediate neighbours is very marked. In Belgium the monarch gives a continuity which has been relatively uncontroversial since the abdication of Leopold III in 1951. The divided communities, and the place of Brussels in the centre of the communal struggle, is reflected in the multiplicity of parties and the constantly changing governments.[36] Belgian prime ministers are still the creatures of rapidly shifting parliamentary coalitions, and many have served several discontinuous terms (see Table 2.2).[37]But the system is essentially a stable one. Ministerial aspirants tend to be drawn from the same small circle of deputies, and the Social Christian Party has dominated the system since the Second World War, despite the existence of language fractions in each of the three major parties and a rising tendency in the 1970s for the electorate to vote for linguistic parties. The 'depillarisation' of Dutch politics has not as yet affected a similar tendency in the Netherlands (see Table 2.3). There too governments remain broadly stable between elections.[38]

> The highly fragmented nature of the Dutch party system ... has not prevented the formation of stable three- or four-party coalitions from the dozen or so parties normally represented, and some ministerial figures become almost permanent fixtures – such as Dr Joseph Luns, foreign minister for eighteen years until 1971. Coalition-building takes several weeks, even months, but this is actually an ingredient for later stability.[39]

The most remarkable resemblance to the rapidly changing governments of the French Fourth Republic, however, is still to be found in Italy, though a single party, the Christian Democrats, has

Table 2.2   Belgium: succession since 1940

Date	Head of State	Head of Government	Government parties
(1934)	Leopold III		
(1939)		Pierlot (CS)	CS,S,L
28.5.40	German occupation		
8.9.44		Pierlot	Exile government
26.9.44	Charles (Regent)	Pierlot	Liberation
11.2.45		Van Acker (S)	C,S,L,Comm.
1.8.45		Van Acker II	S,L,Comm.
11.3.46		Spaak II (S)	S
31.3.46		Van Acker III	S,L,Comm.
1.8.46		Huysmans (S)	S,L,Comm.
12.3.47		Spaak III	CS,S
26.11.47		Spaak IV	CS,S
10.8.49		G. Eyskens (CS)	CS,L
29.4.50		Eyskens II	Caretaker
8.6.50		Devieusart (CS)	CS
11.8.50	Baudouin (Acting)		
15.8.50		Pholien (CS)	CS
17.7.51	Baudouin		Abdication of Leopold III
15.1.52		Van Houtte (CS)	CS
22.4.54		Van Acker IV	S,L
25.6.58		Eyskens III	CS
6.11.58		Eyskens IV	CS,L
2.9.60		Eyskens V	CS,L
25.4.61		Lefevre (CS)	CS,S
28.7.65		Harmel (CS)	CS,S
20.3.66		Vanden Boeynants (CS)	CS,L
28.6.68		Eyskens VI	CS,S
21.1.72		Eyskens VII	CS,S
22.1.73		Leburton (S)	CS,S,L
4.5.74		Tindemans (CS)	CS,L
3.6.77		Tindemans II	CS,S,FDF,VU
20.10.77		Vanden Boeynants II	Caretaker
3.4.79		Martens (CVP)	CS,S,FDF
18.5.80		Martens II	CS,L,S
16.10.80		Martens III	CS,S
6.4.81		M. Eyskens (CVP)	CS,S
20.12.81		Martens IV	CS,L

Key: C   = Conservative
Comm. = Communist
CS   = Christian Social, that is, CVP and Parti social chrétien (PSC)
CVP   = Christlijke Volkspartij

Table 2.2 *continued*

FDF	= Front démocratique Francophone
L	= Liberal
S	= Socialist
VU	= Volksunie

Sources: Gordon L. Weil, *The Benelux Nations* (New York: Holt, Rinehart & Winston, 1970); *The Annual Register; Keesing's*.

Table 2.3   The Netherlands: succession since 1940

Date	Head of State	Head of Government	Government parties
(1898)	Wilhelmina		Death of Willem III
(1939)		de Geer (CHU)	CHU,S
14.5.40	German occupation		
3.9.40		Gerbrandy (KVP)	Exile government
9.2.45		Gerbrandy	
5.5.45	German surrender		
25.6.45		Schermerhorn (KVP) and Drees (PvdA)	PvdA,KVP
27.5.46		Beel (KVP)	KVP,PvdA
6.8.48		Drees (PvdA)	KVP,PvdA,CHU VVD
6.9.48	Juliana		Abdication of Wilhelmina
14.3.51		Drees II	KVP,PvdA,CHU,VVD
1.9.52		Drees III	KVP,PvdA,CHU,
12.10.56		Drees IV	ARP
19.5.59		De Quay (KVP)	KVP,VVD,ARP,
23.7.63		Marijnen (KVP)	CHU
14.4.65		Cals (KVP)	KVP,PvdA,ARP
22.11.66		Zijlstra (ARP)	KVP,ARP
3.4.67		de Jong (KVP)	KVP,VVD,ARP,CHU
22.6.71		Bieshuvel (ARP)	KVP,VVD,ARP
8.8.72		Bieshuvel II	CHU,DS'70
11.5.73		den Uyl (PvdA)	PvdA,KVP,ARP, PPR,D'66
17.12.77		Van Agt (CDA)	CDA,VVD
30.4.80	Beatrix		Abdication of Juliana
15.9.81		Van Agt II	CDA,PvdA,D'66
4.11.81		Van Agt III	CDA,PvdA,D'66
29.5.82		Van Agt IV	CDA,D'66
4.11.82		Lubbers (CDA)	CDA,VVD

Table 2.3 *continued*

Key: ARP = Anti-Revolutionary Party
       CHU = Christian Historical Union
       D'66 = Democrats '66
       DS'70 = Social Democrats '70
       KVP = Catholic People's Party
       PPR = Radical Political Party
       PvdA = Labour Party
       SD   = Social Democrats
       VVD = Alliance for Freedom and Democracy (Liberals).

CDA (Christian Democratisch Appel) was formed from Catholics (KVP), Anti-Revolutionaries and Christian Historicals in 1977.
Sources Gerald Newton, *The Netherlands: An historical and cultural survey, 1795–1977* (London: Ernest Benn, 1978); Gordon L. Weil, *The Benelux Nations* (New York: Holt, Rinehart & Winston, 1970); *The Annual Register*.

dominated politics there ever since the break-up in November 1945 of the short-lived tripartite government of the 'Resistance' period (see Table 2.4). Tripartism continued for a further 19 months, but there was no vigorous reforming period, and government marked time until April 1947, when Alcide de Gasperi, the leader of the Christian Democrats (DC), having secured their consent to the peace treaty and the Lateran Pacts, felt strong enough to dispense with the support of the Left by attacking them in a radio broadcast. This action forced the Communists (PCI) into opposition. But though the DC were left as a minority government, they were as a result able to use abundant Marshall Aid to confront the Communist-Socialist People's Bloc. In the elections of April 1948 they were therefore able to gain an overall majority on 49 per cent of the votes cast and so consolidate their own position as Italy's major governing party, with the support of the smaller parties of the centre-Right.[40]

In the meantime, on 2 June 1946, Italy had held a referendum on the monarchy and voted for a republic. The House of Savoy had been too closely identified with the Fascist period for its own good, and though Vittorio Emmanuele III, who had made it possible, had already abdicated (9 May), the departure of the relatively untainted Umberto II and his permanent banishment from Italy (he was not allowed back even to die in his native land) made it much easier for others to remain. The looseness of the monarchical constitution had made it easy for Mussolini to extend his power quite legally; it was Mussolini's fall rather than his rise that initiated a shift of regime,

Table 2.4   Italy: succession since 1940

Date	Head of State	Head of Government	Cause
(1900)	Vittorio Emmanuele III		Death of Umberto I
(1922)		Mussolini (F)	Cooptation
25.7.43		Badoglio (NP)	Dismissal of Mussolini
22.4.44		Badoglio II	Resistance
8.6.44		Bonomi (DdL)	
12.12.44		Bonomi II	
21.6.45		Parri (Pd'A)	
10.12.45		De Gasperi (DC)	
9.5.46	Umberto II		Abdication of Vittorio Emmanuèle
18.6.46	Republic proclaimed		Referendum
28.6.46	De Nicola (NP)		Provisional
13.7.46		De Gasperi II	
3.2.47		De Gasperi III	Tripartite
31.5.47		De Gasperi IV	PCI,PSI dropped
15.12.47		De Gasperi V	
11.5.48	Einaudi (PLI)		Election
24.5.48		De Gasperi VI	Legislative elections
27.1.50		De Gasperi VII	
26.7.51		De Gasperi VIII	
15.7.53		De Gasperi IX	Legislative elections
24.8.53		Pella (DC)	Vote
18.1.54		Fanfani (DC)	Failed in vote
10.2.54		Scelba (DC)	
29.4.55	Gronchi (DC)		Election
6.7.55		Segni (DC)	
19.5.57		Zoli (DC)	
1.7.58		Fanfani II	Legislative elections
15.2.59		Segni II	
25.3.60		Tambroni (DC)	Caretaker
26.7.60		Fanfani III	
6.5.62	Segni (DC)		Election
21.2.62		Fanfani IV	PSI return
21.6.63		Leone (DC)	Legislative elections
23.11.63		Moro (DC)	Centre-left
22.7.64		Moro II	
7.8.64	Merzagora (DC)		Acting
16.12.64	Saragat (PSI)		Election
23.2.66		Moro III	
19.6.68		Leone II	Legislative elections; caretaker

Table 2.4 *continued*

Date	Head of State	Head of Government	Cause
12.12.68		Rumor (DC)	
5.8.69		Rumor II	
27.3.70		Rumor III	
5.8.70		Colombo (DC)	
24.12.71	Leone (DC)		Election
26.2.72		G. Andreotti (DC)	Caretaker
26.6.72		G. Andreotti II	Legislative elections
7.7.73		Rumor IV	
14.3.74		Rumor V	
20.11.74		A. Moro IV	
11.2.76		A. Moro V	Single party
29.7.76		G. Andreotti III	Legislative elections; National unity
11.3.78		G. Andreotti IV	
3.7.78	Pertini (PSI)		Election
4.8.79		Cossiga (DC)	Legislative elections; centre-left
4.4.80		Cossiga II	
1.8.80		Forlani (DC)	
28.6.81		Spadolini (PRI)	P2 scandal
23.8.82		Spadolini II	Socialists return
1.12.82		Fanfani V	Socialists withdraw
9.8.83		Craxi (PSI)	Legislative elections
1.7.85	Cossiga (DC)		Election*

* President Pertini resigned immediately his successor had been elected.
Sources: S. J. Woolf (ed.), *The Rebirth of Italy 1943–50* (London: Longman, 1972); P. Farneti, *The Italian Party System (1945–1980)* (London: Frances Pinter, 1985); *The Annual Register*.
Key: DdL = Labour Democrat
   F   = Fascists
   NP   = Non-party
   Pd'A = Action party
   PLI = Liberal Party
   PRI = Republican party
   PSI = Socialist party

rather than simply a change of government.[41] And de Gasperi himself, and his fellow Christian Democrats of the People's Party (*popolari*), had been among the substantial non-Fascist majority of the Chamber who had voted full powers to Mussolini on 16 December 1922.[42]

Though a provisional President was elected in June 1946, it took a long time to agree the new Republican Constitution and the April 1948 elections, therefore, were the first held under it. Like all elections since they were held under the Imperiali largest remainder system, which favoured a multiplicity of parties, though with a national cut-off point that eliminated the very smallest. The Constitution, on the other hand, made governments responsible to the Assembly and gave the President, as nominal head of state, the role of choosing in turn the candidates for the premiership. As Mattei Dogan points out, however, his role in choosing other members of the Cabinet is to counsel and to advise, but not to select.[43]

With the Communists firmly ruled out as possible electoral partners, and the Socialists divided on the issue of reform versus revolution, the DC was therefore able to monopolise political power. From 1945 to 1982 it 'supplied all the Prime Ministers and most of the ministers in the various Italian governments'.[44] From 1948 to 1960, when it was dominated first by de Gasperi and then (1954–9) by Amintore Fanfani, it governed in coalition with the smaller centre parties. In 1960 the persistence of the extreme right, and the suspicion that the DC was too tolerant towards it, led to strikes and disturbances in several major cities. The incumbent government collapsed. After 1962, when the DC came under the domination of Aldo Moro (Prime Minister 1963–8), it undertook the 'opening to the left', and successfully coopted the Socialists (PSI) in a centre-Left grouping, but not before the Republic had undergone a really serious crisis, which raised the spectre of a Gaullist-type takeover.

The details of the crisis are still shrouded in secrecy. In August, the President, Antonio Segni, suffered a major stroke which left him partially paralysed. The President of the Senate, Cesare Merzagora, was appointed acting President until Segni eventually submitted his resignation at the beginning of December. It is known, however, that in July an ambitious general, General de Lorenzo, had conspired to overthrow the centre-Left government by force,[45] and the President was believed to be implicated. Moro, then Prime Minister, offered the general the embassy to Brazil, and the President, who after the assassination of President Kennedy had become increasingly nervous, was declared incapable of performing his functions.[46] The coalition survived, though Italy continued to be unique among Western European states in the persistence of the far Right, and in the early 1970s this, and the success of the centre-Left governments, was in turn to lead the Communists to reconsider their position.

In 1974 the defeat of the centre-Left coalition in a referendum on abortion, followed by a sudden rise in support for the Communists in the local elections of June 1975, served notice that the deconfessionalisation of Italian politics was under way. After a rapidly shifting series of coalitions with the centre-Right, in 1976 the DC obtained the agreement of the Communists to rule alone and in 1978 the Communists formally entered the ruling coalition for the first time since 1947.[47] On the same day the leader of the DC, Aldo Moro, who had, with the Eurocommunist leader of the PCI, Enrico Berlinguer, successfully brought about this 'Historic Compromise',[48] was kidnapped and subsequently murdered by the far-left Red Brigades (Brigate Rosse), after his fellow politicians had abandoned him to his fate.[49]

Even this serious crisis, which in January 1979 led the PCI to withdraw its support for the Andreotti government, did not polarise the fragmented Italian party system into the 'consociational' forms found in Belgium and the Netherlands.[50] Instead the centre was again reshuffled, with the main benefit going to the previously divided Socialists,[51] who gained first in new members and then in support. In 1983 their leader, Bettino Craxi, emerged as Prime Minister, after the DC monopoly had been broken the previous year by two successive coalitions headed by Giovanni Spadolini, of the Republican Party.[52] A significant role in this important departure, as in all coalition building, was necessarily played by the incumbent President, Alessandro Pertini, who had been elected to succeed Giovanni Leone (1971–8) in July 1978.

The significance of the presidency – generally understated by commentators – is reflected in the complexity of the electoral process by which he or she emerges. The president is chosen by an electoral college of the two Houses of Parliament sitting together. On the first three ballots a two-thirds majority is needed to elect; thereafter a simple majority suffices. This produces some odd results. In 1955 Gronchi was elected without the support of his own party. In 1962 the election of Antonio Segni (DC) was relatively uncontroversial. But in 1964 it took 21 ballots to elect the Social Democrat, Giuseppe Saragat. The DC claimed they were entitled to serve out the balance of Segni's term, and only on the last ballot did the socialist leader Nenni withdraw in favour of his party candidate. In December 1971 there were 22 inconclusive ballots. By the sixth the former DC prime minister Fanfani had been outstripped by the Socialist de Martino, backed by the united Left. In the seventh to tenth ballots the

DC effectively abstained, reappearing for the last time in the eleventh to back Fanfani, who still came second. De Martino, however, failed to gain enough support in the centre to cross the necessary threshold of 505 votes, and his support began to erode. The DC then sought an alternative, 'compromise' candidate, more attractive both to the centre and to the far Right, and in the last two ballots the new candidate, Leone, obtained 503 and 513 votes respectively in each case against a new Socialist candidate, the veteran Pietro Nenni.[53]

The election of July 1978 could hardly have taken place in more difficult circumstances. Both Leone and the incumbent Prime Minister, Andreotti, were tainted by scandal. The effect of the kidnapping of Aldo Moro, the unchallenged candidate for the presidency in December, had been to consolidate the Grand Coalition and it led to the speedy confirmation of the fourth Andreotti government. But his death was speedily followed by recrimination between all parties, in the course of which the Communists withdrew their support from Leone, who promptly resigned six months before the end of his term. The early balloting showed sympathy for Aldo Moro, whose widow received a scattering of sympathy votes, but they also showed that this time no Christian Democrat could muster a majority. At this point the Socialists proposed Giuliano Vassalli. Both the DC and the Communists were prepared to accept a Socialist as a compromise, but Vassalli's equivocal role as lawyer for Eleonora Moro ruled him out, and the major parties rallied instead behind the candidature of another Socialist, the 82-year-old Alessandro Pertini, a former hero of the Resistance and urban guerrilla leader during the German occupation of Rome, who had been the first to reject the idea of negotiation with the Red Brigades when it had been floated by his party leader, Bettino Craxi.[54] On the sixteenth and final ballot he finally received the votes of his own party, the Socialists, and hence four-fifths of the votes cast, with only the neo-Fascists remaining in opposition.

Pertini turned out to be not only 'the most popular Italian President, but the most popular political figure in the republic's history'.[55] Only a week before the next election, at the age of 88, he announced his decision not to run for a second term. In his place the 1011 electors chose the incumbent President of the Senate, Francesco Cossiga, a former university professor of law and Sardinian Christian Democrat, on the first ballot, in which he received 753 votes. This surprisingly decisive outcome was the result of a pre-election agreement and he received the support of the Communists as well as the DC.[56] Like his predecessor, Cossiga was and is widely respected for his independence of mind. He had resigned from the Cabinet of the day over their handling of the Aldo Moro affair, but in 1979 became the country's youngest Prime Minister, and at the age of 56 was also the youngest President.[57]

The Italian system has therefore surmounted the problem of prime ministerial succession in a fragmented, complex party system, and has done so largely because the parliamentary system, maddening as it is to many Italians and most outside observers,[58] has become well institutionalised. With the help of the EEC it can indeed claim to have been very successful in providing for major economic growth and development within a regional framework which has shown a considerable degree of independence from national politics. The parties provide a well-defined ladder for rising to high political office, all four of the longest-serving DC prime ministers having been Secretary General of their party: de Gasperi, Fanfani, Moro and Rumor. On the other hand, Andreotti reached the premiership entirely through long service in lesser Cabinet offices, assisted by his significant position on the Right of the party's six internal factions.[59] In the stability of the system the presidential office has played a significant role, and the office itself has escaped criticism, despite the evident deficiencies of some of its incumbents and the fact that succession to it has been integrally bound up with the major question of the survival of the Italian state and Constitution.

THE GERMAN FEDERAL REPUBLIC

France had been invaded, but maintained a government in exile which assumed power; Italy, invaded and defeated, retained the monarchy for long enough to bring about an orderly transition to the provisional government of the Republic. In neither case was legitimacy of the post-1945 government seen as being derived from that of the defeated regime. In the case of Germany after 1945, however, two distinct regimes were to emerge, both claiming legitimate succession from the unified Germany of the past. There were considerable problems: on the one hand few could be found to mourn the passing of the Weimar Republic; on the other, the question of at what point the legitimate succession had been broken was further confused by the fact that, from the point of view of the international order and its boundaries, the Allies had already committed themselves to respect the frontiers of the Third Reich as they had been in 1937, though this was not in practice what they actually did.

A major regime change had occurred in united Germany with the fall of the Empire in 1918. The Empire had never been a true parliamentary democracy; it was governed from Prussia by the emperor's appointee, the chancellor. The Weimar Constitution replaced the emperor as titular head of state with a popularly elected president who had extensive powers of appointment, dismissal and the ability in Article 48 to take emergency powers to act in a crisis. The rise of Hitler, therefore, had been initially constitutional, and the use of emergency powers by his predecessors as chancellor paved the way for the Enabling Act of 1934 which swept away the Weimar order and made the will of Hitler as Führer the sole basis of the fascist state.[60] A similar, though shorter, lag occurred in 1945, when the allies found it expedient to maintain the structure of the Reich for several days after the end of hostilities in order to carry out the formal processes of surrender to the satisfaction of the Soviet Union. Only then was the existing order entirely superseded by occupation government.

When the West German Parliamentary Council met at Bonn in 1948 to draft the Basic Law for the new (West) German state, it retained much of the Weimar Constitution.[61] Major changes were intended to strengthen federalism, weaken the power of the President, and make the survival of the government less dependent on the day-to-day majority in the Bundestag. Specifically, almost all the political powers of the President under the Weimar Constitution were transferred to the Chancellor as head of government. The Chancellor was responsible to the parliamentary majority, but could not be dismissed by them except by a resolution nominating a specific successor: the 'constructive vote of no-confidence'.

The first Chancellor of the Federal Republic, Konrad Adenauer, had served as President of the Parliamentary Council.[62] A Catholic Rhinelander, who in the early days of the Weimar Republic favoured a federal constitution, Adenauer had served as Lord Mayor of Cologne from 1917 until his dismissal by the Nazis in 1934, and been recalled by the allied military government to resume his place as the head of government of the devastated city. He was catapulted into the national politics he had always previously avoided by his abrupt dismissal for alleged incompetence on 6 October 1945 by the British chief administrative officer for North Rhine, Brigadier John

Barraclough.[63] Thereafter he took a major role in forming a West German Federal state free from the baneful influence of Prussia, which was now in East Germany. The only German political party that had consistently opposed Hitler, the Social Democrats (SPD), seriously misjudged their appeal.[64] The fact was that they had with the partition of Germany lost much of their former support in the Protestant industrial cities of the East, making it possible for the new Catholic 'union' (the term 'party' being avoided because of its unfortunate associations with the Nazis), the Christian Democrats (CDU/CSU) led by Adenauer,[65] to gain a narrow majority of seats in the new Bundestag: 139 to 131 for the SDP, with 52 seats going to the Liberal Free Democrats (FDP), 15 to the Communists, 12 to the refugee German Party (DP) and 53 divided among a considerable number of smaller, mainly Right-wing parties (see Table 2.5).

Having decided in advance on coalition with the FDP and the refugee DP Adenauer, at the age of 74, was elected Federal Chancellor in September 1949 by only one vote. He had already made the personal decision to nominate as the first Federal President Theodor Heuss, of the FDP. As in Italy or in France under the Fourth and early years of the Fifth Republics, the President of the Federal Republic (*Bundespräsident*) is not directly elected. He or she is chosen by an electoral college called the Federal Assembly, consisting of the members of the Bundestag and an equivalent number of persons elected by proportional representation by the governments of the Länder including West Berlin. An absolute majority is needed on the first two ballots; thereafter a simple majority suffices.[66]

Heuss, a Swabian, whom Adenauer had to defend against his colleagues for his views as a freethinker, was a university professor who saw his role as essentially non-partisan, and resigned from his party after his election.[67] He also had a very notable sense of humour, a great asset for someone who has to act the role of a constitutional president.[68] His interpretation of that role was to be of great significance for the future. He was re-elected in 1954 virtually unanimously, but was debarred by the Basic Law from serving for more than two terms. As the 1959 elections approached the CDU did not have a majority in the Federal Assembly and the SPD nominated a strong candidate, their lively and witty spokesman on foreign affairs, Professor Carlo Schmidt. Taking the opportunity to rid himself of his able Finance Minister, Professor Ludwig Erhard, the architect of the so-called 'German miracle', Adenauer secured his nomination by the CDU. The parliamentary leaders of the CDU,

Table 2.5   West Germany: succession since 1940

Date	Head of State	Head of Government	Cause
(1934)	Hitler		Self-chosen
(1933)		Hitler	Cooptation
30.4.45	Dönitz	Dönitz	Nominated
23.5.45	Allied occupation: arrest of Nazi government		
1.9.48	Parliamentary Council met		
23.5.49	Basic Law promulgated		
12.9.49	Heuss (FDP)	Adenauer (CDU)	Legislative elections
6.9.53		Adenauer	Legislative elections
1.7.54	Heuss		Re-elected
15.9.57		Adenauer	Legislative elections
1.7.59	Lübke (CDU)		Election
17.9.61		Adenauer	Legislative elections
16.10.63		Erhard (CDU)	Resignation of Adenauer
1.7.64	Lübke		Re-elected
19.9.65		Erhard	Legislative elections
1.12.66		Kiesinger (CDU)	Grand Coalition
1.7.69	Heinemann (SPD)		Election
21.10.69		Brandt (SPD)	Legislative elections
19.11.72		Brandt	Legislative elections
1.7.74	Scheel (FDP)		Election
16.5.74		Schmidt (SPD)	Resignation of Brandt
3.10.76		Schmidt	Legislative elections
1.7.79	Carstens (CDU)		Election
5.10.80		Schmidt	Legislative elections
1.10.82		Kohl (CDU)	Secession of FDP
6.3.83		Kohl (CDU)	Legislative elections
1.7.84	Weizsäcker (CDU)		Election

Source: The Annual Register.

however, thought of Erhard as Adenauer's natural successor as Chancellor, and instead saw an excellent opportunity to move the 84-year-old Chancellor 'upstairs'. Surprisingly Adenauer at first accepted, but not with the idea of maintaining the constitutional nature of the office; for a time it appears that he seriously thought of following the example of his friend de Gaulle and turning the post back into an active one. When he found that Erhard would be his successor as Chancellor he abruptly changed his mind, and no one in his own party dared challenge him.[69]

Instead the CDU nominated a near nonentity, Heinrich Lübke, who had been Minister of Agriculture since 1953, and of whom Adenauer himself said to a Western diplomat: 'Do you know who that is, two along from you? It is my new Minister of Agriculture, and he is even stupider than the last one.'[70] Lübke was an honest President, who despite an inept turn of phrase maintained the dignity of the ceremonial office and was re-elected in 1964 by a large majority on the first ballot. He was succeeded in 1969 by a Social Democrat, Dr Gustav Heinemann. Heinemann, however, had originally been a member of the CDU and had indeed served for some months in Adenauer's first Cabinet as Minister of the Interior. But as a pacifist, he resigned from it in 1950 in opposition to its policy of rearmament which he rightly saw would end all hope of German reunification.[71] He formed a new neutralist party, which failed to gain support, and then joined the SPD, becoming again a Cabinet minister. Despite this record – or because of it – he obtained only a narrow majority of six votes on the third ballot, the only occasion so far on which more than two ballots have taken place. The key factor was the refusal of support by five Right-wingers of the FDP led by their former leader Erich Mende, but despite this the Heinemann election was politically significant in showing that the bulk of the FDP were by then prepared to enter a coalition with the SPD.[72]

Though the office of Federal President is non-partisan, the elections for it have been keenly contested, and the rotation of the office between the parties in its early years owed at least as much to the shifting balance of the Bundestag as to any ideal of non-partisanship. By 1959, with Adenauer at the height of his power, the SPD were forced to make substantial concessions to the centre to maintain their hopes of returning to power. The Bad Godesberg programme abandoned the party's traditional Marxist base and substantially modified the SPD's traditional position on state ownership, pacifism and anti-clericalism. In 1961, with Adenauer's grip failing, the CDU lost ground in the Bundestag and became increasingly dependent on their coalition partners, the FDP. Two years later, after the *Der Spiegel* affair, the Right-wing Minister of Defence, the Bavarian Franz-Josef Strauss, had to resign and Adenauer was finally persuaded to retire and make way for Erhard. Even then Adenauer retained sufficient vigour to undercut his successor by relentless and savage criticism. Erhard, long believed by many members of his own party to be a 'rubber lion' (*Gummi-Löwe*), was soon in difficulties, and in 1965, though the CDU recouped much of their losses, the SPD made substantial gains. Soon afterwards the FDP, squeezed between the two leading parties, withdrew from the coalition and went into opposition. Faced with a vote of no confidence, the CDU elected a new leader, forcing Erhard to resign, and the new CDU Chancellor, Kurt-Georg Kiesinger, minister-president of the Land of Baden-Württemberg, headed a 'Grand Coalition' with the long-feared SPD.

The 'Grand Coalition' was of immeasurable significance in making the SPD appear once more a serious governing party, and specifically by giving its leading figures active experience in Federal Ministries. Its leader, Willy Brandt, became Foreign Minister and spearheaded a drive for improved relations with the Eastern bloc countries. Brandt had been a refugee from the Nazis who had escaped to Norway in 1933. He had returned to Berlin after the war and risen to become governing Mayor, and as such a significant international figure at a time of high tension between the super-powers. His many opponents on the Right waged a ceaseless campaign against him, casting slurs on his illegitimate birth and hinting at treason, but he remains a highly respected international statesman.[73] In the 1969 elections the SPD for the first time passed the 40 per cent mark and Brandt was able to form a government without the CDU in coalition with the FDP.[74] In 1972 stresses in the FDP, caused by the further pursuit of Brandt's *Ostpolitik*, led to a constructive vote of no confidence. Some of the SPD members deliberately withheld their votes to force an early election, in which the coalition successfully maintained its position, though in 1974 Brandt himself resigned when a member of his personal staff, Günter Guillaume was arrested and convicted on charges of spying for East Germany.

His successor as Chancellor, the pragmatic Helmut Schmidt, was a striking and controversial figure. A Hamburger, he had – unusually for an SPD politician – military experience and a strong commitment to the NATO alliance; he was equally committed to détente and the European Community; he was in addition an exceptional parliamentarian and public speaker.[75] He proved able to maintain the life of the coalition into the 1980s, aided by the growing conservatism of CDU voters who failed adequately to back the new leader, Helmut Kohl, in 1976. This defeat led to the decision of the CDU to nominate the even more conservative Strauss as their candidate for the chancellorship in 1980. As some of their leaders may have hoped, he did even less well than Kohl and his failure ended his chances; he returned to his native Bavaria. But Schmidt's weakening health was accompanied by increasing irascibility and a loss of direction for his government.[76] In 1982 the FDP, whose conservative leadership were becoming increasingly concerned about the erosion of their support in the Land elections and the danger of falling below the critical 5 per cent mark which would give them seats in the Bundestag, decided they had nothing further to gain from the SPD. Schmidt considered organising a vote of no confidence against his own government, which would have enabled an early election at which the signs were the FDP might be annihilated, but held back when advised that the manoeuvre would be at best of dubious constitutionality. The FDP were therefore free to pick the best moment to switch sides. Irritated, Schmidt sacked the four FDP ministers and faced the consequences before the Bundestag. There on 1 October 1982 the FDP supported the CDU leader, Helmut Kohl, in a constructive vote of no confidence against the government of which they had lately been members. Kohl obtained 256 votes, seven more than were needed, and became Chancellor. At the elections on 6 March 1983 the CDU/CSU gained 48.8 per cent of the poll and the FDP struggled back from danger to take 7 per cent.[77]

This complex pattern inevitably played a major role in determining the outcome of later presidential elections. In 1974 the FDP exacted part of their price for supporting the SPD government by the nomination of Walter Scheel, their former leader and Vice Chancellor under the 'small coalition' (SPD/FDP). The CDU nominated Richard von Weizsäcker, widely regarded as their chief ideologist and a former president of the Protestant Church Assembly, who had been elected to the Bundestag in 1969.[78] Scheel was the first President to be elected at the first ballot, and, less happily, the first President of the Federal Republic to have held nominal membership of the Nazi Party in his youth (Kiesinger was the first Chancellor to have done so.) Scheel's opponent and later successor, von Weizsäcker, who shared the same disability, has since become the first Federal President publicly to admit and to apologise for the complicity of the German people in the atrocities of the Nazi period.

By 1979 the CDU had gained substantially in the Land elections and had an overall majority in the Federal Assembly, and Scheel refused to run for a second term. The SPD nominated Annemarie Renger, President of the Bundestag from 1972 to 1976, but she was heavily defeated by the CDU candidate, Karl Carstens, the incumbent President of the Bundestag. Carstens, then aged 65, had been a CDU member since the 1950s, and had served under Schröder at the foreign and defences ministries before being appointed State

Secretary to Kiesinger in 1967. A north German from Bremen, he was persuaded by his regional colleagues to stand for the Bundestag in 1972, and in the following year had made his reputation by an impressive speech on *Ostpolitik*.[79] He was elected to the presidency with an absolute majority on the first ballot: 528 votes, nine more than were needed.[80] It was Carstens whose support Schmidt would have needed if he were to engineer a dissolution of the Bundestag, and it is testimony to the extent to which the non-political nature of the office has by now been accepted that his reluctance was generally seen as a genuine concern for the obvious intent of the authors of the Basic Law. The election of von Weizsäcker in 1984, however, confirmed that, if the general requirements of relative neutrality still held, the rotation of the office between the parties had at least for the time being come to an end.

The West German pattern, therefore, is one of relative stablility compared with its neighbours France and Italy. Transfer of power between the parties, eased in 1966 by the formation of the Grand Coalition, occurred in 1982 entirely constitutionally and with the minimum of bitterness, given the difficult circumstances. For high political office a strong power base is essential, as is membership of one of the three major political parties represented in the Bundestag. The federal structure makes municipal or state office an important training ground for federal leadership, and in a parliamentary system ministerial office in Bonn seems a necessary step to the chancellorship. Yet the need under the Basic Law for a party to name a chancellor before each election has resulted in the 'Americanisation' of the electoral process and very high visibility for party leaders, whether successful or not, and hence it is difficult to identify a clear career hierarchy for German political leaders in the way that can be done for French or Italian leaders. For the presidential office, at least, experience in the Bundestag and a measure of impartiality between the parties still seem to be the most important characteristics.

CONCLUSION

In Italy, as in Belgium and the Netherlands, and in West Germany and Ireland, to a more limited extent, governmental succession during the period under review has regularly involved the formation of coalitions, and is accompanied, characteristically, by shorter or longer periods of crisis during which negotiations take place. Apart from the brief attempt of Mr Heath to negotiate for a coalition with Mr Jeremy Thorpe in 1974, there has been no comparable episode in Britain since the Second World War.

The office of the presidency, however ceremonial in other respects, plays a necessary role in the major republics of Europe in facilitating this process and directing it where intervention may seem to be of value. Sometimes such interventions may be unexpected, as in the formation of the fifth Fanfani government in Italy, which acted in retrospect as a necessary bridge between the age of DC dominance and the emergence of the new socialist-led coalitions of the 1980s. Awareness of the significance of this role has in turn made the Italian presidency itself a keenly contested office, which despite the previous taint of scandal has recovered and extended its influence to a surprising extent in recent years.

The ceremonial presidency is not, and can never be, non-political. Rotation between the parties in both Italy and West Germany has, however, helped to form a political consensus behind the exercise of its limited functions. Strikingly the outcome of the legislative elections in France in 1986 has once more confirmed the tendency for even the strong presidency of the Fifth Republic to revert towards the system of parliamentary democracy pioneered in the nineteenth century. Though the socialists emerged from the elections as the largest single party, President Mitterrand accepted the resignation of Laurent Fabius, and called on Jacques Chirac, as leader of the RPR, to form a coalition Right-wing administration. Though both parties stated their agreement on the division of powers between president and prime minister, and the president exercised his prerogative to veto Chirac's first nominees for the Foreign Ministry and Defence, he seemed at the same time to be consistent with socialist tradition in France acting in the spirit of the Third rather than the Fifth Republic by acceding to Chirac's request for extraordinary powers to legislate by decree the initial phases of an anti-socialist economic policy. It remained to be seen whether the experiment in 'cohabitation' would last, and, if not, how it would be terminated. The Constitution of the Fifth Republic, after all, does not make explicit provision for a prime minister to be dismissed. The experience of France before De Gaulle shows that powers, once surrendered, are very hard to recover, and the orderliness of political succession does not ensure that power accompanies the transfer of offices.

Notes

1. Jack Hayward, *The One and Indivisible French Republic* (New York: Norton, 1973) p. 6.
2. M. J. Sydenham, *The First French Republic 1792–1804* (London: Batsford, 1974) pp. 18–19.
3. On the Committee of Public Safety see R. R. Palmer, *Twelve Who Ruled: The Year of Terror in the French Revolution* (Princeton, NJ: Princeton University Press, 1941).
4. Martin Lyons, *France under the Directory* (Cambridge: Cambridge University Press, 1975).
5. Sydenham, *The First French Republic*, pp. 158–9.
6. Gordon Wright, *Raymond Poincaré and the French Presidency* (New York: Octagon, 1967) pp. 1–17.
7. D. W. Brogan, *The Development of Modern France 1870–1939* (London: Hamish Hamilton, 1940) p. 198.
8. Anatole France, *Penguin Island*, trans. by A. W. Evans (London: John Lane, The Bodley Head, 1927) p. 145.
9. William L. Shirer, *The Collapse of the Third Republic: An inquiry into the fall of France in 1940* (London: Heinemann and Secker & Warburg, 1970) p. 529.
10. On the sequence of governments of this period see André Siegfried, *De la IIIe à la IVe République* (Paris: Bernard Grasset, 1956). On the fall of the Vichy Government see Walter Stucki, *La Fin du Régime de Vichy* (Neuchatel: Editions de la Baconnière, 1947).
11. D. W. Urwin, *Western Europe since 1945: A short political history* (London: Longman, 1981) p. 43.
12. On de Gaulle's earlier career and views see Alexander Werth, *De Gaulle, a Political Biography* (Harmondsworth: Penguin, 1965).
13. For the unpredictable behaviour of de Gaulle during this crucial period, and the effect on his would-be supporters, see Gordon Wright, *The Reshaping of French Democracy* (London: Methuen, 1950) p. 134ff.
14. Philip M. Williams, *Crisis and Compromise: Politics in the Fourth Republic* (London: Longman, 1964) pp. 196–201.
15. Ibid., pp. 201–2.
16. William G. Andrews, *Presidential Government in Gaullist France: A study of executive–legislative relations 1958–1974* (Albany, NY: State University of New York Press, 1982) p. 4.
17. James H. Meisel, *The Fall of the Republic; Military revolt in France* (Ann Arbor, Mich.: University of Michigan Press, 1962).
18. Andrews, *Presidential Government*, pp. 127–9.
19. Ibid., p. 12.
20. For the text of the Constitution see S. E. Finer (ed.), *Five Constitutions* (Brighton: Harvester, 1979) pp. 279ff. Art 89 (p. 303) specified that the Parliament had first to pass a bill before the matter could be submitted to referendum. See also J. R. Frears, *Political Parties and Elections in the French Fifth Republic* (London: C. Hurst, 1977) pp. 242–3.

21. Andrews, *Presidential Government*, p. 25.
22. See also Philip M. Williams, 'Gaullist grandeur: myth and reality', in his *Wars, Plots and Scandals in Post-War France* (Cambridge: Cambridge University Press, 1970) pp. 207–10.
23. Stanley H. Hoffman, 'Succession and stability in France', in Arend Lijphart (ed.), *Politics in Europe: Comparisons and interpretations* (Englewood Cliffs, NJ: Prentice-Hall, 1969) pp. 150–64.
24. Nora Beloff, *The General Says No: Britain's exclusion from Europe* (Harmondsworth: Penguin, 1963).
25. Patrick Seale and Maureen McConville, *French Revolution 1968* (London: Heinemann with Penguin, 1968).
26. Hayward, *The One and Indivisible French Republic*, p. 81.
27. Ibid., pp. 84–5.
28. P. M. Williams, 'The Mitterrand affair', in his *Wars, Plots and Scandals*, pp. 74–7.
29. Andrews, *Presidential Government*, p. 95.
30. Ibid., pp. 96–8.
31. Cf. Jean Bothorel, *Histoire du septennat giscardien, I: Le Pharaon; 19 mai 1974–22 mars 1978* (Paris: Bernard Grasset, 1983).
32. Frears, *Political Parties*, pp. 33–6, 58–85.
33. Alex N. Dragnich and Jorgen Rasmussen, *Major European Governments* (Homewood, Ill.: Dorsey, 6th edn, 1982), pp. 280–1.
34. Hayward, *The One and Indivisible French Republic*, p. 82.
35. Ibid., p. 42. On the importance of local politics in French political succession see also Henry W. Ehrmann, *Politics in France* (Boston, Mass.: Little, Brown, 2nd edn, 1971) p. 143.
36. Gordon L. Weil, *The Benelux Nations: The politics of small-country democracies* (New York: Holt, Rinehart & Winston, 1970) pp. 98–113.
37. Wilfried Dewachter, 'The circulation of the elite under macro-social crises. Analysis of the Belgian case', paper presented to Planning Session on Political Succession, ECPR Joint Sessions of Workshops, Freiburg, March 1983.
38. Gerald Newton, *The Netherlands: An historical and cultural survey 1795–1977* (London: Ernest Benn, 1978) pp. 210ff.
39. Gordon Smith, *Politics in Western Europe: A comparative analysis* (London: Heinemann, 1972) pp. 193–4.
40. Urwin, *Western Europe*, pp. 82–3, 111–2.
41. Denis Mack Smith, *Mussolini* (London, Weidenfeld & Nicolson, 1982) pp. 52–8; S. J. Woolf (ed.), *The Rebirth of Italy 1943–50* (London: Longman, 1972).
42. Mack Smith, *Mussolini*, p. 58.
43. Mattei Dogan, 'Le sélection des ministres en Italie: Dix règles non-écrits', *International Political Science Review*, 2 (1981) pp. 189–209.
44. Gianfranco Pasquino, 'Italian Christian Democracy: a party for all seasons?', in Peter Lange and Sidney Tarrow (eds), *Italy in Transition: Conflict and consensus* (London: Frank Cass, 1980) pp. 88–109.
45. Elizabeth Wiskemann, *Italy since 1945* (London: Macmillan, 1971) p. 59.

46.	Robert Katz, *Days of Wrath: The public agony of Aldo Moro* (London: Granada, 1980) p. 71.
47.	Peter Lange, 'Crisis and consent, change and compromise: dilemmas of Italian communism in the 1970s', in Lange and Tarrow, *Italy in Transition*, p. 110.
48.	Sidney Tarrow, 'Historic compromise or bourgeois majority? Eurocommunism in Italy, 1976–9,' in Howard Machin (ed.), *National Communism in Western Europe: A third way for socialism?* (London: Methuen, 1983) pp. 124–53.
49.	See Katz, *Days of Wrath*, for details.
50.	Giuseppe Di Palma, *Surviving Without Governing: The Italian parties in parliament* (Berkeley, Calif.: University of California Press, 1977) pp. 219ff.; cf. Giovanni Sartori, *Parties and Party Systems: A framework for analysis* (Cambridge: Cambridge University Press, 1976).
51.	See David Hine, 'Social Democracy in Italy', in W. E. Paterson and A. H. Thomas (eds), *Social Democratic Parties in Western Europe* (London: Croom Helm, 1977) pp. 67–85, and 'The Italian Socialist Party under Craxi: surviving but not reviving', in Lange and Tarrow, *Italy in Transition*, pp. 133–48.
52.	Hans Daalder, foreword to Paolo Farneti, *The Italian Party System (1945–1980)*, ed. S. E. Finer and Alfio Mastropaolo (London: Frances Pinter, 1985) p. xxiv.
53.	Smith, *Politics in Western Europe*, pp. 356–8.
54.	Katz, *Days of Wrath*, pp. 245–6, 292–5.
55.	*Guardian*, 24 June 1985.
56.	*Guardian*, 25 June 1985.
57.	*Guardian*, 18 and 24 June 1985.
58.	See for example Di Palma.
59.	Farneti, *The Italian Party System*, pp. 163–4.
60.	William L. Shirer, *The Rise and Fall of the Third Reich; A history of Nazi Germany* (London: Pan, 1968) pp. 245–50.
61.	For text of Basic Law see Finer, *Five Constitutions*, pp. 195ff.
62.	Biographical details from Terence Prittie, *Konrad Adenauer, 1876–1967* (London: Tom Stacey, 1972).
63.	Konrad Adenauer, *Memoirs, 1945–53*, trans. Beate Rahm von Oppen (London: Weidenfeld & Nicolson, 1966) pp. 31–2; Prittie, *Konrad Adenauer*, pp. 106–9.
64.	Douglas A. Chalmers, *The Social Democratic Party of Germany; From working-class movement to modern political party* (New Haven, Conn.: Yale University Press, 1964) pp. 16ff.
65.	Arnold J. Heidenheimer, *Adenauer and the CDU: The rise of the leader and the integration of the party* (The Hague: Martinus Nijhoff, 1960); Geoffrey Pridham, *Christian Democracy in Western Germany; The CDU/CSU in government and opposition, 1945–1976* (London: Croom Helm, 1977) pp. 21–55.
66.	Dragnich and Rasmussen, *Major European Governments*, p. 393.
67.	Prittie, *Konrad Adenauer*, pp. 142, 271.

68.   On his state visit to London in 1958 he was congratulated by a British official on the cheers that had greeted him in the Mall. He replied: 'Eighty-five per cent of the cheers were for the Queen and another ten per cent for the horses. The remaining five per cent were for me – but they came from Germans.' (*Sunday Telegraph*, 28 July 1985.) See also Ralf Dahrendorf and Martin Vogt (eds), *Theodor Heuss, Politiker und Publizist* (Tübingen: Rainer Wunderlich, 1984).

69.   Prittie, *Konrad Adenauer*, pp. 271ff.

70.   Ibid., p. 278.

71.   Ibid., p. 162.

72.   For a detailed account of the period see Arnulf Baring, *Machtwechsel: Die Ära Brandt–Scheel* (Stuttgart: Deutsche Verlags-Anstalt, 1982). Tony Burkett, *Parties and Elections in West Germany; The search for stability* (London: C. Hurst, 1975), pp. 114–5, notes that seven more FDP members must have withheld their support without declaring it publicly.

73.   Ibid., p. 101. For his views on Ostpolitik at this period see Willy Brandt, *A Peace Policy for Europe*, trans. Joel Carmichael (London: Weidenfeld & Nicolson, 1969).

74.   Burkett, *Parties and Elections*, pp. 122–8.

75.   For Schmidt's views see *inter alia* Helmut Schmidt, *The Balance of Power; Germany's peace policy and the super powers*, trans. Edward Thomas (London: William Kimber, 1971).

76.   Jonathan Carr, *Helmut Schmidt, Helmsman of Germany* (London: Weidenfeld & Nicolson, 1985).

77.   Ibid., p. 190.

78.   Pridham, *Christian Democracy*, p. 235.

79.   Ibid., p. 232.

80.   Dragnich and Rasmussen, *Major European Governments*, p. 394.

3 Political Succession during the Transition to Independence: Evidence from Europe

John Coakley

The process of political succession at the level of the formal political elite may in general be placed in one or other of three categories:

1. governmental succession, where a peaceful transfer of power is effected from one portion of the elite to another, or, depending on circumstances and matters of definition, from one elite to another, within the framework of an authoritative set of rules;
2. regime succession, where a portion of the elite or a counter-elite captures power by means of a (not necessarily violent) coup, in which the new rulers provide an alternative constitutional framework to justify their accession to power;
3. state succession, where a regional counter-elite captures power from the traditional elite of the centre.

It is the object of this chapter to examine the mechanics of political succession in the third category, using evidence drawn from the experience of the new states that appeared in Europe after the First World War. During the turbulent years in which the peace treaties were negotiated, the map of Europe was substantially redrawn and the new ruling elites had to face the formidable problem of establishing the territorial identity of their new states. The manner in which these elites came into prominence and the shape of the political entities which they governed form the basis of the analysis carried out here.

This exercise in comparison is made more manageable by narrowing the focus to European states that were born in the immediate post-war period, where the international environment and, to some degree, the political cultural climate are held constant. Because of the variety of new political entities which then appeared, however, further selection is necessary. The most complex of the categories into which the new states may be divided is represented by the Kingdom of the Serbs, Croats and Slovenes (renamed Yugoslavia in 1929). Here the ruling elite of an independent state, Serbia, provided the momentum for a process of political integration with another independent state, Montenegro, and portions of the former Austro-Hungarian Empire. The new state of Romania was a creation of a similar type, though it retained the name of its core region: it consisted of a union of the independent Kingdom of Romania with the formerly Hungarian region of Transylvania. A second category is represented by the new Republic of Poland, which consisted of a union of territories drawn from three empires, the Russian, German and Austro-Hungarian. The third category consists of regions which seceded from multinational empires: Finland, Estonia, Latvia and Lithuania from the Russian Empire; Czechoslovakia from the Austro-Hungarian Empire; and the Irish Free State from the United Kingdom. This third category necessarily implies a fourth, the states that remained when the peripheral regions had seceded: the Russian Republic, Austria, Hungary and a slightly smaller United Kingdom.[1]

In order to reduce difficulties of comparison, the discussion in this chapter will concentrate on the third category: the relatively simple cases of straightforward peripheral secession. The states in question all fall in the more northerly part of Europe and have certain additional features in common: a culturally and ethnically hetero-geneous population, a strong nationalist movement based on the revival of an indigenous culture, and political challenges to this movement from two directions, Left and Right. The presentation of the political succession process will, then, begin with a consideration of the socio-economic and cultural conditions in the territory in question, go on to an examination of the movement for national independence, and look at its outcome from three perspectives: the bourgeois states that ultimately succeeded in establishing themselves, the attempts by reactionary elements to establish states that would allow them to retain a greater degree of power and the efforts of revolutionaries on the Left to establish states on a more radical basis. In conclusion, an effort will be made to generalise about the nature of the conflict between these perspectives and about the political succession process in these rather special cases.

THE IMPACT OF SOCIO-ECONOMIC AND CULTURAL VARIATION

In all cases except that of Finland the independent states were entirely new territorial units that departed from the main lines of pre-war administrative boundaries. For this reason statistical data from pre-war censuses cannot usefully be used; instead, data from the first post-war censuses are used in Table 3.1 as indicators of the cultural diversity and level of social development in the new states.

The most important point to note is the ethnic diversity of the new states. In general, language was the crucial factor in determining ethnic identity, and hence in structuring political loyalty, except in Ireland, where religion tended to play this role. In the other cases, the great bulk of the population spoke the distinctive language of the country; as a consequence of a massive language shift in the eighteenth and nineteenth centuries, the great bulk of the Irish population spoke English. Not all the ethnic minorities were of equal importance. It is possible to identify in each case a formerly dominant, privileged minority – not necessarily the largest minority in terms of numbers – which regarded the new state in which it found itself with more or less hostility. Irish Protestants, Swede-Finns, Baltic Germans, Germans in Czechoslovakia and Germans and Poles in Lithuania found themselves politically impotent in territories whose economic, cultural and political life they had dominated. In addition, in four cases, spatial concentration of this minority had aggravated majority–minority relations. Swedish-speakers in the Aaland Islands of Finland and Germans in the border areas of Czechoslovakia were included against their wishes in the new states, to which their loyalties remained questionable. In Ireland and Lithuania, by contrast, the comparable areas (Ulster and Vilnius) were excluded from the new states, but at the cost of antagonising the majority of the population: *Irlanda irredenta* and *Lituania irredenta* became powerful foci of nationalist sentiment. It should also be noted that in two cases, the 'majority' population was itself divided along centre–periphery lines. Nominally Catholic, economically progressive Czechs found their fate linked with that of deeply religious but economically backward Slovak Catholics, while Protestant, economically developed northern Latvia had little in common with the Catholic, underdeveloped southern province of Latgale. The languages of the two peripheries, Slovak and Latgallian, though they

Table 3.1	Population and social structure of new European states at first post-war census, 1920–6

	Finland (1920)	Estonia (1922)	Latvia (1925)	Lithuania* (1923)	Czechoslovakia (1921)	Ireland (1926)
Area (000 km²)	388	48	66	56	140	69
Population (000)	3 365	1 107	1 845	2 171	13 613	2 972
Nationality,† language (%):						
Eponymous	88.7	87.6	73.4	80.1	64.8	4.4
German	0.1	1.7	3.8	4.1	23.6	–
Russian	0.1	8.3	10.5	2.3	3.5	
Jewish	–	0.4	5.2	7.1	1.4	–
Swedish	11.0	0.7	–	–	–	–
English	–	–	–	–	–	95.6
Other	0.1	1.3	7.1	6.4	6.7	–
Religion (%):‡						
Catholic	0.0	0.2	22.6	80.5	76.3	92.6
Protestant	98.3	79.1	58.0	9.6	7.3	7.0
Orthodox	1.6	19.0	13.9	2.5	0.5	0.0
Jewish	0.1	0.4	5.2	7.3	2.6	0.1
Other, none	0.0	1.3	0.3	0.1	13.3	0.3
Other (%):§						
Urban	16.1	27.4	34.3	15.8	n.a.	31.8
Agrarian	65.1	58.8	61.0	76.7	39.6	53.0
Literate	99.2	94.4	85.3	69.0	93.0	n.a.

*	Includes Klaipeda/Memel territory (data from 1925).
†	Refers to ethnic nationality except in Ireland and Finland (habitual language); the Irish figure is an estimate based on the Irish-speaking population resident in Irish-speaking districts.
‡	'Orthodox' includes Old Believers and Greek and Armenian Catholics.
§	Because of different defining criteria cross-national comparisons must be treated cautiously.
Source: Calculated from statistical yearbooks or censuses of the states in question.

could be regarded as dialects of Czech and Latvian, were sufficiently different from these to accentuate the cultural distinctiveness of the periphery.

It will be clear from Table 3.1 that the economies of the six states were predominantly agrarian, except for Czechoslovakia (but even there almost half of the population was engaged in agriculture). The populations were substantially literate, with near-universal literacy except in Lithuania, Latgale and Slovakia. It should also be pointed out that in terms of economic and social development the new states compared very favourably, in general, with the states from which they had seceded. This was outstandingly true of the relationship between Finland, Estonia and Latvia and the remainder of Russia, and of Czechoslovakia and the remainder of the former Austro-Hungarian Empire. Ireland, of course, constitutes an exception, having traditionally been one of the more backward areas of the United Kingdom.

Rather more important, however, than the high proportion of farmers in the working population was the extent to which the agrarian sector remained deeply divided economically, socially and politically. The abolition of serfdom and the introduction of formal equality before the law had removed institutional barriers to the purchase of land by tenants, but social change lagged far behind legal reform. A small, culturally distinct group retained a disproportionate hold on landed property even by the end of the First World War, and market forces had deposited by its side a new class of wealthy 'grey barons' drawn from the majority population. The small Swedish-speaking (in Finland), German-speaking (in Estonia, Latvia and Czechoslovakia), Polish-speaking (in Lithuania) and Protestant (in Ireland) landed gentry thus found themselves in uneasy alliance with a class of conservative owners of new property anxious to slow the pace of the agrarian revolution.

THE PRE-WAR NATIONALIST MOVEMENTS

Although the new states were born directly out of the social and political transformation of Europe during and immediately after the First World War, the nationalist movements had longer roots.[2] What is striking, however, is the fact that in each case the moderate nationalist movement of the pre-war period, which stood simply for autonomy, was radicalised or replaced by a much more extreme, overtly separatist movement. This transition coincided with the later years of the war but became obvious only in the domestic political realignments of 1917–18.

The transition to political extremism was least obvious in the case of Finland. Governed as a Grand Duchy in a personal union with Russia since being separated from Sweden in 1809, it had a constitution and representative institutions of its own. The Romanov dynasty governed its Russian dominions autocratically as Tsars; paradoxically, the same individuals governed Finland as constitutional rulers in their capacity as Grand Dukes. Especially after 1863, when the Diet began to meet regularly, limited popular consultation in the legislative process was possible and this was greatly extended with the transformation of the Diet in 1906 into a unicameral parliament directly elected by universal suffrage by means of proportional representation. The political forces that emerged in 1906 changed little in electoral strength between then and 1918: a Finnish Party, representing conservative interests and adopting an attitude of pragmatic collaboration with the Russians; a Young Finnish Party, more liberal in orientation and committed to upholding the Finnish constitution; a Swedish People's Party, representing the Swedish-speaking minority and also insistent on the need to protect Finland's constitution; and two parties which defined their identity in terms of class defence, the Social Democratic Party and the small Agrarian Party. Despite variation in the intensity of their hostility to Russian interference, the leadership of Finland's political parties in the pre-war period shared a concern to preserve Finland's constitution. Finnish political nationalism was, then, essentially negative: it was geared towards preservation of the status quo, resisting Russian attempts at unconstitutional intervention which peaked in the 1899–1905 and 1910–17 periods.

By contrast to Finland, the Baltic provinces of Russia came very late to the experience of mass involvement in politics. While the Russian provincial administrations were in general agencies of the central government, the three Baltic provinces enjoyed a rather special status. Estland, Livland and Kurland had been allowed to retain their ancient *Landtage* or diets even after their incorporation into Russia in the eighteenth century.[3] The Baltic diets remained, however, representative essentially of the landed aristocracy and therefore of the Baltic German elite, a small minority that enjoyed a political influence in the Russian Empire out of all proportion to its size. Although the Estonian and Latvian majorities could eventually wield some political power by capturing control of local administrations, they were without influence at provincial level and *a fortiori* at the level of the Empire. The introduction of a parliament (*Duma*) elected indirectly by mass suffrage raised some prospect that Estonian and Latvian nationalism, which had been developing in the late nineteenth century in a cultural direction, could find political expression; demands for autonomy grew in frequency after 1905. The elections to the first (1906) and second (1907) Dumas indeed showed some evidence of this. But when the electoral system of that insubordinate body was altered to increase the influence of conservative forces Estonian and Latvian representation virtually disappeared, as the results of the elections to the third (1907) and fourth (1912) Dumas showed. Estonian and Latvian nationalist demands for autonomy within the Empire thus continued to go largely unheard.

Lithuania contrasted in many respects with the Baltic provinces. Unlike the ethnic homelands of the Estonians and Latvians, Lithuania had enjoyed independent statehood in mediaeval times. Linked with Poland in a personal union since 1386 and in a closer form of unity from 1569 onwards, it was transferred to Russia as part of the third partition of Poland in 1795. As among the Estonians and Latvians, nationalism was expressed initially primarily in cultural terms, being directed at the creation of an alternative to the dominant Polish cultural forms. Overt political nationalism was born in 1905, when an assembly of Lithuanians in the historic capital, Vilnius, framed a demand for autonomy for Lithuanian-speaking areas. By aligning themselves with other local minorities, Lithuanians fared rather better than their Estonian and Latvian counterparts in Duma elections, but the ineffectiveness of the Duma, their small numbers and the fact that (like the Estonians and Latvians) they were allied to larger Russian parties prevented any progress in the direction of Lithuanian autonomy.

In Czechoslovakia it is more appropriate to speak of two nationalist movements than of one. Before 1918 the western provinces of Bohemia, Moravia and Silesia had constituted lands linked to the remainder of the Habsburg Empire initially through the person of the emperor and subsequently through the additional presence of common representative, administrative and advisory institutions. As each province also had its own autonomous organs of government, Czech nationalist demands focused on the need to protect and extend this autonomy within the Empire. After toying in the middle of the nineteenth century with the idea of restructuring the Empire into an ethnic federation with boundaries determined in effect by patterns of language usage, by the end of the nineteenth century Czech nationalists demanded recognition of the historic integrity and autonomy of their three provinces and the assertion of their linguistic rights against German domination. This implied the inclusion of a very large German minority in the Czech-controlled areas. Slovakia, by contrast, was an ill-defined region of Hungary distinguished by the fact that most of its inhabitants were Slovak-speaking Slavs. The nationalist movement there developed only slowly, and was essentially anti-Hungarian. Though some Slovak nationalists emphasised their common ethnic identity with the Czechs, most recognised Slovak distinctiveness but acknowledged the reality that progress could be made only in collaboration with the Czechs.

Ireland had lost its status as an autonomous kingdom linked to Britain through the person of the monarch in 1801, when the Act of Union created a new unitary state, the United Kingdom. A broadly-supported nationalist movement in the 1830s and 1840s demanded reversion to the position before the Union, but the stronger mass nationalist movement that began to dominate Irish political life in the 1880s was more modest in its demands. Its policy of 'home rule' for Ireland implied merely the establishment of a subordinate legislature and government in Dublin, but this Nationalist (Home Rule) Party nevertheless enjoyed unparalleled electoral dominance until the outbreak of the war. Unlike the other European cases discussed above, linguistic or cultural revivalism played only a minor part as a factor in mass nationalist mobilisation. The more radical Sinn Féin party, dating from the beginning of the twentieth century, linked the notion of linguistic revivalism with political opposition to the Union but obtained negligible popular support.

Although extreme nationalist viewpoints could have been heard immediately before the war, the great body of middle-class public opinion in each of the six countries, then, favoured no more than autonomy. In general, too, this view was shared by the parties of the Left, the socialist, social democratic or labour parties. There were important variations from country to country in the political context within which these demands were asserted and thus in the extent to which they could be construed as radical from the point of view of the existing regime. At one extreme, Finnish nationalism was essentially conservative and defensive, seeking to protect the constitutional status quo. At the other, Estonian, Latvian and Lithuanian nationalism called for the creation of new political entities which, even in the case of Lithuania, were without precedent. Czechoslovakia and Ireland fell into an intermediate position, canvassing for the return of what was seen as an autonomy that had been lost. The war years, however, brought about a profound change in political attitudes, a consequence both of a military defeat of established political structures and of a social psychological transformation. Groups which a few years earlier would have been satisfied with autonomy now demanded independence, and change in the international balance of power permitted this to be realised.

THE FORMATION OF THE NEW STATES

The states that were to emerge victorious after the war were all the creations of middle-class elites.[4] In only one case, that of Finland, was there substantial continuity with the old regime. There the March revolution in Russia had terminated the phase of Russian interference in Finland's internal affairs, and a government representative of the strength of the parties in the Diet was appointed.[5] Conservative Finnish constitutional theorists held that the abdication of the Tsar had resulted in the passing of his powers as Grand Duke of Finland to the Russian Provisional Government, but the November revolution pushed the Right into support for indepen- dence and the Bolsheviks' policy on nationalities permitted this to be realised. On 15 November 1917 the Diet declared itself in possession of supreme power in Finland; on 5 December 1917 it declared Finland an independent state; and this was accepted by the new Russian Bolshevik government on 2 January 1918. A coalition of the non-socialist parties took control of the new state.

In the Baltic provinces and in Lithuania events were even more directly conditioned by the two Russian revolutions of March and November 1917. An additional factor of the greatest importance was the Russo–German conflict during the First World War, which left the Baltic area divided between the two countries, and the post-war decision of the victorious powers to leave the German army in temporary occupation of Russian territories with a view to containing the Bolshevik threat.

In Estonia, the Russian Provisional Government moved quickly after the March revolution to confer autonomy. A law of 13 April 1917 extended the borders of Estland province to include the Estonian- speaking districts of Livland and provided for an autonomous local administration. This included an elected Provincial Council, in the elections to which the Right won control, and an administration headed by the Mayor of Tallinn. The authority of the Provincial Council was undermined by the growing extent of Bolshevik influence at local level and in city and rural soviets, though the results of the elections to the Russian Constituent Assembly in November

1917 and to an Estonian Constituent Assembly in January 1918 showed that opponents of the Bolsheviks retained a majority among the electorate. The accession of the Bolsheviks to power in Russia in November 1917, however, led to the disbandment of the Provincial Council on 28 November; but immediately before this the Council effected a paper coup, declaring itself the sole repository of supreme power in Estonia and appointing a Committee of Elders as an interim government. When the tide of war flowed against the Bolsheviks in early 1918, the Council of Elders was able to use the short interlude between Russian withdrawal and German occupation to declare once more Estonia's independence on 24 February 1918. Following German defeat in the war and near-mutiny by German troops in the Baltic provinces, the Estonian Provincial Council was permitted to meet and again proclaimed the existence of the Estonian Republic on 13 November 1918. The German military authorities agreed to the formation of a provisional government on 19 November 1918, but by 10 December the advancing Red Army had captured more than half of Estonia. The fall of Tallinn was prevented by the assistance of Russian White soldiers, Finnish volunteers and a British naval detachment, and by mid-February 1919 the Red Army had been pushed out of Estonia. The establishment of the new bourgeois state was confirmed when it proved possible to hold elections for a Constituent Assembly in April 1919.

In Latvia the indigenous strength of the Bolsheviks and the external influence of the Germans formed the backdrop to the creation of the new state. Following the German advance into Russia in 1915, Kurland came under German military administration. The German military authorities permitted the establishment of a *Landesrat* for Kurland in 1917, but this body was dominated by Baltic German interests. In the Latvian-speaking areas on the other side of the front line demands for autonomy began to be coordinated into a realistic programme after the March revolution of 1917, but the Russian Provisional Government was slow to respond. The Latvian Council which was eventually conceded proved much less effective than its Estonian counterpart and it was overthrown by the Bolsheviks shortly after its first meeting in September 1917; power shifted instead to a Soviet of Workers and Landless Peasants, in anticipation of the November revolution in Russia proper. Following German occupation of the rest of Latvia in September 1917 bourgeois demands for autonomy were articulated through an *ad hoc* Latvian National Council, which was permitted by the German authorities to proclaim a Republic of Latvia on 18 November 1918 and to set up a provisional government. This body never succeeded in asserting its authority, as it lacked control over an armed force. It was, instead, compelled to bargain with the Germans, and to promise Latvian citizenship to German members of a volunteer militia, the *Baltische Landeswehr*. The proto-government was eventually driven from Riga by the advancing Russian forces in January 1919, overthrown by a German-sponsored coup in April 1919 and re-established in July 1919 only on Allied insistence.

Lithuania had come entirely under German control by September 1915 and the bourgeois nationalist forces there worked in alliance with the occupying authorities. The Germans permitted the meeting of an assembly of Lithuanian nationalists on 18–22 September 1917; this body elected a 'National Council' and called for the establishment of a Lithuanian state. On 11 December 1917 this Council declared Lithuania independent but linked to Germany, and on 10 February 1918 it repeated this declaration without mentioning the German connection. As Germany moved only slowly to recognise the new state, the Council proclaimed itself the government of Lithuania in July 1918 and invited a German Catholic Duke to become king. The occupying authorities refused to sanction this, and the Lithuanian National Council was powerless to act against their wishes. As it depended on the German army for military support, it was unable to put up a resistance to the advancing Bolsheviks, who occupied Vilnius in January 1919. An army was, however, created with the aid of German volunteers, and by the latter part of 1919 the Bolshevik forces had been driven out.

The dissolution of the Habsburg Empire in 1918, following its defeat in the war and under pressure from the irreconcilable demands of its nationalities, thrust independence on the Czechs and made it possible for the Slovaks. Even before the end of the war, a 'Czechoslovak' National Committee, consisting of representatives of all Czech parties in proportion to their strength in the Austrian *Reichsrat* in 1911, had been formed. Following the disintegration of the Austro-Hungarian army, this Committee declared Czechoslovak independence on 28 October 1918. With a hastily-recruited volunteer army it was able to enforce its writ over the Czech provinces, but the occupation of Slovakia, carried out against Hungarian resistance, was completed only in January 1919. The subordinate role of Slovakia reflected the underdeveloped nature of nationalism there and set the stage for relations with the Czechs over the next two decades.

The end of the war promised to bring autonomy to Ireland also. A

Home Rule Act had finally become law in 1914 but its implementation had been suspended on the outbreak of war. An armed rebellion by a secret separatist organisation (the ancestor of the contemporary IRA) in 1916 had been easily crushed, but nationalist reaction to the harsh measures taken against the rebels and a growing radicalisation of public opinion in the later years of the war resulted in a huge transfer of electoral support from the Nationalist Party to the formerly insignificant Sinn Féin in the British general election of 1918. Sinn Féin's increased popularity coincided also with the party's adoption of more extreme policies; it now demanded the establishment of an independent state. In an attempt to give effect to this, the newly-elected Sinn Féin Members of Parliament abstained from attendance in the British parliament and instead established their own illegal parliament, or Dáil. Following a guerrilla war in 1919–21 Sinn Féin succeeded in 1922 in securing statehood within the British Commonwealth for all except the north-eastern portion of the country, but failed to win complete formal independence. The Dáil became the parliament of the new state, the Irish Free State, and a government answerable to it took office.

The new bourgeois states clearly enjoyed the blessing of the Western powers, modified in the East European case by caution in view of the possibility of the restoration of a counter-revolutionary Russia to its pre-war territorial limits. The precarious new governments were able eventually to set down roots and, with material and sometimes military support from abroad, to define the constitutions of more enduring regimes.

THE CHALLENGE FROM THE RIGHT

Attention has been drawn above to the existence of an entrenched ethnic minority which, in varying degrees, had a vested interest in preventing untrammelled majority rule in the independent states which nationalist leaders proposed to create. It is not surprising that these groups tended to participate in externally-promoted efforts at the construction of an alternative, conservative state where their interests would be safeguarded.[6]

Finland might be seen as an exception to this tendency. There the Swedish-speaking minority had been even more insistent than the majority on the need to preserve Finland's autonomous status, but it was motivated more by aversion to Russian dominance than by support for Finnish majority rule. Indeed, a section of the Swedish-speaking population looked to Sweden rather than to Finland as its motherland; the Swedish-speaking Aaland Islands succeeded in obtaining special autonomy in 1920. A small section of the Finnish elite (of the type represented by General Mannerheim, leader of the Finnish 'White' forces) would have liked to preserve the status quo, which would have demanded the restoration of Tsarist Russia. When it became clear that this would not be possible, the transfer of the Tsar's powers as Grand Duke to a new King of Finland was proposed. This attempt to establish an hereditary monarchy was reinforced by the new state's dependence on Germany for military assistance; this close alliance was reflected in the selection on 9 October 1918 of a German prince, Friedrich Karl of Hesse, as king-designate.

The pattern in Lithuania showed some similarities to that in Finland. Reference has already been made to the German-sponsored initiative at the establishment of a Lithuanian state. It was initially envisaged that this state would have as its head a German Duke, and on 4 June 1918 the Lithuanian Council invited Wilhelm von Urach, Duke of Württemberg, to assume the throne. Difficulties in internal German domestic politics prevented this settlement taking effect in the short term and Germany's defeat in the war made the proposal unrealistic in the long term, as in Finland. A second type of threat with which the new Lithuanian state was faced came from Polish designs on what could be regarded as part of Poland's 'national territory'; but, although attempts to revive the old Polish–Lithuanian Commonwealth of the eighteenth century in a new Greater-Polish Republic failed, Poland succeeded in annexing Vilnius, the historic capital of Lithuania.

The most ambitious of the German-sponsored efforts at extending control over conservative regimes in neighbouring territories was the proposed establishment of a United Baltic Duchy. On 8 March 1918 the German-dominated *Landesrat* of Kurland offered the crown of the Duchy to Kaiser Wilhelm in a move that would have ensured the province's integration with Germany, and a little over a month later a United Council of the more northerly Baltic provinces, summoned under German tutelage, proposed the establishment of a hereditary monarchy uniting the three provinces in a personal union with Germany. Although it proved impossible to effect a union, the

German government recognised the Baltic area as an independent state in October 1918; its *Landesrat* met to elect a provisional government and it established its own militia force using German volunteers, the *Baltische Landeswehr*. The collapse of German military control in the Baltic was accompanied by a last-ditch effort to install a pro-German government in Latvia. This was the short-lived Niedra government in 1919, which, with German assistance, temporarily displaced the Latvian nationalist government of Ulmanis.

Although the new Czechoslovak state did not face a serious threat from the Right, there had been a russophile strand in Czech nationalism which until 1917 looked to the establishment of a separate state of a conservative kind: a monarchy under the Romanov dynasty. The Russian revolution quickly ended this prospect. The collapse of the Habsburg Empire was too complete to permit its more conservative elements to fight an effective rearguard action, Kaiser Karl's manifesto of 16 October 1918, authorising the federalisation of the Austrian part of the Empire, was immediately seized on by the German Austrians, who on 21 October 1918 declared the existence of an independent German-Austrian state. Although its boundaries were drawn along ethnic lines, this state would have resulted in dismemberment of the historic Czech territories; but it did not represent a serious threat to the prospect of a separate Czechoslovak state.

Unlike the other cases, the pre-war ruling group in Ireland belonged to the winning side in the First World War and was thus able to resist Irish demands for independence without too much external interference. The guerrilla campaign of 1919–21, however, forced the British government to undertake some kind of policy of containment. The result was the concession of autonomy to Ireland in 1921, but in the form of two distinct regimes rather than one. The largely Protestant north-eastern areas were to become the new British autonomous province of Northern Ireland; the rest of the island became Southern Ireland. Northern Ireland, indeed, lasted until 1972 as a conservative regime based on the 1921 settlement; but domestic support for the proposed new autonomous province of 'Southern Ireland' was too slight to allow the experiment ever to get off the ground.

The ultimate collapse of the German monarchy following its defeat in the war effectively terminated the prospect of a line of buffer-states from Finland to Lithuania under hereditary rulers drawn from Germany, despite the influence of the German troop concentrations that remained in the Baltic area until 1919 in the guise of defenders of the people against Bolshevism. For a mixture of reasons, ranging from the local balance of military forces to the international balance of diplomatic power, Czechs and Lithuanians were able to hold their own against neighbouring states with claims on their territory, though Polish military occupation of the historic Lithuanian capital of Vilnius left the new Lithuanian state with a lasting grievance. The proposed new state of Southern Ireland also collapsed quickly; it was insufficient to satisfy nationalist demands for separate statehood.

THE CHALLENGE FROM THE LEFT

The most significant threat to the stability of the new states was from the Left in the case of the four borderlands of Russia, where Bolshevism struck roots of varying depth and revolutionary workers' states were established and enjoyed some claim to constitutional legality. Finnish Social Democrats had won a parliamentary majority in the elections of 1916, and on the abdication of the Tsar the Social Democrats took the view that his powers as Grand Duke now passed not to the Russian Provisional Government but to the Finnish Diet. Although they refused to recognise the dissolution of the Diet by the Provisional Government in 1917, they contested the general election that followed but lost their majority. The party was eventually forced by increasing working-class radicalisation into direct action, and on 28 January 1918 it established the Finnish Socialist Workers' Republic whose writ extended over most of southern Finland. After a bloody civil war, however, the Workers' Republic was overthrown by the white forces.

Estonia had already been granted autonomy by the Russian Provisional Government in April 1917, and, following the Bolshevik takeover in Petrograd, the Executive Committee of Estonian Soviets assumed power. Though displaced by the advancing German army in February 1918, Bolshevik power was re-established at the end of the year when the Red Army beat back the Germans and the 'Estonian Labour Commune' was proclaimed on 29 November 1918. The future of this new, radical Estonian state was, however, determined by the outcome of the broader White-Red conflict, and by the end of January 1919 the Bolshevik government had lost control over the entire territory of Estonia.

Bolshevism was strongest of all in Latvia, and Latvian social democrats were in the vanguard of the revolutionary movement in Russia itself.[7] In the election to the Russian Constituent Assembly of 1917 in the portion of Latvia not under German control the Bolsheviks won 72 per cent of the poll.[8] The German advance and conquest of the remaining areas of Latvia, completed by February 1918, temporarily ended Bolshevik rule; but the Red Army was more successful than in Estonia and on 4 December 1918 a Latvian Socialist Soviet Republic was formed. It was able to retain control of most of Latvia until June 1919 and of a smaller portion until the beginning of 1920, but eventually suffered the same fate as its Estonian counterpart.

Bolshevism had always been much weaker in Lithuania than in the two other Baltic territories, but the advancing Red Army had occupied more than half of its territory, including the capital, Vilnius, by January 1919. A Lithuanian Socialist Soviet Republic was established but, reflecting the modest degree of local support for the political radicalism it represented, it was converted the following month into a Lithuanian–Belorussian Socialist Soviet Republic. This experiment also went down in military defeat, when the Poles captured Vilnius in April 1919 and the Lithuanian Right-wing forces had captured the rest of the country by the autumn.

No comparable Left-wing movements sought to seize power in the other two cases. Czech social democracy was removed from the radicalism of Eastern Europe, but there were, nevertheless, echoes of Soviet-style revolt in Slovakia, where a short-lived Slovak Soviet Republic was declared on 25 May 1919. In Ireland there was a violent threat to the state from the Left, but it was characterised more by its emphasis on extreme nationalism than on social reformism. The Sinn Féin parliamentary representatives who met in Dublin in 1919 and declared the country an independent republic were unable to maintain the existence of their new state in the face of British power on the island. In the 1921 'Treaty' with Great Britain, their representatives were conceded independent status within the British Commonwealth. This precipitated a secession by extreme republicans, who refused to recognise the 'British-imposed' dissolution of their illegal parliament, the Dáil, in 1922. After a bitter civil war in 1922–3 the anti-Treaty forces were defeated.

An important contrast between the Right- and Left-wing challenges to the new states should be noted. The new states that emerged from the turmoil of the 1917–23 period were regarded by their Right-wing opponents as having been definitively established. The threat from this direction consequently dissipated relatively quickly, as the prospect of establishing a reactionary regime seemed to disappear. Although fascism and Right-wing authoritarianism did become potent forces later, at least in Finland and in the Baltic states, the social bases of these movements were in general different from those of the old Right of the 1917–21 period. By contrast, the Left continued to proclaim its legitimacy and to castigate the new states which, they alleged, were established and sustained by foreign support. The new Communist regimes introduced in Estonia, Latvia and Lithuania in 1940 thus claimed continuity with the Soviet republics of 1918–19. In Ireland, similarly, the anti-Treaty leadership eventually vested the executive authority of the 'Republic of Ireland' in the Army Council of the IRA, which, in the view of its supporters, constitutes to the present the sole legitimate government of the island.[9]

CONSOLIDATION OF THE NEW STATES: CIVIL WAR AND ITS AFTERMATH

It will be clear, then, that the political succession process in the six cases under analysis here was anything but neat. The bourgeois states that were eventually to triumph faced serious threats from both Left and Right. These are summarised in Table 3.2, in which the competing regimes that claimed legitimate succession to the old regime are listed in simplified form.

Although there has been a tendency for both sides to deny that any civil war took place and to refer instead to a 'war of liberation' directed against alien forces and domestic fifth columnists, it is clear that the outcome of the political succession process in all cases except that of Czechoslovakia (where the dispute was over territory rather than over the exercise of central authority) was determined by the relative military strength of the competing forces. The military balance was in turn a function of two factors: the power of the local supporters of a particular regime and the extent to which they could depend on assistance from foreign allies. The presence of external forces has been noted above. The main external agents were the Russian government in supporting the Left in Finland and the Baltic states; the Germans in supporting the Right in the same states; the British in supporting the Right in Ireland and in Estonia and Latvia; and local support of one Right-wing regime for another, as in

Finnish support for the Estonians, Estonian support for the Latvians
and Polish support – though for reasons which few of the recipients
welcomed – for the Lithuanians.

Table 3.2   Competing successor regimes, 1917–23

Country	Leftist regime	Bourgeois state	Rightist regime
Finland	Finnish Socialist Workers' Republic (1918)	Republic of Finland (1918–)	Kingdom of Finland (1918)
Estonia	Estonian Labour Commune (1918–19)	Republic of Estonia (1918–)	United Baltic Duchy (1918)
Latvia	Latvian Socialist Soviet Republic (1918–19)	Republic of Latvia (1918–)	United Baltic Duchy (1918)
Lithuania	Lithuanian–Belorussian Socialist Soviet Republic (1918–19)	Republic of Lithuania (1918–)	Kingdom of Lithuania (1918)
Czechoslovakia	[Slovak Soviet Republic] (1919)	Republic of Czechoslovakia (1918–)	Republic of German–Austria (1918)
Ireland	Republic of Ireland (1919–23)	Irish Free State (1922–)	Southern Ireland (1921)

While the military power balance was important, one
circumstance that played into the hands of the conservative
governments of each of the new states was the incompletely-resolved
agrarian problem. The radical land redistribution measures of the
post-war period were in some instances merely the last stage in the
breaking-up of large estates (Finland, 1918–22; Czechoslovakia,
1919; Ireland, 1923), but in others their effects were more immediately
far-reaching (Estonia, 1919; Latvia, 1920; Lithuania, 1922). In all
cases, the sponsoring governments could claim credit for measures
that won more support than they alienated, and this was a critical
factor in one case, Latvia. There the conservative peasants found the
scheme of the government of the embryonic Republic of Latvia to

introduce a radical measure of peasant proprietorship preferable to the collectivist policies of the Latvian Socialist Soviet Republic.

The civil wars had two types of consequence for the victorious bourgeois states. The first was that they disrupted the forces of the Left. The Left-wing social democrats of Finland, Estonia, Latvia and Lithuania had been decisively defeated by military force and their new Communist parties were not permitted to function openly in the new states, and the Right-wing social democrats who cooperated with the new states represented only a fraction of their movements' former strength. In Ireland, the anti-Treaty Sinn Féin rump split in 1926, dissidents under de Valera forming the pragmatic Fianna Fáil Party, which was prepared to recognise the *de facto* regime. The Left-wing republican socialists tended to remain in the Sinn Féin camp.

Second, the civil wars helped to bring about a consolidation of the forces of the Right. Much though they might have disliked the new bourgeois states, the formerly privileged minorities found them the lesser of two evils; they were certainly preferable to the Left-wing republics. Thus the Baltic Germans played a role in defending the new states of Estonia and Latvia, and Irish Protestants collaborated with the pro-Treaty government of William Cosgrave and his new, conservative, Cumann na nGael party. The position of the Swedish-speaking minority in Finland was similar, despite the existence of a small, Left-wing Swedish-speaking working-class element. In Czechoslovakia, by contrast, the bitter relations between Czechs and Germans were not tempered by the catharsis of a joint struggle for survival against Bolshevism, and the linguistic division continued to coincide with a clear-cut political gulf.

CONCLUSION: PARALLELS IN THE POLITICAL SUCCESSION PROCESS IN NEW STATES

The cases of state succession examined here might be said to be untypical: they took place in a period of international turbulence after a global war and in an atmosphere of popular volatility and social revolution. It is, however, precisely in such periods that old regimes tend to collapse and new states are born. To what extent is it possible to generalise about the mechanics of state succession in such contexts on the basis of the cases examined? Three points emerge.

The first is that the succession process is typically contested. With the removal or diminution of external influence the power of local traditional elites, which owed their position to their links with the central ruling group, is placed in jeopardy. Especially if the old regime is itself in the throes of a revolution at the centre, as in the case of the Austro-Hungarian and Russian empires, it may be impossible to impose a set of rules to govern the succession process; but even at the best of times regimes naturally do not possess an agreed procedure for bringing their own existence to an end and effecting an orderly transfer of power to new elites. The ultimate criterion in determining which group succeeds is military strength.

Second, the involvement of foreign states appears to be usual. The power-vacuum which competing groups seek to fill attracts the interest of neighbouring countries and of the great powers. This arises in part because of the natural tendency of states to seek to extend their influence and secure the appointment of friendly governments; this tendency is particularly strong if the new state might constitute a buffer between great powers or power blocs. There are, however, other factors that may encourage foreign governments to intervene. They may fear a mimetic effect in their own countries if the established order is too deeply shaken; if they are revolutionary states, they may wish to export revolution; or they may have decided to intervene (either with or without an invitation) on grounds of community of interest or ethnic solidarity with one of the competing groups.

Third, whatever the outcome of the contest, the legality of the succession process is likely to be sufficiently ambiguous to allow the defeated side to claim a 'moral victory' and to continue to proclaim its own legitimacy. Civil war between rival governments claiming jurisdiction over the same territory typically ends in victory for one side; but the defeated side may inherit a myth which is transmitted from generation to generation, based on the legitimacy of its succession, the heroic sacrifices endured in seeking to uphold this and the unfair or unpatriotic tactics of its enemies. The group which seizes the mantle of political succession immediately after independence, then, may have to continue looking over its shoulder because of threats from both Left and Right.

Notes

1. In the cases of Russia and the United Kingdom the distinction between the metropolitan territory and the periphery is clear, but the Habsburg Empire is more complex. The interpretation here is based on the assumption that since 1867 there were two core territories, Austria and Hungary.
2. For accounts of the evolution of nationalist movements in the countries in question see E. Jutikkala, *A History of Finland* (London: Thames & Hudson, 1962), J. H. Jackson, *Estonia* (London: George Allen and Unwin, 2nd edn, 1948), Alfred Bilmanis, *A History of Latvia* (Princeton, NJ: Princeton University Press, 1951), Alfred Erich Senn, *The Emergence of Modern Lithuania* (New York: Columbia University Press, 1959), C. A. Macartney, *The Habsburg Empire, 1790–1918* (London: Weidenfeld & Nicolson, 1969) and F. S. L. Lyons, *Ireland since the Famine* (London: Collins/Fontana, rev. edn, 1973).
3. Estland and North Livland were Estonian-speaking; Kurland and South Livland were Latvian-speaking.
4. On developments around the period of independence see the works cited in note 2 and also D. G. Kirby, *Finland in the Twentieth Century: A history and an interpretation* (London: C. Hurst, 1979), Georg von Rauch, *The Baltic States: The years of independence: Estonia, Latvia, Lithuania 1917–1940* (London: C. Hurst, 1970), Malbone W. Graham, *New Governments of Eastern Europe* (New York: Henry Holt, 1927), and Victor S. Mamatey and Radomir Luza (eds), *A History of the Czechoslovak Republic 1918–1948* (Princeton, NJ: Princeton University Press, 1973).
5. Note that to maintain consistency of dates the events in Russia that are commonly known as the 'February' and 'October' revolutions are here identified according to the months in which they took place according to the Western calendar (March and November).
6. On the most obvious area of external intervention see Stanley W. Page, *The Formation of the Baltic States: A study of the effects of great power politics upon the emergence of Lithuania, Latvia and Estonia* (Cambridge, Mass.: Harvard University Press, 1959).
7. Andrew Ezergailis, *The 1917 Revolution in Latvia* (Boulder, Colo.: East European Quarterly, 1974).
8. Calculated from O. H. Radkey, *The Election to the Russian Constituent Assembly of 1917* (Cambridge, Mass.: Harvard University Press, 1950) pp. 78–80.
9. The Irish Free State changed its name in 1937 to 'Eire' or 'Ireland'; in 1949 it declared itself the 'Republic of Ireland', but this should not be confused with the 'Republic of Ireland', embracing all of the island, which the IRA claims has been in existence *de jure* since 1919.

4 Political Succession in the Ottoman Empire and Modern Turkey

C. H. Dodd

How political leaders succeed one another in office, or indeed, how one government or one political regime succeeds another are clearly important questions in political science, if not ones frequently studied with any specificity. The succession of *persons* to high office is, however, a major and enduring preoccupation with students of authoritarian and totalitarian regimes. Students of more open systems are primarily concerned with political succession through elections and other institutional means of reaching high office, but also with interruptions in those processes through the assertion of class or group interest and influence, as with that of the military, or even with foreign influence.

Within a study of the rise of political leaders and their continuance in office emphasis may be placed on the occupancy of the very highest positions, but attention may also legitimately be directed to high-ranking and influential members of the bureaucracy and to political party leaders, if they are acknowledged to have significance in the political and governmental system. To broaden the concerns of political succession in this way is also, however, to suggest that interest has also to be taken in not only how one *government or political elite* succeeds another, but also how one *political regime* succeeds another, even though this would appear to be a consideration of revolution, not political succession, which suggests a degree of continuity. A regime which supplants another, and is completely different with respect to its personnel and their social provenance, its policies, the nature of its political institutions, its ideology and basic values, is clearly revolutionary and should not be considered as coming under the scope of political succession. Yet some alleged revolutions do not go much beyond a change of persons, policies and, sometimes, institutions. A number of cases of apparent revolution, or regime change, can therefore profitably be considered by reference to the concept of political succession. Indeed to do so may well throw into sharper relief the enduring characteristics of the political system in question.

To study political succession in Ottoman and Turkish political development is immediately to be aware that succession within closed authoritarian regimes, between closed and more open regimes, and between different forms of open regime, has to be taken into account. This chapter is principally concerned with political succession in modern Turkey (which entails both intra-regime and inter-regime change) but also with some of the problems faced by the Ottoman Empire. It will be suggested when considering political succession in modern Turkey that certain developments in modern Turkish democracy have greatly disrupted the operation of the normal procedures of political succession found in liberal and democratic societies.

In liberal and democratic societies the problem of political succession is generally provided for by electoral processes in relation to which political parties perform recruiting and policy-making functions. However, the necessity of political succession is never as simple as this model suggests. This is because groups like churches, unions, business associations, or indeed even the bureaucracy and the military, will play an important role in advancing candidates for political office. Even foreign governments, or economic organisations, may exert an indirect but nevertheless important influence in helping forward those candidates it would be in their interest to see in high office.

If these considerations apply in more open societies, blurring the liberal and democratic vision of political succession, they can apply with even more force in authoritarian political systems, where groups like the military, the bureaucracy or the religious institutions may powerfully affect the choice of political leaders. However, there is no warrant for assuming that in all authoritarian regimes it is not the political ruler who actually rules and is most influential. There have been despotic, or near-despotic, regimes where in the question of political succession personality looms particularly large. It is much less predictable than in those states where groups or political organisations are predominant. The Ottoman Empire suffered greatly from problems of political succession, especially when the power of the Sultan was unchallenged. Nor were they satisfactorily solved either in later Ottoman times or during the inter-war Atatürkist period, when Turkey had a single-party regime.

THE OTTOMAN AND ATATÜRKIST REGIMES

If no plans can be made by a ruler for political succession on his demise there will almost inevitably be strife, which may well spread outside governing circles. The strongest wins and occupies power. This was the system which operated in the days of the classical Ottoman Empire – when sons fought one another for the succession – but eventually and logically this gave way to the practice whereby the son who momentarily seized power had his brothers strangled. In 1603 the system was modified, and brothers were not killed but kept in strict isolation, a device which ensured that the Ottoman Empire eventually became bereft of virile leaders. This process was accelerated when the rule became established that the Sultan's eldest brother, rather than his son, should succeed, for the brother would have enjoyed a restricted but indulgent life for a longer period than a son would normally have done. This produced stability in the succession; it was known who would succeed, but he was unlikely to be a troublesome aspirant to power during the life-time of a ruler. Stability was achieved at the cost of political dynamism.

The Ottoman Empire found an unsuccessful means of overcoming the difficulties posed by political succession in autocratic regimes. A moment's reflection shows how difficult these succession problems are. In the case of the tyrant who does not care who succeeds him and whose aim is simply not to be usurped, the problem is at its simplest. After he dies there is simply a struggle of lesser or greater magnitude. However, if the ruler (a revolutionary leader, for example) wants to see either his policies, or his supporters, or both, to continue to be effective after his death, considerable difficulties immediately arise. After all, to nominate a successor is to invite usurpation: and in the case of a revolutionary regime, like that of Mustafa Kemal Atatürk, when the experience of the recent overthrow of governmental authority is all too fresh, coups easily follow on coups. Whether a ruler in such a situation will hold on to office will depend on many factors.

A leader of unparalleled prestige, like Kemal Atatürk, charismatic to a degree, skilful in politics, supported by the military and by a single party, does not find it all that difficult a task to maintain himself in power. But even Mustafa Kemal Atatürk was extremely careful not to encourage any one person to challenge him. His obvious successor was İsmet İnönü, his doughty lieutenant in the struggle for independence, but Atatürk was careful to remove him from the premiership for long periods, first in 1930, and then later, shortly before his own death in 1937. It was only in the last few weeks of his life that Atatürk openly named İnönü as his successor, knowing full well that the principles of the revolution he had inaugurated would be safest in his hands. İnönü owed his succession partly to Atatürk's nomination but also, however, to the respect in which he was held in the bureaucracy, the party and army. He was massively elected into office on a free vote in the Grand National Assembly, a body where these sections of society were dominant. The fact that at the time potential rivals held the offices of Chairman of the National Assembly and even of the premiership (Celal Bayar) carried very little weight in the succession stakes. By his policies Atatürk successfully ensured that no candidate for the succession was favoured by him until his very last days and especially the most obvious and the most popular.

This must be a classic tactic for any autocratic ruler and not too difficult to carry out provided potential successors do not have the backing of powerful groups in society. In the case of Atatürk's Turkey there was just a danger that İnönü, influential in party bureaucracy and army, could become a rival, and therefore, just possibly, an untimely successor. There was no very great danger of this occurring, but the experience underlines the fact that in autocracies in developed societies succession must depend to a large extent on the political strength of groups in that society and how they are manipulated, rather than formal appointment to office. Indeed, even in the classical years of the Ottoman Empire the power of the military had to be reckoned with, and also that of the established religious institution of Islam. The jurisconsults who manned this institution (the *ulema*) had no formal say in deciding who should succeed, but if a Sultan was unpopular with the soldiery, the soldiers could, and did, ask the head of the *ulema* whether the Sultan was to be considered on moral grounds fit to be Sultan. If the answer was no, he could then legitimately be deposed and another set up in his stead. The fact that the head of the religious institution was appointed by the Sultan made the frequent operation of this procedure less than likely, but it did nevertheless occur.

It is so far evident that in both the Ottoman Empire and in the Republic of Kemal Atatürk the problems of political succession to the highest political office are typical of patrimonial regimes. The difficulties were partly personal and partly connected with the presence of powerful groups in society. The discussion so far has, however, been centred on succession to the highest office of state, whereas much political initiative stems from the ruling elite necessary for any large society. It is therefore important to move the discussion down a rung and ask what the conditions of succession to political power were for this elite in Ottoman and Atatürkist times.

THE OTTOMAN AND ATATÜRKIST ELITES

In the early Ottoman Empire the military and the religious institutions were welded together in the common purpose by the vitality of the Sultan, whose classic task comprised the expansion of the domains of Islam and the subjugation of the infidel. When the Sultans' vitality declined – and opposition to Ottoman expansion became more effective – the military or the religious institution might well have come to occupy the centre of the stage replacing the personal power of the Sultan, but this did not happen. It was not because there was either a landed aristocracy or a commercial middle class to take over power. A hereditary aristocracy had never been allowed to emerge and commerce was in the hands of Christians and Jews, who did not qualify for any formal place in the scheme of governance. What occurred was the expansion of the civil bureaucracy for which many young recruits were forcibly recruited from the sons of Balkan Christian peoples. They, like recruits for the military (the Janissaries) had 'slave' status, their lives and property being at the disposal of the Sultan. But they were well chosen from among able recruits and in the absence of powerful rivals in society they managed the Empire. Within this bureaucracy there was much mobility, little regard for status as such (all slaves being of equal non-status before the Sultan), much intrigue and rivalry, but an overall stability which resulted from the security enjoyed by the class of officials if not, at first, by the persons themselves who composed the class.

During the nineteenth century, however, there were two particularly important developments for these officials both as a class and as persons. For during that century with the enforced reform of the military in the early years, and notably in 1826 when the now corrupted Janissaries were destroyed, the military was eclipsed for a long time as a force in government. The new model army that was created took some time to assert itself politically. The need for modernisation of the state to face up to the competition from Europe also led to governmental disenchantment with the Islamic institution, whose members mostly preferred to ignore, rather than come to grips with, the threat from the West. The role of the religious institution was therefore progressively weakened during the nineteenth century. On the personal side a great boost to the position of bureaucrats was given by Western-inspired legislation which guaranteed rights of life and property to all. It now became more possible for leading bureaucrats to establish powerful adminstrative dynasties. They constituted an entrenched class, still internally fluid, devoted to the modernisation of the Ottoman state and without any group, or class, rivals to challenge their power. When a liberal and religious opposition arose in the mid-nineteenth century it came, and could only come, from the lower ranks of the bureaucracy itself. It led to no more than the abortive Constitution of 1876, after which many of the disillusioned liberal critics of the Ottoman Empire in the nineteenth century were found places in the administrative machine.

This increasingly westernised and modernising bureaucracy carried through the policies of the Young Turk and Atatürk revolutions without much challenge appearing to their power. Nor did the revival of the military's prestige with their success in the War of National Liberation (1919–23) result in the removal of the higher bureaucracy from the centre of the stage. Atatürk had the military take a secondary place and even in 1961 the military listened to the civilian intelligentsia in the making of a new Constitution. It was being said as late as the 1960s that Turkey, like the Ottoman Empire, was still being governed by the triumvirate of officials, officers and *ulema*. The only difference was that the *ulema* were replaced in modern Turkey by the academic intelligentsia brought up in accordance with the principles of Atatürkism. Despite regime change a large measure of stability in political succession had been maintained.

MODERN TURKEY

In 1946 Turkey took important steps towards creating a liberal and democratic political system. By 1950 a rival to Atatürk's People's Party had appeared strong enough to gain victory at the polls. As a result the Democrat Party occupied power, winning subsequent elections (in 1954 and 1957) until it was ousted by a military junta in 1960. With regard to political succession the Turks seemed by 1950 to have solved the problem of how to obtain a change in top leadership by radical (for Turkey) liberal and democratic means. İsmet İnönü stepped down to be succeeded as President by Celal Bayar, with Adnan Menderes soon to become Prime Minister. The leaders of the new party in power, it has to be noted, were in fact former and quite prominent members of the People's Party, so a certain continuity in leadership was preserved. The new party, with an internally recruited leadership, carried on many of the policies of the previous government, though with greater emphasis on economic entrepreneurilism and religious freedom. In these policies they were not extreme, however. They did not dismantle the state economic enterprises; neither did they allow a religious revival, save in superficial respects.

It was by and large the case that the transition to a multi-party system between 1946 and 1960 was accompanied by what was overall an orderly process of political succession. The new political elite in the Democrat Party did not depart greatly in policies or style from that which it had supplanted, for the People's Party was itself becoming more liberal and less aggressively secularist. Yet before long some quite considerable changes began to occur in the political elite which showed that political succession to the most important political roles was not necessarily going to be as smooth as hitherto. It has been observed by one student of the period that 1950 led to the development of severe intra-elite conflict in Turkish politics. A new elite, or part-elite, was emerging that was, in this view, beginning to challenge the hegemony of the Atatürkist bureaucratic and military elite. It was noted that only 13 per cent of the deputies in the National Assembly in 1954 were of bureaucratic or military background, whereas in 1920 they had formed 38 per cent of the whole membership. The deputies were also becoming more local, many more born and brought up in the constituencies they represented.[1] However, although intra-elite conflict became a reason for gross political instability by the late 1970s, it cannot convincingly be attributed to a division between the major party recruitment along occupational or class lines. Both major parties have broadened their membership and both have become heavily 'professional' in the occupational background characteristics of their deputies in parliament. It is for other reasons to do with the transition to a liberal and democratic system that political succession has proceeded anything but smoothly, as the military interventions of 1960, 1971 and 1980 bear witness.

However, before discussing the relationship between Turkish liberal-democracy and political succession, the fortunes of the bureaucratic elite since Atatürk's days need to be examined. As we have seen, they were the major promoters of Ottoman and Atatürkist development. It might therefore be expected that they could continue under conditions of multi-party politics to provide that leadership for the Turkish state which has so often been provided for France by the French administrative elite.

The conditions necessary for the continued predominance of the administrative elite appeared generally to be favourable in Atatürk's Republic. By Young Turk times recruitment to a developing civil service had widened to embrace a large circle of professional parental occupations – from journalistic, teaching and military backgrounds – though three-quarters of the bureaucracy then in office had still come from bureaucratic and military backgrounds. This homogeneous administration carried much responsibility in Atatürk's Republic, even although recruitment to these top positions from those of purely military and bureaucratic background was by then reduced to some 50 per cent. However, in the Atatürkist Republic the School of Political Sciences at Ankara University continued to perform the task of the Ottoman Civil Service school out of which it had developed. The natural career of those graduates was the Civil Service, and indeed during this period graduates of the School provided 21 per cent of parliamentary deputies between 1920 and 1946 and 28 per cent of Cabinet ministers. Succession to the top political and administrative posts raised no real problems.[2]

By 1964 a study showed half of the highest officials still had official or military backgrounds,[3] but it was clearly the case that by the 1960s the bureaucracy was ceasing to become a desirable profession and the graduates of the Political Science School (now Faculty) were looking elsewhere for better-paid jobs in the developing private sector. They also profited from a development in the public service sector which saw the growth of a variety of administrative agencies rather loosely tied to the central structure and which allowed extra-ordinary salaries to be paid. Moreover, the fact that Turkish Civil Service structure is basically decentralised to ministries prevented the emergence of a strong bureaucratic pressure group now needed to defend bureaucratic interests, which had hitherto not been subjected to any threat. There is enough evidence to show that by 1960 this Atatürkist administrative elite had become sufficiently dissatisfied with their position and salaries to welcome the military coup of that year. The coup was seen by many as a reassertion of Atatürkism against the trends towards the irresponsible political entre-preneurialism of rising elements in society which was encouraged by competitive politics. After the 1960 revolution the Atatürkist adminis-trative elite could not easily be preserved in power and influence. However, its main political arm, the People's Party, began to turn Left-of-centre, when Right-of-centre and economically liberal parties mostly dominated the political scene. In other words, a long-established chain of political succession by the bureaucratic elite was being broken.

The question then arises whether another regular system of political succession has been created by the creation of a liberal and democratic political system, a system which in principle provides few problems of political succession. In fact, the problem of political succession is one that a liberal and democratic system is intended to solve. The termination of office of political leaders and the political elite in parliament after a specified number of years, and the need for re-election in order to continue in office, make the point clearly enough. And, of course, there is in some forms of the system the possibility of overthrow of leaders in mid-term. Neither usually does the bureaucracy have any right to formulate policy, even if in practice this is often the case and much real power lies in their hands. Yet whilst liberal and democratic systems usually provide a reliable means for solving the problem of political succession they only have to go wrong for great difficulties to emerge. Turkey is a case in point.

In the first place too rapid a rate of political succession is normally destabilising politically. The three military interventions in Turkish politics in 1960, 1971 and 1980 were particularly disruptive of stability. Large numbers of Democrat Party politicians were effec-tively excluded from politics by the military in 1960, and two of their leaders were hanged. In 1980 *all* former deputies and political leaders were banned from politics for five years and ten years respectively. This was hugely disruptive of political continuity and ensured that the inexperienced assumed high office. But in addition to these extraordinary instances of military intervention there have been other factors at work. First, a procession of coalition governments of various mixes has ensured a remarkably high rate of turnover in the highest offices of state; this occurred particularly in the 1970s. Second, the rate of turnover among deputies in parliament has also been high with less than half the deputies of any one parliament subsequently being elected to the next, this applying about equally to the two major parties. The Right-of-centre Justice Party showed the greater stability, but in the 1969 government only one-quarter of its members had belonged to the immediately previous 1965 government. In the People's Party the situation was even more fluid. In 1977 an abortive 25-member Cabinet contained only seven out of the 1973 Cabinet. In 1978 the Prime Minister, Bülent Ecevit, chose only four members of the 1973 government.

These discontinuities in political succession at the top political levels encouraged an even worse degree of discontinuity in succession to the highest administrative posts. We have seen why the higher Civil Service has lost its pre-eminence in Turkish political life. But in the 1970s the position of its top leadership was in addition repeatedly undermined by the replacement of higher officials on each (frequent) change of government. Moreover large numbers of subordinate officials were also moved around or dismissed. It has been observed that in the Rightist coalition governments of that era 'each ministry was brought under the complete jurisdiction of an individual political party' and 'the coalition members were each heavily engaged in unrestricted patronage and nepotism. Never before in Turkish political development had the civil servants been reshuffled in such an arbitrary fashion.'[4] The prime reason for this disruption of the highest bureaucratic leadership was the virulent nature of the struggle between and among the political parties which arose from personal animosities and a widening ideological divide. The People's Party went further to the Left, and in conditions of electoral balance the Right-wing and Islamic parties exerted an inordinate degree of influence over the Right-of-centre Justice Party government. In such conditions the politicisation of the bureaucracy could not be prevented.

CONCLUSION

By way of summary and conclusion it can be seen that the Ottoman Empire at its height was not able to create a smooth and effective mode of political succession. The Empire did, however, manage to assert the predominance of a bureaucratic elite which guaranteed not personal but corporate political succession. In this assertion of its place as the unrivalled *de facto* holders of power the bureaucracy was greatly assisted by the decline of the political influence of the military and the religious institution, due to their inappropriateness to the changing conditions of the nineteenth-century international world which placed the Ottoman Empire in considerable danger. This bureaucratic elite arranged political succession without difficulty and came particularly into its own in the Atatürk Republic which existed until 1946. In this period they extended their influence into the new single-party political structure and into the Assembly. The struggle for political succession in these conditions was set in personal terms. After the abolition of the religious establishment by Atatürk and his success in returning the military to barracks there were no forces available to make political succession more than a matter of choice of the person best suited to develop the aims of the Atatürk revolution and to gain the support of the party and bureaucracy.

With the transition to a liberal and democratic regime after the Second World War the problem of political succession would appear to have been solved. However, the singular development of the Turkish political system, partly causing, but partly caused by, successive military intervention has rendered political succession problematic and has greatly undermined the hitherto stabilising position of the bureaucracy. Political succession, it would appear, is best achieved in conditions of liberal democracy, but when anti-systemic parties have to be involved and are influential the dangers to smooth processes of political succession are considerable. A revolution is not to be regarded as an act of political succession if it imposes new leaders with new values and new institutions and some-times from different economic and social groups or classes. But the Young Turk and the Atatürkist revolutions provided a greater measure of political succession, both in respect of persons, the classes from which they came, and the policies they adopted, than did changes induced by the liberal and democratic system. The disruption of the processes of political succession may partly be laid at the door of the military. Their intervention in 1960, 1971 and 1980 certainly brought about instability in the highest levels of leadership. Their desire to start afresh has been most disruptive. However, when they occupied power the military did not impose massive policy changes. They intervened to bring stability to a system in which regularities in the process of political succession were mainly being eroded by the operation of the party system in social and economic conditions which showed that liberal and democratic systems do not necessarily always provide the most satisfactory means of achieving a stable system of political succession.

Notes

1. See F. Frey, *The Turkish Political Elite* (Cambridge, Mass.: MIT Press, 1965), especially Ch. 13.
2. J. S. Szyliowicz, 'Elite recruitment in Turkey: the role of the *Mülkiye*', *World Politics*, 23 (1971), pp. 371–98.
3. C. H. Dodd, *Politics and Government in Turkey* (Manchester and Berkeley: Manchester University Press and University of California Press, 1969), Ch. 18.
4. Metin Heper, 'Recent trends in Turkish politics: end of a monocentrist polity?', *International Journal of Turkish Studies*, (1979–80) pp. 102–13.

5 Political Succession in the Soviet Union: Building a Power Base[1]

Peter Frank

In competitive, multi-party political systems, a newly-elected prime minister enjoys great authority when forming a government. There may be certain self-imposed constraints (such as the need, as some prime ministers see it, to have at least token representation of various interests from within the victorious party), or constraints arising out of the electoral process (such as coalition building), but in general an incoming leader has a fairly free hand.

It is not so in the USSR. There, because of the absence of an orderly, regular, well-understood mode of removing or re-endorsing incumbent leaders, a new leader is uncommonly restricted at the onset of his period of rule (although this generalisation may require some qualification in the case of Gorbachev). So far, Soviet leaders have either died in office (Lenin, Stalin, Brezhnev, Andropov, Chernenko), or have been ousted (Khrushchev). Thus the newcomer is put in place by his predecessor's team – he inherits a government, rather than creates a new one – and because he owes his position to them in the short to medium term, he must be careful not to alienate their support. That is one reason why there is a tendency in Soviet politics for a 'cult of the individual' to be followed by a period of 'collective leadership'. (See Table 5.1.)

Another consequence is that much of the new leader's energy is expended upon painstakingly building a power base, and since the distribution of power at the apex of the party structure is shifting and ill-defined, it means that the new leader must seek to change the composition of the Politburo and Secretariat by replacing rivals and opponents with 'his' men. Estimates differ as to how long this process takes (and in any case it varies according to the unique circumstances of each succession), but Brezhnev needed about ten years, much more than the life of a government in Britain.

Table 5.1   Political succession in the Soviet Union since 1940

Date	Head of State*	General Secretary CPSU†	Head of Government‡	Chairman of the Supreme Defence Council
(1938)	Kalinin			
(1922)		Stalin		
6.4.41			Stalin	
12.3.46	Shvernik			
7.3.53	Voroshilov	Malenkov	Malenkov	
14.3.53		Khrushchev		
8.2.55			Bulganin	
27.3.58			Khrushchev	
7.5.60	Brezhnev			
15.7.64	Mikoyan			
14.10.64		Brezhnev	Kosygin	
9.12.65	Podgorny			
16.6.77	Brezhnev			Brezhnev
23.10.80			Tikhonov	
12.11.82		Andropov		
5.83				Andropov
16.6.83	Andropov			
13.2.84		Chernenko		
11.4.84	Chernenko			Chernenko
11.3.85		Gorbachev		
3.85				Gorbachev
2.7.85	Gromyko			
27.9.85			Ryzhkov	

* Chairman of the Presidium of the Supreme Soviet.
† First Secretary 1953–66: CPSU = Communist Party of the Soviet Union.
‡ Chairman of the Council of People's Commissars to 1946; thereafter Chairman of the Council of Ministers.
Sources: Isaac Deutscher, *Stalin; a political biography* (Harmondsworth: Penguin Books, 1966); John Dornberg, *Brezhnev: the masks of power* (London: André Deutsch, 1974); Martin McCauley (ed.), *The Soviet Union after Brezhnev* (London: Heinemann, 1983); R. W. Pethybridge, *A History of Postwar Russia* (London: Allen & Unwin, 1966); *The Annual Register*.

The prudent General Secretary does not leave it at that. The longer he holds office, the lower down the party apparatus he is able to place his clients. Crucial in this respect is the Central Committee (CC), for it is from this body that the Politburo's and his own authority derive in formal, statutory terms. Moreover, the CC, as was demonstrated in 1957 and, to a somewhat lesser degree, again in 1964, may occasionally play a real role in leadership politics. Also the willing cooperation of CC members may be vital in securing the implementation of policies: as Brezhnev put it in his speech to the twenty-fifth Congress in 1976 when referring to the republic and regional party first secretaries, 'One can say without exaggeration that upon them rests the chief responsibility for putting policy into effect in the localities.'[2]

Yet it is not easy for a General Secretary to alter the composition of the CC. The party *Statutes* stipulate that the Congress, which meets usually every five years, elects the CC, which in turn elects the Politburo, Secretariat, and General Secretary (although *de facto* it is a process of selection from above). Between congresses, the CC may expel members (something that it does very rarely) or promote candidates to full membership. Otherwise, any major turnover must wait upon a congress, which may be awkward for an incoming General Secretary if one is not due for some time. The twenty-sixth Congress was held in 1981; Andropov succeeded Brezhnev in November 1982 and was clearly anxious to make changes which *inter alia* were bound to antagonise important groupings within the CC. Chernenko may also have felt handicapped by having inherited a CC not entirely of his own making (although given his closeness to Brezhnev and Andropov's short tenure in office, he may have found it more congenial than did his predecessor). Gorbachev was lucky: Chernenko died just in time for him to put his stamp upon the CC elected at the twenty-seventh Congress in February–March 1986.

The CPSU General Secretary, as head of the CC Secretariat, has overall responsibility for the selection, training and placement of cadres. It is this function that invests the post with much of its power. Among the most important cadre appointments are the party *obkom* (provincial committee) first secretaries, who together constitute one of the main groupings within the CC.

Under Stalin, these men wielded enormous power throughout their territorial areas of competence; but, like everyone else at that time, they were vulnerable to the preposterous allegations that periodically swept the country. According to Khrushchev, in 1937–8 'in almost all krais, oblasts and republics there allegedly existed "rightist Trotskyite, espionage–terror and diversionary–sabotage organisations and centers" and that the heads of such organisations as a rule – for no known reason – were first secretaries of oblast or republic communist party committees or central committees'.[3]

It was Khrushchev's rejection of arbitrary mass terror as a method of rule that afforded the *obkom* first secretaries (and many other occupational groups, of course) the prospect of relatively stable careers. But Khrushchev was astute enough to realise that to secure his own position he had to pack the CC with his supporters, and the CCs elected at the twentieth Congress in 1956 and the twenty-second Congress in 1961 bore witness to his manipulation. Then his judgement slipped. Intent upon trying to infuse the Soviet political system with the vitality needed to achieve his laudable but ambitious aims, Khrushshev began to experiment with party and state structures. For some, it was a time of great opportunity; for others (most especially those already holding office in the *apparat*, such as the incumbent *obkom* first secretaries), it was a period fraught with uncertainty and declining influence. Having failed to protect his rear by electing a new CC dominated by the beneficiaries of the 1962 'bifurcation' reform,[4] Khrushchev was ousted in October 1964 by his Politburo colleagues supported by his erstwhile appointees in the CC.

Brezhnev learned the lesson. He began by reversing Khrushchev's 'harebrained schemes', as his reforms and organisational innovations were pejoratively termed, and followed this by offering assurances to the *apparat* that their tenure, unless promoted, was permanent. At the first Congress following his accession to the General Secretaryship (the twenty-third, in 1966), Brezhnev condemned the frequent reorganisations and restructurings of recent years and criticised the constant turnover of cadres that had given rise to their feeling of insecurity.[5]

That these sentiments were no short-term, tactical bid for support is evidenced by Brezhnev's returning to the same theme at subsequent congresses. Ten years later, at the twenty-fifth, he reminded his audience:

The party has firmly committed itself to a caring, solicitous attitude towards its cadres. Gone are the unwarranted chopping and changing and frequent turnover of officials, a question that was raised as far back as the XXIII Congress. Now the transfer of cadres takes place only when the interests of business require it; when there is a need to strengthen this or that sector of work.[6]

In the meantime, at that twenty-fourth Congress in 1971, Brezhnev had marked the establishment of another practice that was to continue throughout his entire period in office. His message now was that as well as security of tenure, personnel changes when they did occur would draw upon local cadres. Instead of drafting officials from the central *apparat* to fill vacancies at regional level, promotions would be made from within the *oblast* party organisation. The applause with which the audience greeted this part of his speech showed that the message had been understood and was welcome:

> Many new comrades with good political and specialist training have been promoted to head party and soviet organs in the localities, including first secretaryships of republics, communist party central committees, and *krai* and *oblast* committees. In so doing, the Central Committee has been consistent in following the line of promoting local officials, the sending of people from the centre to fill these posts occurring only in exceptional circumstances. This way of selecting and posting cadres meets with the approval and support of party organisations and all communists. (*Applause*)[7]

Brezhnev held to his policy of stability of cadres throughout his entire 18-year period in office. It undoubtedly won him considerable support within the party apparatus: in that sense, he was a genuinely popular leader. Initially, following Stalin's predations and Khrushchev's constant reshuffling, stability was a political virtue. But too secure a guarantee of tenure, particularly in the absence of any broader accountability, led to complacency, and then to inertia. By 1982, the party apparatus, especially at the regional level, had become elderly, smug, parochial, and very often corrupt to boot. That was part of Brezhnev's legacy to Andropov.

Andropov had two reasons to want to shake up the apparatus. First, he had to make haste to consolidate his own position; and, second, being desperately short of time, he needed to ensure the willing cooperation of the regional *apparat* in putting into effect certain policy innovations. Not that Andropov's policies were particularly radical; but he did demand a more vigorous, dynamic style of leadership, one free from the taint of corruption.

In the 15 months that he was leader, Andropov effected a substantial renewal of cadres, all the more remarkable in the light of his own serious illness. There were changes in the composition of the Politburo, some brought about by death and others by promotion from candidate to full membership. Several heads of department in the Secretariat were replaced, but perhaps the greatest turnover occurred amongst the *obkom* first secretaries.

Chernenko's appointment as General Secretary following Andropov's death in February 1984 was a victory for the 'Old Guard', for those elderly cadres, set in their ways, who owed their appointment originally to Brezhev and who had felt threatened by Andropov's invigorating style of leadership. For 13 months – until Chernenko, too, expired – the USSR marked time (although beneath the surface, politics were seething). Gorbachev, who as a result was in effect the 'second General Secretary'[8] in the collective leadership and in charge of cadres, was able to make some changes at the *oblast* level, but certainly not to the extent that he would have liked. However, between his appointment as General Secretary in March 1985 and the convening of the twenty-seventh Congress a year later, 46 *obkoms* found themselves with new first secretaries. Together with the appointments that he and his mentor Andropov had been able to make earlier, this changeover contributed to ensuring Gorbachev a very substantial degree of support in the CC: a power arrangement that must serve him for another five years.

Study of the manipulation of appointments reveals a great deal of the workings of Soviet leadership politics and of the Soviet political process in general. Such manipulations are the visible tip of the iceberg of organisational manoeuvring that goes on within the closed CPSU structure and which is far removed from popular participation. It provides glimpses of the relative standing of Soviet leaders and of the fortunes of their current policy priorities. Moreover, as well as retrospectively throwing light on Brezhnev's, Andropov's and Chernenko's style of leadership, study of personnel change at the provincial level also contributes to any assessment of Gorbachev's institutional strength and hence of his chances of receiving active support for the attainment of the ambitious goals that he has set for the Soviet Union. It is with such considerations in view that the following analysis is made.

There are two occasions when – to use a navigational metaphor – it is possible 'to take a fix' on the main party–state apparatus. One is when there is an election to the USSR Supreme Soviet; the other is at a party congress. Prior to each of these events, the party undergoes a period of statutory 'account and election procedure' (*otchetno-vybornaya kampaniya*). It is a time when the apparatus is momentarily settled and stable, and thus a convenient juncture for the student of Soviet politics to utilise for analytical purposes. For example, every *obkom* first secretary is a member of the USSR Supreme Soviet: they can all be identified at the same point in time, just when any process of turnover is likely to have come to a halt.

The other occasion is when a party congress is held. It is then that a new CC is elected, and although not every *obkom* first secretary (to use the same example) is a member, most are, and again it is an opportune moment to take a fix.

The last elections to the Supreme Soviet in the Brezhnev period were held in March 1979; the last party congress (the twenty-sixth) in February 1981. Supreme Soviet elections were held again on 4 March 1984, but the election-and-report conferences took place in December 1983 and January 1984, and thus were completed before Andropov died. Neither Supreme Soviet elections nor party congresses were held during Chernenko's time in office; but the twenth-seventh party congress was convened a little over a year after Gorbachev's accession to the General Secretaryship (see Table 5.2).

Table 5.2   Periodisation of Soviet succession, March 1979–March 1986

Periodisation	Length (approx)
I 4 March 1979 (Supreme Soviet elections) to 23 February 1981 (XXVI CPSU Congress)	2 years
II February 1981 (XXVI Congress) to 10 November 1982 (Brezhnev's death)	1 year 8 months
(Periods I and II represent the last 3 years 8 months of Brezhnev's time in office.)	
III 10 November 1982 (Brezhnev's death) to December 1983 (start of *oblast* conferences)	1 year 1 month
IV December 1983 (start of *oblast* conferences) to 9 February 1984 (Andropov's death)	2½ months
(Periods III and IV represent the 15 months when Andropov held office.)	
V 9 February 1984 (Andropov's death) to 10 March 1985 (Chernenko's death)	1 year 1 month
VI 10 March 1985 (Chernenko's death) to 25 February 1986 (convening of XXVII Congress)	12½ months
(Periods V and VI represent Gorbachev's time in office.)	

In the two years between the elections to the USSR Supreme Soviet in March 1979 and the convening of the twenty-sixth party congress in February 1981, there were only 12 changes of *obkom* first secretary (out of a total of 155:[9] please refer to Table 5.3). One first secretary died; two retired, and since neither was exceptionally elderly (56 and

63), it is possible that they were dropped (as may have been the case with the two who simply faded from public view). But for the remaining seven officials, change of position resulted in either no loss of status or, as usually happened, in promotion. All this group came from the Russian Soviet Federative Socialist Republic (RSFSR) or the Ukraine; all were already full members of the CC. Five were transferred into state ministerial posts; another, I. I. Sakhnyuk, moved to Moscow from Kharkov in the Ukraine to head the newly created CC Department of Agricultural Machine-Building; while F. A. Tabeev, hitherto first secretary of the Tatar *obkom* and the only non-Slav amongst them, was, in November 1979, appointed ambassador to Kabul, shortly before the Soviet invasion of Afghanistan.

In all these 12 cases, the new first secretary was a local cadre, usually the former *obkom* second secretary, or the chairman of the parallel soviet's executive committee (*oblispolkom*), a post that falls within the *party* career structure.

Table 5.3   Turnover of CPSU *obkom* first secretaries, March 1979–March 1986

Period	No. of changes (N = 155)	Of which CC full members	Candidate members	CRC members	None of these
I	12 (7.7%)	8	1		3
II	12 (7.7%)	3	3	1	5
I + II	24 (15.4%)	11	4	1	8
III	18 (11.6%)	12			6
IV	17 (11.0%)	9		1	7
III + IV	35 (22.6%)	21		1	13
V	14 (9.0%)	7	2		5
VI	46 (29.7%)	26	2	1	17
V + VI	60 (38.7%)	33	4	1	22

In short, Brezhnev's assurances on both stability and favouring local cadres are amply supported by the empirical evidence.

There are some signs, however, that cadres policy in the 20 months prior to Brezhnev's death was beginning to fray. One must be cautious about generalising too much, since of the 12 changes that occurred in this second period, six were in Kazakhstan alone. Nonetheless not one of these changes resulted in promotion and, indeed, in three instances it was made publicly and explicitly clear that the first secretary had been dismissed for unsatisfactory performance.[10] Moreover, in most cases in this period, the incoming first secretary was not a local cadre, but had been drafted in from outside the *oblast* in question.

Although Andropov succeeded to the CPSU General Secretaryship in November 1982, he lacked what in Soviet terms is a vital political resource: he had never had the opportunity to exercise patronage over appointments that carried with them membership of the CC and thus constitute the kind of power base that an aspiring Soviet leader ideally needs. It is true that he had served in the regional party apparatus just after the Second World War; but however vital its strategic importance, Karelia offered few opportunities to build up a network of clients comparable with, say, Khrushchev's Ukraine or Brezhnev's Dnepropetrovsk 'mafias'. Andropov's subsequent term in the central *apparat* in Moscow involved relations with foreign Communist parties and, useful though this was (together with his service as Soviet ambassador to Hungary in the late 1950s) in broadening his range of experience, it afforded little chance to exercise patronage. Similarly, his 15 years at the head of the security police had given him unrivalled access to information (some of which he was to put to good use in the leadership contest), but there was a limit to how far he could deploy KGB clients about the party–state apparatus.

Consequently, Andropov not only had to begin building his power base almost from scratch following the death of Brezhnev, he had to do so in competition with a defeated, yet still ambitious rival, Chernenko, who was identified closely with his patron's popular cadres policy.

That Andropov managed to replace over one-fifth (22.6 per cent) of the incumbent *obkom* first secretaries in only 15 months was a considerable achievement, more especially since 21 of the 35 officials involved were full members of the CC. However, more detailed scrutiny of the changes suggests that it would be unwise to overemphasise the significance of these changes.

To begin with, none of this group of *obkom* first secretaries was sacked ignominiously, although N. V. Bannikov at Irkutsk in Siberia was pensioned off only five weeks after *Pravda* had published a report criticising him personally for shortcomings in agriculture in the *oblast*,[11] while G. P. Pavlov (Lipetsk *obkom*) went into retirement without being accorded the Politburo's appreciatory recognition, a practice that had become standard following Andropov's accession. Four more first secretaries retired 'honourably', and since their ages were 68, 69, 71 and 74, there was an at least plausible reason for their political demise. Another two retired on health grounds (aged 60 and 65) and were thanked by the Politburo for their services. One *obkom* first secretary, G. I. Chiryaev (Yakutsk), died. In two instances ('transferred to other work') it has not been possible to ascertain what happened to the outgoing official: these should probably be regarded as demotions.

The remaining ten CC-full-member transfers were all promotions: hardly the stuff of an Andropovian purge! Three such former *obkom* first secretaries joined the ministerial apparatus (two at all-Union, the other at republic level); three moved into the *apparat* of the Committee of Party Control (an important institution in the context of the discipline campaign begun by Andropov) which following Arvid Pel'she's death in May 1983 has been headed by M. S. Solomentsev, and at least one of those promoted, M. G. Voropaev (formerly at Chelyabinsk) was his client, not Andropov's. One of the former Ukraine *obkom* first secretaries moved to Kiev to join the republic CC secretariat, while another, V. N. Taratuta (Vinnitsa), was posted to Algeria as Soviet ambassador; possibly not a promotion, but certainly involving no loss of status. That leaves two personnel changes to account for: both are extremely significant.

The CPSU General Secretary controls local party cadres through the CC Department of Organisational-Party Work, so whoever heads that department has a key role to play in that process, and it is essential that the leader should be able to rely upon him absolutely. Since 1964 (from 1965 as a member of the Secretariat), this position had been held by I. V. Kapitonov who, although never accorded even candidate membership of the Politburo, was nonetheless closely identified with Brezhnev's cadres policy, and had close relations, too, with certain other members of the leadership; notably V. V. Grishin, first secretary of the Moscow city party committee. At the end of April 1983, it was announced that the head of the cadres department was now E. K. Ligachev, since November 1965 the first secretary of Tomsk *obkom*.[12]

Ligachev had no obvious career links with Andropov, or with any of Andropov's likely supporters. But he *did* have connections dating from the early 1960s with A. P. Kirilenko, for much of the preceding 18 years considered to be a probable successor to Brezhnev and the secretary and full Politburo member with general oversight of personnel appointments, especially in the RSFSR. Kirilenko had had ample opportunity to create his own network of clients; but with his political demise at the end of 1982 (probably as a consequence of Chernenko's machinations) those clients found themselves without a patron. Conversely, Andropov was a 'patron' without clients: it made political sense for him to select amongst Kirilenko's appointees when filling vacancies, particularly if the officials concerned shared his outlook and political preferences.[13] Ligachev, who otherwise might have languished in his Siberian outpost indefinitely, was no doubt glad to become the loyal executor of Andropov's cadres policy. Further, the departure early in July 1983 of N. A. Petrovichev to be chairman of the State Committee for Professional-Technical Education and who since June 1968 had been first deputy head of the Department of Organisational-Party Work and closely identified with Kapitonov, and his replacement by E. Z. Razumov, hitherto a deputy head, who also had links earlier in his career with Kirilenko, seemed to consolidate Andropov's hold over the crucially important areas of personnel appointments. Ligachev's promotion to full secretary status at the CC plenum in December 1983 was apparently additional confirmation of this; although rumours[14] that Gorbachev had by then acquired broad responsibility for cadres under Andropov, coupled with Andropov's prolonged absence from public view, raises the question as to whose policy it was, and thus in whose interests it was being carried out.

It is tempting to conclude that Andropov's interests and Gorbachev's were at that time identical, at least with respect to cadres policy; and this may well be correct as far as Ligachev was concerned. But the same can hardly be said for the translation in June 1983 of G. V. Romanov from his first secretaryship of the Leningrad *obkom* to Moscow to join the all-Union Secretariat. The fact that he now met the vital criterion of being simultaneously both party secretary and a full member of the Politburo made him automatically a contender for the succession should Andropov resign or die, particularly as only two others fitted the bill, Gorbachev and Chernenko. Be that as it may, it was certainly the case that Romanov's loss of his *obkom* first secretaryship involved no demotion, but rather a substantial increase in political stature.

At the same June 1983 plenum that appointed Romanov to the Secretariat, V. I. Vorotnikov was made a candidate member of the Politburo. A former *obkom* first secretary and from 1975 to 1979 a first deputy chairman of the RSFSR Council of Ministers, Vorotnikov had been sent to Cuba as Soviet ambassador, a move that was widely construed as a demotion (he was, incidentally, also a Kirilenko client). But in July 1983 he was brought home, almost certainly at Andropov's instigation, to assume the first secretaryship of the Krasnodar kraikom[15] in place of S. F. Medunov, one of the three dismissals in the later Brezhnev period. Obviously now an Andropov client, Vorotnikov, a few days after his promotion to candidate member of the Politburo (ironically at the same plenum that expelled Medunov from the CC for corruption), was appointed chairman of the Council of Ministers of the RSFSR, thus filling the vacancy caused by Solomentsev's move to the Committee of Party Control. Six months later, at the December 1983 plenum, Vorotnikov was accorded full membership of the Politburo: an astonishing rate of promotion.

If the career destinies of the outgoing *obkom* first secretaries suggest a somewhat contradictory picture of, on the one hand, enhanced support for Andropov yet, on the other, not to perhaps such an extensive degree as would appear from superficial analysis of quantitative change, what about the *incoming* replacements? Did they conform to the Brezhnevite stability-of-cadres pattern by virtue of their being drawn from amongst local personnel? Or were the new Andropov appointees sent in from the centre?

Again, the picture is mixed and it is not possible to draw an unambiguous conclusion from the empirical evidence. In six out of the 21 cases involving full members of the CC, the new *obkom* first secretary had been brought in from a different *regional* party organisation, but only three had been sent from the centre (two former CC inspectors and an RSFSR ex-minister). But 12 replacements were local cadres in the Brezhnevite sense: six had been party second secretary in the same *obkom*; four, chairmen of the parallel *oblispolkom* or its equivalent in the case of an autonomous soviet socialist republic (ASSR); and two had been first secretaries of the capital-city party committee of the ASSR on which the *obkom* was based.[16]

Soon after coming to office in November 1982, Andropov's health began to deteriorate. His physical appearance worsened alarmingly; he had to be supported by aides when meeting the Finnish President in June 1983, and at the Supreme Soviet session later that month he was unable to go to the rostrum, so delivered his speech from his seat. Last seen in public on 18 August, when he received a group of visiting US senators in the Kremlin, Andropov died on the morning of 9 February 1984, just 15 months after coming to power.

Andropov was succeeded as CPSU General Secretary on 13 February 1984 by Konstantin Ustinovich Chernenko. Thirteen months later, on 10 March 1985, Chernenko died and was replaced the next day by Mikhail Sergeevich Gorbachev. In the interim, there had been only one change in the composition of the central party leadership: on 20 December 1984, Marshal Ustinov, Minister of Defence of the USSR and a full member of the Politburo, died (his successor as minister was Marshal S. L. Sokolov, but he was accorded candidate membership of the Politburo only in April 1985 after Gorbachev's accession).

Fate had been kind to Gorbachev. Had Chernenko held on for just a few more months, Gorbachev would have been denied the opportunity to make his mark on the new, revised party programme, the revised party statutes, and, most important of all in an immediate sense, on the composition of the new CC to be elected at the forthcoming congress in February 1986. It is true that Gorbachev, as part of a deal with the 'Old Guard', acted as almost a joint General Secretary during Chernenko's time in office and, as such, undoubtedly was able to exert considerable influence upon appointments. But that is not the same as having the title, status and authority of General Secretary, and thus a much freer hand in the placement of cadres. The timing of Chernenko's death, coming so soon after the deaths of two previous General Secretaries, was favourable to Gorbachev also in the sense that the very age and decrepitude of the old Brezhnevite residue in the leadership created a situation in which Gorbachev was able to act decisively on appointments to an extent that previous leaders would have found impossible at the same stage in their incumbency.

In the 12½ months that Chernenko was General Secretary there were 14 changes of *obkom* first secretary. However, the fact that one of these came about as the result of the death of the incumbent, and that out of seven more there were only three retirements (the other four being simply transfers of existing first secretaries), suggests that Gorbachev's room for manoeuvre was quite limited in the face of Chernenko's preference to leave the situation alone. Moreover, those who retired were aged 62, 69 and 73. One 'retirement' that *can* probably be attributed to Gorbachev was that of I. A. Bondarenko, first secretary of Rostov *obkom* since 1966. He was pensioned in July 1984 and thanked by the Politburo for his service to party and state in an announcement published in *Pravda*.[17] His replacement was A. V. Vlasov, hitherto first secretary of the Chechen-Ingush *obkom*, who was appointed to the Rostov post at a meeting of the *obkom* attended by Ligachev, in his capacity as head of the CC Department of Organisational-Party Work. Later, the real reason for Bondarenko's 'retirement' emerged: Rostov *oblast* was awash with corruption (and the implication that Vlasov had been drafted in to clean it up was confirmed indirectly in January 1986 when he was appointed to the post of Minister of Internal Affairs of the USSR in succession to Fedorchuk, a Brezhnev–Chernenko client).

If Gorbachev managed to effect only a handful of real changes in the 13 months that Chernenko held office, he certainly moved quickly in the slightly shorter period that elapsed between his becoming General Secretary and the convening of the twenty-seventh congress, a period during which there were 46 changes of incumbent *obkom* first secretary (30 per cent of the total). However, impressive though this clearing-out was, once again, a word of caution is necessary. In a couple of instances, the first secretary *was* dismissed for 'shortcomings' in his work (for example, V. P. Esin in the Navoi *oblast*, Uzbekistan, and A. Askarov, first secretary of Chimkent *obkom* in Kazakhstan who, using state funds, had built himself a luxuriously furnished dwelling and hunting lodge while a nearby children's hospital remained uncompleted for lack of resources). Four secretaries were transferred to 'other work' and, given that their whereabouts are now unknown, it may be assumed that they, too, were dropped. In one case, retirement was due to ill health, and in another it has not been possible to ascertain the cause of the first secretary's leaving office. But in 18 instances, the reason for leaving office was given as retirement on pension, and closer investigation shows that the *average* age of this group was 66, with the distribution as follows:

Aged 60–64	6
Aged 65–70	9
Aged 70 and over	2
Age not ascertained	1
Total	18

Now, it may be that these 18 first secretaries would have preferred not to have retired at that juncture, and that in Brezhnev's or Chernenko's day they would not have been called upon to do so. Nonetheless, in the great majority of cases, retirement was not intrinsically unreasonable, given their advanced age. In other words, while Gorbachev was undoubtedly clearing out the *obkom* stratum, he was at the same time careful to pick 'soft' targets.

The remaining 19 (out of 46) changes are accounted for by either promotions or horizontal transfers without loss of status, a significant number of them into the governmental apparatus (where Gorbachev's axe has cut deepest of all), again suggesting that the turnover at party *obkom* level, while substantial, should not be exaggerated. Indeed, part of the pattern that has emerged under Gorbachev is of a new, vigorous, determined party leader cutting into the dead wood of ministerial inertia and self-interest who is at the same time seeking to reinvigorate his party apparatus. In that latter respect, it is noticeable that Gorbachev has reversed the practice established by Brezhnev: instead of favouring local cadres against the centre, Gorbachev has tended to send functionaries from the CC apparatus (particularly CC inspectors) out from the centre and into the provinces to take control of the regional organisations there. In other words, Gorbachev has been reasserting the political control of the centre over the periphery, a control that had been weakened dangerously during the years of 'stability of cadres'.

However, there is yet another twist to this game of *apparat* snakes and ladders. While the centre has been re-establishing control over the periphery, 'healthy' elements from the periphery have been brought to the centre in order to overwhelm and oust the 'Old Guard' and to energise the top party leadership. Some have come as ministers in the governmental apparatus (such as V. S. Murakhovskii, sometime patron of Gorbachev, then – the positions reversed – his client and successor in Stavropol, who was brought to Moscow in November 1985 to head the new State Agro-Industrial Committee of the USSR). Others have been given Politburo and/or Secretariat status (please see Tables 5.4 and 5.5).

It has been a complex process, and one which must have absorbed a great deal of Gorbachev's attention and energy (although he has been assisted greatly by having Ligachev as his stern, loyal executor). Yet the point about Soviet politics, and the point with which this chapter began, is that General Secretaries, unlike prime ministers

Table 5.4 Politburo and Secretariat of the CPSU CC (as at 6 March 1986 following the plenum that day of the CPSU CC at the close of the twenty-seventh Congress)

Politburo full membership	Secretariat
Gorbachev, M. S.	Gorbachev (Gen. Sec.)
Aliev, G. A.	
Vorotnikov, V. I.	
Gromyko, A. A.	
Zaikov, L. N.	Zaikov
Kunaev, D. A.	
Ligachev, E. K.	Ligachev
Ryzhkov, N. I.	
Solomentsev, M. S.	
Chebrikov, V. M.	
Shevardnadze, E. A.	
Shcherbitskii, V. V.	
Candidate membership	
Demichev, P. N.	
Dolgikh, V. I.	Dolgikh
El'tsin, B. N.	
Slyunkov, N. N.	
Sokolov, S. L.	
Solov'ev, Yu. F.	
Talyzin, N. V.	
	Biryukova, A. P.
	Dobrynin, A. F.
	Zimyanin, M. V.
	Medvedev, V. A.
	Nikonov, V. P.
	Razumovskii, G. P.
	Yakovlev, A. N.

and presidents in competitive party systems, have a far from free hand in forming a government. Much of the skill, therefore, lies in a Soviet leader's ability to place his supporters in key positions, notable amongst which are the *obkom* first secretaryships. It is something that he *must* do as quickly as possible, for it is a necessary precondition to his securing his place in office and to putting into effect his policy preferences. By March 1986, Gorbachev had cleansed and reordered his party and ministerial apparatuses. Literally and metaphorically, he now had to deliver the goods.

Table 5.5   Politburo and Secretariat of the CC of the CPSU
(as at 6 March 1986)

	Date (month/year) of first appointment to:		
	Full member Politburo	*Candidate member Politburo*	*Secretariat*
Gorbachev, M. S.	10/1980		11/1978
Aliev, G. A.	11/1982	3/1976	
Vorotnikov, V. I.	12/1983	6/1983	
Gromyko, A. A.	4/1973		
Zaikov, L. N.	3/1986		7/1985
Kunaev, D. A.	4/1971	4/1966	
Ligachev, E. K.	4/1985		12/1983
Ryzhkov, N. I.	4/1985		11/1982 (–10/85)
Solomentsev, M. S.	12/1983	11/1971	12/1966 (–71)
Chebrikov, V. M.	4/1985	12/1983	
Shevardnadze, E. A.	7/1985	11/1978	
Shcherbitskii, V. V.	4/1971	10/1961	
Demichev, P. N.		4/1966	10/1961 (–74)
Dolgikh, V. I.		5/1982	12/1972
El'tsin, B. N.		2/1986	7/1985 (2/86)
Slyunkov, N. N.		3/1986	
Sokolov, S. L.		4/1985	
Solov'ev, Yu. F.		3/1986	
Talyzin, N. V.		10/1985	
Biryukova, A. P.			3/1986
Dobrynin, A. F.			3/1986
Zimyanin, M. V.			3/1976
Medvedev, V. A.			3/1986
Nikhonov, V. P.			4/1985
Razumovskii, G. P.			3/1986
Yakovlev, A. N.			3/1986

Notes

1. An earlier version of this chapter, following its presentation to the
    Workshop on Political Succession at the Joint Sessions of Workshops
    of the ECPR at Salzburg, April 1984, was published in mimeographed
    form in May 1984 as Discussion Paper No. 2 by the Centre for Russian
    and Soviet Studies at the University of Essex. Since then it has been
    substantially revised and updated.
2. USSR, *XXV s''ezd KPSS* (Minutes of the XXV Congress of the
    CPSU), 1976.

3. T. H. Rigby (ed.), *The Stalin Dictatorship: Khrushchev's 'Secret Speech' and other documents* (Sydney: Sydney University Press, 1968) p. 48.
4. In 1962, Khrushchev divided ('bifurcated', as it was commonly called) the party, state, Komsomol and trade union apparatuses into industrial and agricultural branches. Hence, instead of there being a single *oblast* party organisation, there were usually two, each headed by a first secretary.
5. USSR, *XXIII s"ezd KPSS*, 1966, pp. 88, 90.
6. USSR, *XXV s"ezd KPSS*, p. 96.
7. USSR, *XXIV s"ezd KPSS*, 1971, p. 124.
8. See the *Observer*, 19 February 1984; *Guardian*, 1 March 1984; *The Times*, 2 March 1984.
9. At the time of the USSR Supreme Soviet elections in March 1979 there were 155 party *obkoms*. By March 1984 there were 157, a figure that has stayed constant since then. However, as neither of the two *obkoms* created since 1979 appears in the present analysis, N in all cases is 155.
10. In one instance, that of S. F. Medunov (Krasnodar), the dismissal was almost certainly brought about by Andropov, not Brezhnev. For further discussion of this point, see note 15.
11. *Pravda*, 23 February 1983.
12. *Pravda*, 30 April 1983, p. 2.
13. For an original discussion of this and related points, see Radio Liberty Research Bulletin RL 405/83: 'Andropov in power: the succession reconsidered', by Michel Tatu (first published in French in *Politique Internationale*, October 1983).
14. See, for example, 'Andropov fails to meet party reform target' by Mark Frankland, *Observer*, 5 February 1984.
15. Brezhnev was taking his customary summer holiday, leaving Andropov in charge. It is thought that this afforded Andropov opportunity to effect the change in Krasnodar.
16. In an *obkom* based upon an ASSR, it is usual for the first secretary to belong to the nationality group that gives its name to the republic, and for the second secretary to be a Slav, usually a Russian. To maintain this practice, it is often necessary to draw upon the first secretary of the ASSR's capital city's party committee when a replacement is needed.
17. *Pravda*, 26 July 1984, p. 2.

6 Political Succession in the People's Republic of China: Rule by Purge

Eberhard Sandschneider[1]

The study of political succession in Communist systems has always been characterised by a certain mixture of academic research and crystal-ball gazing. The 'Whither China' literature up to 1976 presented itself more or less as a collective attempt at advanced speculation about who was to succeed Mao Zedong. Assessing the political status and the improving or worsening health of the incumbent, and ruminating about 'the unforeseeable future' in China's power contest were among the primary tasks pursued by China watchers all over the world.[2] Of course, it is tempting to speculate on 'who is going to make it' when top leadership positions – especially in highly centralised and hierarchical systems – become vacant due to death or political struggles.

What about political science and its abilities to forecast future events? As Lucian W. Pye has pointed out,

> social sciences in general are not very good at dealing with succession problems in any non-electoral context. The difficulty is that succession issues are usually resolved by the maneuvering of a few principals at the pinnacles of power, while the social sciences are best only at explaining or predicting behaviour at the two extremes of mass action (sociology) and individual conduct (depth psychology).[3]

Our task of forecasting future developments is further complicated by the basic hostility of Communist systems towards open information on unresolved issues and the resulting lack of information on the rules of the game, on persons, policies, and procedures: not forgetting that in China interpretation of the recent past is still changing as a result of leadership conflicts. It is, however, no exaggeration to regard aspects of political succession as basic constituents of the policy process in the People's Republic of China (PRC). Thomas W. Robinson points out that

> much of the domestic politics of China since 1953, and perhaps significant elements in its foreign policy, were conducted in terms of differences between the chosen successors, Liu Shaoqi or Lin Biao, and their nominator, Mao, or in terms of jugglings for positions among the various groups and personages thought to be contending for the right to wear the mantle of leadership in the post-Mao period.[4]

In other words, at stake was not only the resolution of a leadership conflict involving comparably few top cadres, but also the highly debated overall future orientation of Chinese politics between the Liuistic Scylla of material incentives and evolutionary development, and the Maoistic Charybdis of mass mobilisation and great leaps towards a bright Communist future.

Considering this framework it is no wonder that the piecing together of Chinese succession politics mainly concentrated on answering three questions. Who will be the next dominant leader after Mao? Will the present gerontocracy continue to rule China? What will be the role of functional subsystems such as the People's Liberation Army (PLA) in future succession conflicts? At a time when everyone once again seems to be speculating on who is going to follow Deng Xiaoping, on whether the Cultural Revolutionary Left (the supporters of the so-called Gang of Four around Mao's widow Jiang Qing) is eliminated for good, and why everything will have to be as one predicts it to be, my academic interest is confined here to an analysis of the five most important case studies of political succession in China's recent past: the two unsuccessful attempts of Liu Shaoqi (1959–66) and Lin Biao (1969–71) to secure positions as personal successors to Mao Zedong with the charismatic incumbent still alive, the abortive attempt of Jiang Qing and her Cultural Revolutionary supporters to establish themselves as Mao's heirs (September 1976), and the ensuing conflict between Hua Guofeng and Deng Xiaoping (1977–80) over supreme power in Beijing, which ended – for the time being – with Deng's victory at the Fifth Plenum of the Eleventh Chinese Communist Party Central Committee (CCP/CC) in February 1980.

Forgoing the temptation to indulge in the elaboration of still another keen and (ideally) correct scenario for tomorrow's development, let us look instead at yesterday's scenarios in order to learn by analysis of differences and similarities whether it is possible to work out a basic pattern for political succession in China that might prove more realistic and reliable than mere speculation on the political future of today's contenders. The basic aim of this chapter, therefore, is to seek to answer whether every resolution of a political succession conflict in the PRC is unique, without any comparable aspects, or whether there are basic features or even patterns of political succession that allow reasonable prognoses for future events.

The question, of course, is not new, and there have been many attempts to build models and develop new approaches to bring some light to the politics of succession in Communist systems in general.[5] Analysts of Soviet politics have put forward at least three different models:

1. a totalitarian model, which regards the individual leader's personal and all-encompassing rule as 'paramount in determining the nature of both public policy and political structures';
2. a conflict model, which 'suggests that policy and political structures are shaped by the nature of the conflict between individuals jockeying for political power';
3. a bureaucratic model, which 'places less emphasis upon the individual leader, suggesting that the way in which a system is governed is more a function of rules and norms within the political system'.[6]

For the specific context of Chinese politics, Robinson suggests a distinction between four approaches:

1. an environmental approach focusing 'on such matters as the stage and direction of the Chinese economy, the population–food balance, the Soviet border threat, and the status of Taiwan, rather than on how political decisions themselves are made';[7]
2. a personality approach, particularly discussing 'individuals, personalities, factions, and the generational question':[8]
3. a societal approach, which postulates that society (defined as the social environment, including 'the set of influences that stem from Chinese culture, Chinese history, and the structure and operation of Chinese social-political familial–economic institutions') determines politics;[9]

4. a political approach, which regards politics as 'an atmosphere in which all political actors are immerged and which immutably conditions their every act';[10]

Pye differentiates between three perspectives on the succession question in China:

1. a historical perspective, which we mainly follow in our discussion below;
2. a psychological perspective, focusing on the dominant role of Mao;
3. a generational perspective, which arises from the structures of clearly defined revolutionary generations within the Chinese leadership elite.[11]

However elaborate and sophisticated the approaches described above may be, the state of the art is unsatisfactory because crucial elements of political succession in Communist systems remain unknown to us. From a comparative point of view, one has to take into account the following characteristic features. First of all, there is no exact procedural consensus among the ruling elite either on how to get rid of an incumbent or on exactly how to choose a new one[12] – a problem closely related to the specific feature in Communist systems of life-long tenure in power positions (with the marked exception of Yugoslavia). As a result, succession conflicts have to be solved by elite infighting, which again necessitates the cultivation of power bases from which to start attacks and on which to fall back for political security. In a moment of crisis, however, it is not only the mere existence of a power base but above all the ability to mobilise one's constituencies that is crucial for the outcome of a power contest. Finally, we do not know the exact relevance of issues, of alternative and mutually exclusive policies, and of the aggregation of interests to the outcome of a succession struggle. In other words, are issues dealt with as they come up or are they seized upon or created for the purpose of advancing one's own cause?[13] Although we know that there must be conflicting groups behind the monolithic screen of ideologically prescribed unity, we do not know exactly who belongs to them, or what is the respective political weight of their members until they have been unmasked and criticised by the regime.[14] These, then, are the pitfalls for analysts, leaving them with the dilemma of scant historical knowledge and the innate problem of unpredictability.

After this short excursion into the state of the art, let us return to our previously sketched approach of looking at political succession in China from an historical point of view that will take into account not only how a successor position is reached by a candidate, but also how and with what results it is defended (see Table 6.1). The actual outcome of succession conflicts in the PRC shows that three of the five contenders for Mao's mantle who succeeded in winning the position of successor with Mao's approval sooner or later lost their number two status to their opponents: Liu Shaoqi was purged during the Cultural Revolution, Lin Biao fell victim to a coalition of political enemies in September 1971, and Hua Guofeng was forced to step back by the influence of a rising Deng Xiaoping in February 1980. Some remarks on the fate of the losers will finally lead us to the question of the transition from charismatic to institutionalised rule in China and to possible scenarios for the future.

Table 6.1   PRC: succession since 1949*

Date	Head of State†	Head of Government‡	Head of Party§
9.49		Zhou Enlai	Mao Zedong
10.10.49	Mao Zedong		
4.59	Liu Shaoqi¶		
1.67	vacant		
10.68	Dong Biwu		
1.75	Ye Jianying‖		
7.2.76		Hua Guofeng (acting)	
7.4.76		Hua Guofeng	
10.76			Hua Guofeng
10.9.80		Zhao Ziyang	
12.80			Hu Yaobang
6.83	Li Xiannian		
1.87			Zhao Ziyang (acting)

* Lin Biao, the 'Gang of Four' and Deng Xioaping are not included as none of them ever held one of these three top positions.
† Chairman of the PRC.
‡ Premier.
§ Chairman of the CC of the CCP.
¶ *De jure* until October 1968.
‖ Between 1975 and 1983 the position of Chairman of the PRC was officially abolished and its function taken over by the Chairman of the NPC's (National People's Congress's) Standing Committee.

THE MAKING OF A SUCCESSOR

For any process of political succession in Communist systems we may theoretically distinguish three possible *modes of initiation* that are typical of political systems where there are no clearly defined regulations for the transfer of power, and where – in contrast to systems with constitutionally defined terms of incumbency – life-long tenure of a power position is the rule. These are: succession for political reasons, succession for natural causes (death), and succession after voluntary resignation of the incumbent.[15]

In China the first mode, which assumes the leader is 'forced from power by the political pressures of opponents',[16] was not of great importance during Mao's tenure, although one might regard Mao's position in the period between the failure of the Great Leap Forward and the outbreak of the Cultural Revolution (1959–66) as a politically enforced as well as physically motivated semi-resignation.[17] It did, however, serve as the mode of initiation for the struggle between Hua Guofeng and Deng Xiaoping.

The second mode, succession as a result of the death of the incumbent, clearly initiated one of the major watersheds of Chinese politics after 1949, the succession crisis of September 1976. For the first time the contest was not for the second position after Mao, but for the overall leadership of post-Mao China. The power struggle was correspondingly fierce and intense. It took the winning coalition between moderate party cadres and the military about a month to eliminate the leaders of the Cultural Revolutionary Left in Beijing's top power echelons; the effects of the ensuing mass campaign to eliminate the Left's supporters in middle and lower levels of the party and state are still felt in the present move towards party rectification.

Before Mao's death, the choices of successors presumptive were clearly motivated by the third mode, Mao's voluntary resignation from some of his leadership duties as a result of the basic dilemma he shared with other charismatic or absolute leaders. The unassailability of such leaders to a large extent stems from the absence of an obvious successor candidate and is, of course, endangered once the necessarily growing influence of a 'crown prince' and the possibility of an accelerating shift of loyalties is felt. The advantage of a secure position is matched sooner or later by the need to lay the foundations for a smooth succession by a leader or a leadership group which will follow the established political paths and fulfil the present leader's

options and policies without being restricted in its actions by a
marked lack of authority during the period of transition.

Before 1949 and in the following decade Mao obviously favoured
another option that combined elements of the two modes most
relevant to his tenure. With the cultivation of Liu Shaoqi as
designated – albeit never officially endorsed – successor, he pursued
a leadership arrangement based on a 'two front' policy. In Mao's
own words:

> Originally, for the sake of the state security and in view of the
> lessons in connection with Stalin of the Soviet Union, we created
> two fronts. I was in the second front while other comrades were in
> the first front ... Since I was in the second front, I did not take
> charge of daily work.
>
> Many things were done by others and their prestige was thus
> cultivated, so that when I met with God, the State would not be
> thrown into great convulsions. Everybody approved of this
> view of mine.[18]

However, the dilemma described above and the historical outcome of
Mao's successor choices indicate the innate opposition between
leader and successor-to-be that for Liu Shaoqi and Lin Biao was
instrumental in their respective downfalls. Without reducing the
dynamics of Chinese politics to the Mao-centric statement, favoured
especially by Taiwanese scholars,[19] his attempts to remove powerful
succession candidates from their positions must be regarded as pre-
eminent in shaping the course of Chinese politics in the 1960s and
1970s. We shall have to return to this aspect of succession politics
when we discuss the situation of the successor defending himself. For
our present purpose it is sufficient to underline the enormous impact
Mao personally had on the choice of the second man in the
leadership hierarchy and the importance of Mao's role as the
dominant source of legitimacy.

Legitimacy in China, again, is not defined by objectively established
rules of law or prodecure recognised by all parts and actors of the
polity. The reference to Mao or a depersonalised Mao Zedong
Thought as the one-time intellectual medium for winning powers in
China and the way to preserve power for the CCP today is still indis-
pensable. To date, none of Mao's heirs has tried to establish a
legitimacy of his own without continuing reference to Mao. Even
Deng Xiaoping, the architect of the post-1976 de-Maoisation,

recently intensified the cultivation of an image of a close relationship to Mao and Mao Zedong Thought. In a countrywide study campaign, his *Selected Works*, published on 1 July 1983, were immediately praised by the national press as an outstanding contribution to the revolutionary development of Mao Zedong Thought.[20] An issue of the official *Red Flag* journal[21] pictured Deng with Mao on the front page in a position that during the 1960s was reserved for Lin Biao: a towering Mao in teacher's gesture seems to be instructing an obedient disciple half his size.

Deng's relationship to Mao may be the most problematic of all possible successors so far, but his predecessors also had to compete with Mao for political power and public prestige. From the late 1950s up until the Cultural Revolution, Liu Shaoqi built his own power base in more or less constant conflict with (at least sometimes) a publicly disapproving Mao. Lin Biao, incessantly waving the 'Little Red Book', primarily relied on his image of sworn follower and humble disciple of the great helmsman. Common to both, however, was a strong power base in party and army, respectively.

Jiang Qing, and to a considerable extent Hua Guofeng, had to rely on Mao as their more or less sole source of legitimisation. The lack of a stable institutional background certainly was central to their unstable positions, and this leads us to identify another systemic prerequisite for securing a successor position. Although there can be no doubt about Mao's personal importance, it is somehow inconceivable that Liu Shaoqi with his towering position in the party apparatus, and Lin Biao, the supreme leader of the army – the nation's most powerful organisation at the moment of his demise – could have been purged simply because Mao chose to purge them. There must have been other reasons and these most probably are to be found in some of the characteristics of political power in China.

In a remarkable analysis [22] Lowell Dittmer suggests a distinction between two types of power in China: formal power, that is, 'the power that automatically accompanies certain ranks and posts in the Party or State [or military] hierarchies' and whose bonds of loyalty are easily passed on to the next occupant, and informal power, which 'consists of the long-term, diffuse, and relatively disinterested alliances that an actor collects along his recruitment path into the central decision-making area'. The conceptual distinction lies in the fact that any high official in a figurehead position may have the former without the latter, or a dominant political figure may base his position in large part on a system of informal power without necessarily seeking prominent posts and formal power. The two are, however, 'closely interdependent, and a prudent political actor will strive to acquire both'.[23] This places us at the core of a deeply entrenched factionalism that has been dubbed 'the curse of Chinese politics since the dawn of recorded history'[24] and which, at least since the upheavals of the Cultural Revolution, seems to make up the basic network of power distribution, leadership relations, promotions and purges in China.

The five who aspired to succeed Mao differ widely in acquaintance with and mobilisation of their respective formal and informal power bases. Liu Shaoqi served as the primary representative of the party apparatus between 1949 and 1966–7. His formal power was based on his positions as Chairman of the PRC (taken over from Mao in 1959 and in itself more a state position) and as Vice Chairman of the CCP. These positions were almost ideally complemented by his experience as 'the leading organizer of the network of Communist Party branches, labor unions, and various student and 'front' organisations' that 'formed the skeleton onto which the civilian Party organization was later grafted'.[25] The background of his fellow purge victims during the Cultural Revolution, many of whom had worked together with Liu in the 'white' areas during the 1930s and 1940s, revealed that he must also have acquired a strong local power base in his capacity as former director of the CCP North China Bureau.[26] During his long service in official assignments within almost all important sub-systems of the Chinese Communist institutional network,[27] he succeeded in establishing a web of relationships (the all-important *guanxi* in Chinese political culture) that during the Cultural Revolutionary struggle for power proved extremely resistant to attacks from outside. It even took Mao three years of hard struggles to drag him down.

Lin Biao's formal power base was clearly the army, especially his loyalty group in the Fourth Field Army, the Central Military Organs (with the exception of the General Political Department), and the air force. His political career rested on a combination of factors: his close relationship to Mao, his formal command position as Minister of Defence, his status as a member of the Politburo and CC, and above all his vast network of informal relations based on the system of field army affiliations.[28] Lin Biao's personal rise to the second position in party and state can, of course, only be understood in the overall political context of the Cultural Revolution, which catapulted the army and its predominant leader into control of the nerves of Chinese politics. His record of having made many enemies within and outside the military and his lack of a sufficient informal power base in party and state, however, made him vulnerable to the attacks of a coalition between Mao, old party cadres, succession contenders, and dissenting military leaders in the provinces.[29]

Given the advantage of hindsight, the Cultural Revolutionary Left's position, in comparison with that of Liu Shaoqi and Lin Biao, must be regarded as extremely weak. As the actual outcome in October 1976 shows, its sole source of legitimisation was Mao and disappeared with him. The Left's figurehead Jiang Qing, for example, lacked appreciable service experience in the pivotal positions of party, state, and military because of her highly specialised career experience in the field of culture and propaganda. The failure of the Left's efforts to establish a solid and reliable base within the military [30] and its unsuccessful reliance on the urban militia and the 'revolutionary masses' were the weakest aspects of its attack on opponents between 1973 and 1976. Its strong position in Shanghai, in parts of the labour unions and in the mass media sector could not overcome its unstable network of informal affiliations.

The same holds true, at least in part, for Hua Guofeng, who after the death of Mao was initially invested with the insignia of successorship. A typical party-administration cadre with a local base in Mao's home province, Hunan, Hua first came to prominence as Mao's chosen candidate for the position of premier in February 1976 (he was appointed acting Premier on 7 February, and officially inaugurated on 7 April 1976). Among his principal supporters in the central leadership were the Minister of Defence Ye Jianying and the Vice Premier Li Xiannian, while crucial military support came from the Beijing Military Region under its commander, Chen Xilian.[31] But as a typical 'Cultural Revolutionary upstart',[32] Hua lacked both a well-developed formal base in the centre (admitted only in August/ September 1971) and an appreciable network of informal relations; perhaps with the exception of the public security sector and the Canton Military Region where he served as political commissar (and concurrently first political commissar of Hunan Military District). Again we have to conclude that Hua's successor position was based almost exclusively on Mao's blessing. In October 1976 the story arose, obviously deliberately fostered by Hua and his clients, that on 28 April of the same year Mao had told Hua: 'With you in charge I am at ease' (*Ni banshi wo fangxin*). It is therefore no wonder that the decline of Mao's image was followed by the decline and fall of Hua Guofeng [33] which – if the above quoted version is true – marks the third and final failure of Mao to set the course for an approved successor.

The political career of Deng Xiaoping, for the time being the last candidate for succession once again underlines the importance of the formal/informal network system. Deng's long career path since his return to China in 1924 from studies in France almost ideally combines service in the all-important political, military and economic subsystems.[34] With his local power base in Sichuan, he cultivated two important bases in the Second Field Army and in the Party Apparat which he headed as Secretary General of the CC between 1953 and 1967. The strength of his informal relations system may be clearly shown by the fact that he was twice purged and severely attacked as the 'number two capitalist roader within the party' and twice returned with the help of his followers to the same positions with even more political power. Within a few months of his first rehabilitation in April 1973, he had collected an impressive array of important leadership posts: Vice Chairman of the CCP/CC, member of the Standing Committee of the Politburo, Vice Chairman of the CCP/CC Military Commission, and the Chief of the General Staff of the PLA. In his capacity as Zhou Enlai's representative at numerous official receptions between 1974 and January 1975, he was widely regarded as the most likely successor to Zhou Enlai in case of the premier's death.

However, with the approval of Mao and by unanimous decision of the Politburo, he was again stripped of all official duties in April 1976 and fell back on his informal power network for personal and political security.[35] Perhaps the most interesting and striking example of the working and effectiveness of this informal system is the technique of building up pressure on Hua Guofeng and the party centre as it was used by Deng's long-time followers, Xu Shiyou and Wei Guoqing, under whose protection he was hiding in Canton after his second removal from power. In the name of the party and military organisations of Canton, they openly demanded the rehabilitation of Deng in a letter written on 1 February, 1977.[36] Their joint effort finally led to Deng's official rehabilitation by the Third Plenum of the Tenth Central Committee in July 1977. Nothing works better than firmly established *guanxi*!

The foregoing discussion of the respective power bases of contenders for succession to Mao now leads us to a closely related aspect.

According to Dittmer's analysis, it is not only the mere existence of formal and informal power networks that counts, but above all the ability to mobilise one's constituencies in a period of crisis or whenever a fundamental threat to one's position is anticipated. The traditional technique of mobilising a constituency is to convene meetings or – once already isolated and deprived of the right to convene meetings – by public self-criticism.[37] If in a situation of political antagonisms the necessity to mobilise a constituency is regarded as the last resort for political (and often personal) survival, the moment of truth for formal and informal power networks has come.[38]

As the historical data suggest, therefore, the following features of career pattern and political background strongly influence the development of a successor position:[39]

1. undisputed reference to Mao Zedong Thought as the ideological source of legitimisation;
2. long-standing career experience in important subsystems;
3. membership of the inner leadership core;
4. maintenance of a strong local power base;
5. extensive network of formal and informal power affiliations;
6. ability to mobilise power bases and constituencies.

To these one might add some personal requirements which are extremely difficult to observe objectively, such as close connections to essential leadership groups within the PLA, an instinct for political self-preservation, a 'record of not having made too many enemies',[40] the ability to handle difficult situations and, finally, public approval. The circle of candidates to which one is admitted only by cooptation is limited to the ranks of the Politburo and high echelons of the CCP's CC.

DEFENDING THE CLAIM TO SUCCESSION

It has been pointed out above that a candidate who succeeds in establishing a claim to succession either by common approval (Liu Shaoqi) or explicit party leadership decisions (Lin Biao, Hua Guofeng) immediately and almost inevitably enters a state of vulnerability that is characteristic of his position, especially if he is to follow a dominant charismatic leader. The dangers he has to face are manifold and range from systemic aspects typical of almost all successor arrangements in Communist systems to specific features of Chinese Communism.

The first problem he has to tackle is posed by the inherent tendency of complex organisations towards institutional self-assertion. The balance of power between factions or concurring sub-systems may lead to a joint effort by high- and middle-level cadres to curb the future leader's influence in time, not only to protect themselves 'from the capricious whims of a single individual but also [to] give them[selves] greater scope to exercise their own personal initiatives'.[41] 'Institutional jealousy' may be even further enhanced if it is probable that the appointed individual will promote not only his personal but also his institutional constituency's role in the political decision-making process. The joint effort of civilian party cadres – whether 'moderate' or 'Leftist' in political orientation – to restrain the PLA's influence on national politics before and after 1971 may be cited as one prominent example.

The second and, in the case of China, highly important danger arises from problematic personal and political relations between ruler and heir presumptive. As the cases of Liu Shaoqi and Lin Biao, who were both accused of attempted usurpation, show, the succession candidate may never be safe against a potential change of mind by his patron by which he may lose his primary source of legitimisation. In Myron Rush's word, the 'heir presumptive has a thin line to walk between becoming a robot at the command of the ruler and asserting his own will in ways that may awaken his patron's fears and suspicions. Since heirs are chosen because they are thought to have some capacity for rule, it is no wonder that they have tended to assert themselves.'[42] This relationship between patron and heir is obviously characterised by a closely woven net of political experiences, personal attitudes and psychological incompatibilities.[43] Whatever the exact reasons may be, the dangers for a successor's position become immense the moment the ruler openly defies his former choice.

Although it is obviously much more difficult to change succession arrangements than to institute them, the combined efforts of incumbent and potential succession rivals represent a considerable destabilising factor. Once the conflict becomes perceptible to opponents or breaks out openly, the successor's status normally comes under increasing attack and he himself is exposed to the manifold techniques of undermining and usurping his power. The following delineation of four tactical steps draws on internal documents and the observation of formal events during a power struggle.

First Step: Criticise the Policies Initiated by the Target

The initial stage of the conflict between Mao and Lin Biao after the Ninth Party Congress was characterised by Mao's open disapproval of Lin's propagation of a 'theory of genius' closely connected with the problem of how to fill the position of head of state. Further, Mao criticised the army's and thus Lin's workstyle as 'bureaucratic, subjective and formalistic',[44] and Lin's criteria for the selection of new cadres.[45] Similarly, Deng pushed ahead his preliminary attacks against Hua Guofeng at a PLA 'National Political Work Conference' (27 April–6 June, 1978) by attacking Hua's 'whatever' position[46] and at the same time propagating the opposite theorem of 'Practice is the sole criterion for truth'. After dismantling Hua's concept of rural policies based on the Dazhai model, Deng initiated his overall attack on Mao as Hua's primary source of legitimisation.[47] Such attacks on policies may be taken as tests of the relative strength of contenders for the build-up of future coalitions, and they seem to lay the foundation for an intensification of attacks during the following stages.

Second Step: Undermine the Target's Power Network

The primary technique used at this stage of conflict is to remove identifiable supporters already in office, or to prevent them from gaining further power positions whereby the target's formal and informal network could be increased. The aim of the aggressor clearly is the removal of substantial support and the final isolation of the target. Direct attacks at this stage of confrontation – if used at all – are shrouded by esoteric allusions and the use of historical figures as fictitious objects for indirect attacks on the real target.[48] For reasons of political stability, Lin Biao was not officially mentioned by name for more than six months after his purge, but referred to only as a 'Liu Shaoqi type political swindler'. During the campaign to criticise Lin Biao and Confucius, the Cultural Revolutionary Left clearly aimed at attacking Zhou Enlai by implying he was a modern Confucius. And Deng Xiaoping was referred to only as an 'unrepentant capitalist roader within the party' between January and April 1976.

These examples may suffice to indicate the difficulties encountered in decoding this kind of esoteric communication and may hint
at the caution with which attackers proceed so long as the outcome of
their endeavour seems uncertain. In the case of Lin Biao, the filling of
leadership positions in the newly created Provincial Party Committees between December 1970 and August 1971 was clearly marked by
the conflicting aims of Lin and his opponents. As the final outcome
shows, Lin Biao's Fourth Field Army loyalty group dominated five
provinces, participated in a strong position in two, and held a weaker
position in six provincial leaderships, whereas 14 provinces were
under the dominant influence of his opponents and two under the
domain of the Cultural Revolutionary Left.[49] The first move, against
Lin's regional power base, was followed by a closing-in on his
position in the centre. After the purge of Chen Boda at the Second
Plenum of the Ninth Central Committee (23 August–6 September
1970, at Lushan), the self-criticism of Lin's top military supporters for
their backing of Chen Boda's position at the Plenum, and the two
formal steps of reorganising the CCP Military Affairs Commission
and Beijing Military Region, Lin Biao's position was ready to be
assaulted. The removal of actual or potential supporters and the promotion of Lin's competitors among the military[50] considerably
favoured the process of increasing his isolation.

Again, a similar technique was used by Deng Xiaoping against
Hua Guofeng. Immediately after his second comeback, Deng started
to undermine Hua's stronghold in the party centre. After the dismissal of Wu De and Chen Xilian and their replacement by Deng's
supporters, Lin Hujia and Qin Jiwei, he proceeded to reduce
further the number of Hua's men on the Politburo Standing Committee between the Eleventh Party Congress and the Fourth Plenum of
the Eleventh Central Committee from seven to three or two while he
himself increased the number of his supporters from seven to 13 or
14.[51] The Fifth Plenum (23–9 February 1980) saw the completion of
his endeavours and the almost total isolation of Hua Guofeng. As a
result Hua was forced to hand over the position of premier to Zhao
Ziyang at the Third Plenum of the Fifth NPC on 10 September 1980.
Although he still held the position of Chairman of the CCP/CC and
of the CCP's Military Commission, his base had eroded to such an
extent that the final assault was merely a question of how and
when.

Third Step: Attack the Target Personally

The process of successfully eroding a target's overall power base finally leads to the lifting of the veil over his real identity when the power struggle enters a stage of almost 100 per cent irreversibility. In the case of Liu Shaoqi the transition between the second and third stage seems to have been marked by his demotion from rank two to eight in the Politburo name list at the Eleventh Plenum of the Eighth Central Committee in August 1966. But by confessing his 'errors' and making profound self-criticism, Liu obviously was able to retain his already shaky position for another couple of months.

The best example is again provided by the Deng/Hua conflict. Deng Xiaoping's direct assault on Hua was bluntly launched during a series of nine consecutive and obviously conflict-laden Politburo sessions between 10 November and 5 December 1980.[52] Hua was forced to open self-criticism for his adherence to Leftist policies, for his opposition to the rehabilitation of Deng and other veteran cadres purged during the Cultural Revolution, and for his wrong economic policies. Self-criticism, which may sometimes be useful for political survival in early stages of conflict, now only marked the last step for Hua. Since the verdict was clear, there was no more need to cover the actual conflicts and a remarkably open diction was used in the 'unanimous' resolution of the Politburo:

Comrade Hua Guofeng eagerly produced and accepted a new cult of personality. He had himself called the wise leader, and his own pictures hung beside the pictures of comrade Mao Zedong, accepted poems and songs in his honor, and felt comfortable about this. This situation continued to exist until shortly before this year ...

During the last four years, comrade Hua Guofeng has also done some successful work, but it is extremely clear that he lacks the political and organisational ability to be the Chairman of the Party. That he should never have been appointed chairman of the Military Commission, everybody knows ...

Comrade Hua Guofeng suggested that he should resign his posts, and that, even before the Sixth Plenum, he wanted no longer to lead the work of the Politburo, the Politburo's Standing Commission, and the Military Commission. The Politburo holds that he indeed should concentrate his strength on deliberating his problems, and therefore accepts his opinion that he no longer wants to lead the current work. But before the Sixth Plenum makes a final decision on this, he is still officially the chairman of the Party Center, and he will have to receive foreign guests in the capacity of the Center's Chairman.[53]

Thus the last step was clearly envisaged.

It remains to be said that in the periodically recurring context of highly dramatic factional infighting, the third step may be skipped. The conflict then immediately enters the last stage where a resolution is sought by means of physical coercion rather than by middle- or long-term power manoeuvering. The purges of Lin Biao and the Cultural Revolutionary Left certainly are representative examples of this kind of escalation.

Fourth Step: Purge or Remove the Target

Theoretically, the continuum of 'rectification' methods in the broadest sense of the word ranges from mere self-criticism, demotion, and the loss of power positions to expulsion from the party, criminal prosecution, and, finally, death (including the possibility of political murder). The political outcome of the inner-party struggle over the succession to Mao clearly shows a tendency toward a clustering 'at the coercive end of the continuum'.[54] A speculative answer about the reasons for this 'inhuman' – from a conventional point of view – character of politics in China may relate to the possibility and thus the danger of a 'reversal of verdicts'. As the political career of Deng Xiaoping demonstrates, a purge victim may come back under more favourable conditions and then start an overall revenge campaign (as Deng did with his rehabilitation policy). Even if the former opponent is now dead, his legacy and posthumous rehabilitation must be reckoned with (for example, the rehabilitation of Liu Shaoqi at the Fifth Plenum of the Eleventh Central Committee, 23–9 February, 1980; Liu died in prison in 1969).

Whatever the reasons, the political fate of Mao's successors presumptive so far is a fate of losers. Bereft of protection by supporters, attacked and stripped of political and personal security, their downfall almost inevitably resulted in political *and* personal disaster.

In spite of this formidable threat, the successor presumptive as target for removal attempts is, at least in the initial stages, not totally helpless. The counter-measures at his disposal are, of course, most effective and his chances for survival best during the first stage of attack. The defender's tactics may aim at a diversion of criticism by blurring certain points of the attack, or by pushing ahead other policies in order to break up the coalition of opponents during its process of formation. The successful attempt of the Cultural Revolutionary Left in 1972 to change the verdict on Lin Biao from 'ultra-Leftist' to 'ultra-Rightist' may be quoted as an especially instructive example of efforts to save as much of the Cultural Revolutionary 'Leftist' policies as possible and to remove its own political orientation from the centre of criticism. This more or less passive reaction to the initial tactical manoeuvering of opponents may be successfully complemented by an active ideological counter-attack such as that which characterised the ups and downs of the 'Campaign to Criticise Lin Biao and Confucius' (1973–5).

By making public self-criticism the defender may appeal to the traditional priority for re-education in Chinese Communist political culture, which ever since the rectification campaign of 1942 clearly stressed education, rectification, and redemption rather than punishment as long as the conflict was regarded as 'non-antagonistic'.[55] Once the attack proceeds to the second step of our above typology, the successor's only chance for a successful defence is immediate abandonment of supporters already under direct attack. The nonchalance with which Mao used this method of abandoning former and cultivating future supporters is both noteworthy and well-documented.[56] Liu Shaoqi and Peng Zhen, Lin Biao and Chen Boda, Hua Guofeng and Wu De are others who may be cited from the long list of possible examples. If the defender is not able to stop attacks at this critical stage of conflict development by a general mobilisation of his power network, his chances of preventing the imminent direct attack are close to zero. History shows that once opponents have pushed the confrontation to the level of personal attacks, the defender's political fate is almost certainly sealed. If one assumes at least some truth in Beijing's official version of the death of Lin Biao, it was exactly this dilemma that induced him to seek his survival in a desperate last move by plotting to kill Mao and take over political power by means of a military coup.

The depth of a succession crisis is revealed by the relative strength of these attacks and counter-measures. It ranges from the upheavals of the Cultural Revolution, which involved all parts of Chinese society and heavily shook the foundations of the whole system, to the relatively 'small scale' clashes in the party's top leadership circles in 1971 and 1976 that were normally followed by extensive criticism campaigns aimed at removing the loser's clientele, and to the almost 'orderly' removal of Hua Guofeng by majority decisions in the Politburo and CC. But the observer should be cautious in assuming from the discussion so far that any attack on a successor almost certainly leads to a positive result. Although this is definitely true for the examples presented in this essay, the reader should bear in mind that the successors might have been able to defend themselves successfully by managing attacks in the early stages of a critical confrontation. In Lowell Dittmer's words:

> Power proves itself when contested, and the relative utility of formal and informal power depends upon the intensity of such a contest. If the issue is routine, it is usually allocated to the official in charge of the appropriate functional 'system' for resolution . . . But if the issue defies routine decision-making procedures and provokes intractable opposition, it is likely to be defined as a 'contradiction between the enemy and ourselves' (*ti-wo mao-tun*), in which dissent is deemed illegitimate.[57]

Only under the circumstances of an antagonistic conflict is the vicious circle entered of 'purge or be purged'.

From an historical point of view the question of who is going to dominate political decision-making in China can certainly not be regarded as 'routine' since succession has tended to assume an antagonistic character. As a result we have to conclude that political rule in China all through the 1960s and 1970s was political rule by purge. But what about the future? Will conflicts about top leadership succession continue to assume the dramatic dimensions of the past, or will the ruling elite make greater efforts – last but not least for the sake of its own security – to push ahead the process of institutionalisation and regularisation of politics in China? A tentative approach to answering this question may lie in a look at the stages of political rule in China (see Table 6.2).

TOWARDS A 'TRANSITIONAL CONFLICT SYSTEM'

Attempts to describe Chinese politics in terms of periods of political rule or stages of internal development are numerous.[58] From a broader perspective and in comparison to other Communist systems, especially the Soviet Union, one may arrive at a three-stage model for the development of political rule in China which Jürgen Domes first proposed in the form presented below[59] with reference to Max Weber's sociology of political rule.

Table 6.2   Leadership positions in the PRC, 1977–86

Position	Period	Name	
		Pinyin	*Wade-Giles*
Party			
Chairman	Oct. 76–Dec. 80 (*de jure* June 81)	Hua Guofeng	Hua Kuo-feng
	Dec. 80–Sep. 82	Hu Yaobang	Hu Yao-pang
Standing Committee of Politburo	Since Sep. 82	Hu Yaobang	Hu Yao-pang
		Ye Jianying	Yeh Chien-ying
		Deng Xiaoping	Teng Hsiao-p'ing
		Zhao Ziyang	Chao Tsu-yang
		Li Xiannian	Li Hsien-nien
		Chen Yun	Ch'en Yün
General Secretary of CC	Since Feb. 80	Hu Yaobang	Hu Yao-pang
First Secretary of Central Disciplinary and Control Commission	Since Dec. 78	Chen Yun	Ch'en Yün
Central Advisory Commission	Since Sep. 82	Deng Xiaoping	Teng Hsiao-p'ing
Central Military Commission	Oct. 76–Dec. 80 (*de jure* June 81)	Hua Guofeng	Hua Kuo-feng
State			
President of the PRC	1977–83 Since June 83	Li Xiannian	Li Hsien-nien
Vice President	Since June 83	Ulanhu	Ulanfu
Government			
Premier	Apr. 76–Sep. 80	Hua Guofeng	Hua Kuo-feng
	Since Sep. 80	Zhao Ziyang	Chao Tsu-yang
Chairman of NPC Standing Commission	Mar. 78–June 83	Ye Jianying	Yeh Chien-ying
	Since June 83	Peng Zhen	P'eng Chen
Chairman Central Military Commission	Since foundation in 1983	Deng Xiaoping	Teng Hsiao-p'ing

After a first stage of *charismatic rule*, which is dominated by the 'role of that leader who led the Party to its revolutionary victory', the system enters a stage of *transitional rule* before, finally, the process of bureaucratisation leads to the gradual formation of *institutionalised rule*. In China, the first stage more or less ended by 1959 when Mao's charismatic legitimisation was injured once and for all by the failure of the Great Leap Forward. From the beginning of the 1960s Mao had to compete and bargain with rival politicians and opposing subsystems for the recognition of his political ideals. Since then and until today,the PRC has seemed to have undergone the second stage of transitional rule, which Domes defines in the specific Chinese context as political rule in a *transitional crisis system* that is

> virtually based upon the interplay between the formation of opinion groups and their condensation into factions, of which one comes out as the victor in each intra-elite conflict, only to split up again, for a new crisis cycle to begin. As the former charismatic leader retires more and more to – or is pushed into – the role of legitimator, and several leaders compete on an equal footing after his death, political initiatives are questioned, parcellised, and – with regard to the long-term decisions – paralyzed.

However, if one accepts Domes' description of conflicts during this stage of rule as 'mostly signalled by terminological divergences, removals, expulsions, and occasionally the open rift within the Party', it is tempting to argue that with the ousting of Hua Guofeng the PRC already and at least for the time being has left the pure stage of a *transitional crisis system*. For the first time, a loser was not completely purged or physically eliminated after the resolution of a successor conflict.

Due to obviously strong support among the CCP's rank and file, Hua was even able to retain his CC membership and may thus be waiting in political hibernation for his hour to come. Assuming no drastic changes in his present status, we can perhaps call him the 'Malenkov of China', or if one accepts that Malenkov's demise marked the initial step towards an institutionalised leadership in the USSR (now definitely) proved by the succession processes in recent years), one may suggest that China may have entered a similar stage where conflicts between concurring groups still prevail, where terms of incumbency and transition of power from incumbent to successor are not yet completely regularised, but where succession conflicts do not result in a thorough shake-up and ensuing *crises* for the whole political system. Under these circumstances and – remembering my own caveats concerning unqualified prophesies – one may now tentatively regard the PRC as a *transitional conflict system*.

The way towards further institutionalisation seems open, but the somewhat erratic character of Chinese politics in the past should always remind the observer that another 'reversal of verdicts' might easily lead us back to highly conflict-laden political structures and even – at least theoretically – to the emergence of a new form of charismatic leadership. On the basis of our present data the further development towards bureaucratisation of Chinese politics in accordance with the Soviet experience seems highly probable. In this case, the preponderance of single individuals and the consequent importance of solving top leadership succession questions will continue to lose its relevance. Tomorrow's rule by bureaucratic self-assertion may then, finally, take the place of yesterday's rule by purge.

Notes

1. This article was first presented as a paper at the workshop on Political Succession during the 1984 ECPR Joint Workshop Sessions, held at Salzburg, Austria, 13–18 April 1984. The author wishes to thank the participants of the workshop for their encouraging remarks, Johannes von Thadden for a critical reading of parts of the manuscript, and above all Professor Jürgen Domes for his critical help and many useful comments. Responsibility for the contents remains with the author. The text was first published in *Asian Survey*, 25 (1985) pp. 638–58, and is reproduced here by kind permission of The Regents of the University of California.

   © 1985 by The Regents of the University of California.

2. Harold Hinton, The succession problem in Communist China', *Current Scene*, (1961); Ting Wang, 'The succession problem', *Problems of Communism*, May–June 1973, 13–24; A. Doak Barnett, *China After Mao* (Princeton, NJ: Princeton University Press, 1967) and, by the same author, 'Round one in China's succession: the shift toward pragmatism', *Current Scene*, 15 (1977) pp. 1–10. A critical assessment and further notes on literature are to be found in Thomas W. Robinson, 'Political succession in China', *World Politics*, 27 (1976), pp. 1–38.

3. Lucian W. Pye, 'Generational Politics in a Gerontocracy: The Chinese succession problem', *Current Scene*, 14 (1976), pp. 1–9.

4. Robinson, 'Political succession', p. 2.

5. For an overview, see *Studies in Comparative Communism*, 9 (Spring/
    Summer 1976), which is wholly devoted to the discussion of leadership
    and political succession in Communist systems with some interesting
    attempts at model building.
6. Carl Beck, William A. Jarzabek and Paul A. Ernandez, 'Political
    succession in Eastern Europe', *Studies in Comparative Communism*, 9
    (Spring/Summer 1976) pp. 35–61, esp. p. 36.
7. Robinson, 'Political succession', pp. 8–12. For a general classification
    and a remarkable analysis of approaches used in the China field, see
    Harry Harding, 'Competing models of the Chinese Communist policy
    process: towards a sorting and evaluation', *Issues and Studies*, 20 (1984)
    pp. 13–36.
8. Robinson, 'Political succession', pp. 13–20. For a recent example, see
    William De B. Mills, 'Generational change in China', *Problems of
    Communism*, November/December 1983, pp. 16–35, and fundamentally
    Pye, 'Generational politics.'
9. Robinson, 'Political succession', pp. 20–7.
10. Ibid., pp. 27–35.
11. Pye, 'Generational politics', pp. 2–4.
12. In China, such constitutional rules or procedures, on the one hand, do
    not exist in the Western sense of regulations for a smooth and
    undebated transition of political power and, on the other hand, seem to
    make little difference to the outcome of a power contest. Lin Biao, for
    example, was the only one so far who had the 'guarantee' of his
    designation to succeed Mao written down in the 1969 Party Constitution.
    Exactly two years later he was dead and his name turned into a
    synonym for every imaginable evil. And the CCP had to go through
    another two years of conflicts and compromise until the 1973 Party
    Congress deleted the remnants of the once powerful but unsuccessful
    would-be successor from official party documents and all aspects of
    political life in the PRC.
13. Robinson, 'Political succession', p. 5; Andrzej Korbonski, 'Leadership
    succession and political change in Eastern Europe', *Studies in
    Comparative Communism*, 9 (Spring/Summer 1976), pp. 18–19, and
    Myron Rush, *How Communist States Change Their Rulers* (Ithaca, NY:
    Cornell University Press, 1974) pp. 25–26.
14. David S. G. Goodman, 'China: the politics of succession', *The World
    Today* (1977) p. 134.
15. For a general discussion of 'modes of initiation', see Rush, *Communist
    States*, pp. 19ff., whence my distinction is taken.
16. Ibid., p. 20.
17. For speculations on Mao's faltering health, see Hinton, 'The succession
    problem', p. 1.
18. Speech at a CC Work Conference, 25 October 1966; quoted from Rush,
    Communist States p. 253.
19. See, for example, Chang Chen-pang, 'The succession problem in
    Communist China', *Issues and Studies*, 9 (1983) p. 10ff.; quotation from
    p. 10.
20. *People's Daily*, 4, 7 and 13 July 1983.

21. *Red Flag*, 23, December 1, 1983.
22. Lowell Dittmer, 'Bases of power in Chinese politics: a theory and an analysis of the fall of the "Gang of Four" ', *World Politics*, 31 (1978–9) pp. 26–60, esp. pp. 28–40.
23. Ibid., pp. 29, 30.
24. David Bonavia, *Far Eastern Economic Review*, 15 May 1984, p. 20.
25. Dittmer, 'Bases of power in Chinese politics', p. 30.
26. James P. Harrison, *The Long March to Power: A history of the Chinese Communist Party, 1921–1972* (London: Macmillan, 1972) p. 505.
27. See 'Liu Shao-ch'i' in *Who's Who in Communist China*, I (Hong Kong: Union Research Institute, 1969), and Li Tien-min, *Liu Shao-ch'i: Mao's first heir-apparent* (Taipei: 1975), Chs 2–7.
28. William W. Whitson and Huang Chen-shia, *The Chinese High Command: A history of Communist military politics, 1927–1971* (New York: Praeger, 1973).
29. For an analysis of the coalition behind the fall of Lin Biao, see Ellis Joffe, 'The Chinese Army after the Cultural Revolution: the effects of intervention', *China Quarterly*, 55 (1973) pp. 427–49.
30. See Alan P. L. Liu, 'The "Gang of Four" and the Chinese People's Liberation Army', *Asian Survey* 19 (1979) pp. 817–37.
31. Barnett, 'Round one in China's succession', p. 2.
32. For the term and its definition, see Jürgen Domes, *Politische Soziologie der VR China* (Wiesbaden- Akademische Verlagsgesellschaft, 1980) p. 205.
33. Jürgen Domes, *Government and Politics in the People's Republic of China: A time of transition* (Boulder, Colo.: Westview, 1985) pp. 140–55 and 173–191.
34. 'Teng Hsiao-p'ing', in *Who's Who in Communist China*, II (Hong Kong: Union Research Institute, 1970), pp. 610–12.
35. *Current Scene*, 14 (1976) pp. 24–5.
36. See Domes, *Government and Politics*, pp. 146–7, for an analysis and excerpts of an English translation. The Chinese text was first published by *Zhonggong Yanjiu, Studies in Chinese Communism*, 17 (1983) p. 82ff.
37. See Dittmer, 'Bases of power in Chinese Politics', pp. 26ff., for examples of the outbreak of the Cultural Revolution: and Kenneth Lieberthal, *Research Guide to Central Party and Government Meetings in China, 1949–1975* (White Plains, NY: 1976).
38. Dittmer, 'Bases of power in Chinese politics', pp. 38–9.
39. See Robinson, 'Political succession', pp. 15ff., for a somewhat different classification.
40. Ibid., p. 15.
41. Wang, 'The succession problem', p. 15.
42. Rush, *Communist States*, p. 321.
43. Lowell Dittmer, 'Power and personality in China: Mao Tse-tung, Liu Shao-ch'i, and the politics of charismatic succession', *Studies in Comparative Communism*, 7 (1974) pp. 21–49.
44. *People's Daily*, 5 November 1969, and *Beijing Review*, 14 November 1969.

45. In his instructions of 10 August 1966, on the question of the line of cadres, Lin had advocated the following three criteria for a loyal Maoist: (1) one who supports Mao; (2) one who gives prominence to politics; (3) one who is filled with revolutionary zeal; *Issues and Studies*, 8 (1972) pp. 107–9. In a *People's Daily* editorial of 1 January 1970, Mao's own criteria were published in clear contrast to Lin's: Communist Party members would now have to (1) be loyal to Marxism/Leninism/ Mao Zedong Thought; (2) trust the masses; and (3) be willing to conduct self-criticism after having made mistakes.

46. A pejorative term used for Hua and his supporters, based on the statement, 'Whatever policies Chairman Mao formulated we shall all resolutely defend; whatever instructions Chairman Mao gave we shall all steadfastly abide by.' This was attributed to Hua by a joint editorial of *People's Daily, Liberation Army Daily*, and *Red Flag*, on 7 February 1977. See also Domes, *Government and Politics*, pp. 144–5.

47. For a detailed analysis of Deng's tactics to remove Hua, see Domes, *Government and Politics*, pp. 156–91.

48. For a description of the technique of esoteric allusions, see Peter Michael Jakobs, 'Kritik an Lin Piao und Konfuzius', (Diss., Saarbrücken, 1978, publ. Köln, 1983).

49. Jürgen Domes, *China nach der Kulturrevolution: Politik zwischen zwei Parteitagen* (München: Fink, 1975) pp. 130–1.

50. Ibid., pp. 134–5.

51. Domes, *Government and Politics*, p. 163.

52. Ibid., p. 175.

53. Quoted in ibid., p. 176. The Chinese text is to be found in *Zhonggong Yanjiu (Studies in Chinese Communism)*, 17 (1983) p. 82ff.

54. Frederick C. Teiwes, *Politics and Purges in China: Rectification and the decline of party norms, 1950–1965* (New York: 1979) p. 12.

55. See Mao's 1957 article, 'On the correct handling of contradictions among the people,' (Peking: Foreign Languages Press).

56. Dittmer, 'Bases of power in Chinese politics', p. 32.

57. Ibid., pp. 32–3.

58. For just one representative example, see Bjung-joon Ahn, 'The Cultural Revolution and China's search for political order', *China Quarterly*, 58 (1974) p. 249ff., esp. p. 257.

59. Domes, *China nach der Kulturrevolution*, pp. 334ff.; *Politische Soziologie der VR China*, pp. 237ff.; and recently, *Government and Politics*, pp. 249–53, from which the following quotations are taken.

7 Political Succession and Political Change: The Case of Nigeria

Alan Brier

Political succession, in its broadest sense, has been defined as 'the ways in which political power passes, or is transferred, from one individual government or regime, to another'. In its narrower sense, it refers to orderly arrangements for the transfer of tenure of important offices within a state, which make allowance at the same time for change and for continuity. The extent to which they do so successfully has been suggested as an index of the political maturity of the state in which they operate. The study of political succession is thus primarily concerned with the processes, and accompanying ceremonies, of changes of tenure of important offices of state. There is, however, a productive ambiguity in the formulation offered by Peter Calvert, between 'power' and 'office' as the object of succession, which is particularly evident in the examples offered of the mechanism to be called 'cooptation'. These include the widening of suffrage, with consequent growth of political parties interested in control of the nomination of candidates, and the regulation of military promotions in countries persistently subject to military intervention.

The term cooptation also invites comparison with 'the specific instance of hereditary succession', which calls, at least, for an acknowledgement of the historical priority of dynastic succession in the European state tradition, in however attenuated or symbolic a form it may be considered to persist at present.[1] It is, perhaps, worth recalling that as late as 1914 dynastic states made up the majority of the world's political system[5]. Furthermore, if it is possible to talk in this context both of an elaboration of formal rules of hereditary succession to the office of head of state and of the reduction of this office to a largely symbolic function, then in some sense these changes in the object of succession must have been revealed in the course of the processes of succession, on one or a number of occasions. If, therefore, it is not to remain a mere enumeration of processes, it seems necessary to locate the idea of succession itself more securely within a more general theory of the relationship of political change and political tradition.

There are two main reasons for this suggestion. First, it is necessary to have a secure foundation for the differentiation of important offices and lesser ones, which cannot be a purely empirical distinction although a large element of empiricism may well serve to distinguish the broader categories. Second, it is important to distinguish adequately between greater or lesser degrees of change associated with the process of succession. It has been found useful to apply the methods of structural anthropology to the rituals and cultural significations of successions, to draw attention to the importance of symbols in the transfer of power. Nevertheless it should be noted that just as no two performances of however stylised a form are in practice the same, and the whole point of communication by means of a performance is that they are not, individual acts of succession themselves can be considered analogously to the post-structuralist case of the signature, which is again simultaneously the same and not the same, and which offers a paradigm of representation of the subject involving 'repetition with a difference'. What may, then, serve is an approach to the 'reading of a particular succession somewhat analogous to the analysis of a political discourse, in which, to refer briefly to the approved jargon, the intention is not epistemological (treating of voluntaristic knowing subjects) but to show how speaking/spoken subjects are 'overdetermined by the creativity of constitutive discourses'.[2]

It is, however, not necessary to follow in detail this particular philosophical line to propose that a particular succession has to be understood in the light of the 'constitutive discourse' of the development of modern nation-states. The analogy between culture and language can in any case not be pressed too far. In politics and economics, the relevant subjects are clearly collective, not individual, and the agency of these subjects can clearly transform their structures in a way which is hardly possible with a language. The main point here lies in the treatment which is required of the *interdependence* of structure and subject.[3]

It may be thought desirable, as well as instructive, if the terms in which political succession is discussed are serviceable for the comparative analysis of as wide a range of instances as possible, as well as for the analysis of the historical development and present arrangements of European states. The idea of a 'succession' from colonialism to independence has been somewhat reluctantly, admitted to recent discussions; partly, perhaps, as an extension of linguistic usage, and partly through the acceptance that, in decolonisation, *something*, presumably power or sovereignty, must have passed from its earlier holders to identifiable successors. Leaving aside for the moment the need to distinguish post-colonial states from others, this usage remarks two important features of the processes denoted. Few would dispute that:

> Social and political change in Africa and Asia during the last two centuries has been largely intrusive in nature and exogenous in kind. Within Western Europe, social and political change can be analysed in mainly 'endogenous' terms, or at least as the product of the interplay between its constituent states and nationalities; but in Africa or even Asia since 1800, such an analysis would omit the most important types and sources of change.[4]

But within the radically reconstitutive process of late European colonialism the idea persists that state systems were created which were capable of being passed on, in a modular fashion, while it is increasingly unpopular to claim that the legacy was a beneficial one. It would still be quite popular to hold one of two ideas about how to change such a legal order. One is that good law in one place is good law anywhere else. The other is that laws make little difference to people's behaviour: 'Good men, not good laws make good government.' Both dominated colonial thinking about law and constitutionality, and persisted in modern Africa. Robert Seidman summarises the problem as it affects development after decolonisation:

> Two general propositions oppose these notions. The first [is] denoted the law of non-transferability of law: the same rules of law and sanctions in different times and places cannot induce the same behaviour by the role occupant as they did in their time and place of origin. The second [is] denoted the law of the reproduction of institutions: other things remaining the same, unless the legal order is changed, institutions will continue as they are.[5]

From this the conclusion may be drawn, perhaps, that even in circumstances of radical political disjunction, such as decolonisation or major regime changes, it is both permissible and desirable to keep in mind the possibility that there may also be potentially disabling continuities, which may be identified in the nature of the system within which power passes to other holders: in the terms introduced earlier, in the object of the succession.

The argument put forward so far is completed with one qualification This is that it is the conclusion of the act of succession which represents and confirms the nature of the object of succession, and is effectively the only reliable means of determining what is happening. This both influences and is in turn influenced by the process of succession, so that object and process together constitute what is often called political change or political development. These considerations may not be particularly pressing in cases of 'normal', orderly succession to well-defined offices, when they may safely remain implicit, but are clearly required when the object of succession is itself ill-defined or contested, or when it is subject to rapid or radical change.

COLONIAL SUCCESSION AND STATE SYSTEMS

The concept of political development has always had a chequered history, and was regarded by some critics as having reached a theoretical impasse almost as soon as it began to find a place in comparative analysis.[6] Nevertheless, some 20 years of discussion of the processes of 'modernisation', 'nation-building' and 'political change' in the post-colonial world, far from creating an alternative perspective, has served finally to return the focus of attention to the problems of succession to the 'modular' political forms of (originally) European nation-state systems. There is now a high degree of agreement between diverse traditions of analysis about the need on the one hand to return to the historical uniqueness of the European state tradition, and on the other to reconceptualise the role of politics in newer states which have otherwise tended to be regarded principally as dependent in a system dominated by the European tradition.

One result of the researches of comparative historians has been to correct, and specify, the rather sweeping characterisations of European history, and its consequences for thinking about change in the rest of the world, which used to be presented by modernisation theories. There are two main variants of the theory of modernisation, conceived as a universal form of development which involves a transition from 'traditional' type of society, economy and culture to one which is 'modern'. The neo-evolutionist perspective of Shils,

Einsenstadt, Almond, Apter, Binder and others in the 'political development' school in its universal functional approach pays curiously little attention to the few common threads which can be identified in an otherwise highly heterogeneous picture of social change:

1. the rise of the modern state;
2. the emergence of nationalist thinking and practice;
3. the formation of new social strata, notably bourgeoisies, bureaucrats and intelligentsia.

The 'communications' school, of Deutsch and Lerner, does accord nation-building as such a central role, but treats it as a usually painful and disturbing phase in an attempted transition to a modernity characterised by 'ethnic complementarity' and 'cultural assimilation'. On the whole, this fails to notice the peculiar selectivity of the European historical model itself. ' " 'Nation-building' has entailed "nation-destroying"; or even better, "state-building" has erased or eroded many a variable nation.'[7] Frequently, also, European experience has involved an excess of mobilisation over assimilation. The real significance of Herder's assertion, 'Denn *jedes* Volk ist ein Volk; es hat *seine* nationale Bildung wie *seine* Sprache', made at a time when this was certainly not the case in practice, lies in its connection between old languages and new post-revolutionary models of linguistic community, in European humanism's expansion of the concept of time into 'homogeneous empty time' suitable for inhabitation by emerging nations.[8]

This is to require a substantial qualification, too, of the analysis offered by Tilly and others of the emergence of the European state-system out of absolute monarchy, with its concept of sovereignty within, and in the external defence of, it's own territory. Of the various special factors in a 'bid for statehood' Tilly concludes that 'war made the state and the state made war'.[9] This to a large extent obscures the basis of the continuation of another of his specific factors – the homogeneity of, or the ability to homogenise, the territorially incorporated populations – into the era of nationalism through what Seton-Watson has called 'official nationalisms.'

These nationalisms were historically 'impossible' until after the appearance of popular linguistic-nationalisms, for, at bottom, they were responses by power-groups primarily, but not exclusively, dynastic and aristocratic, threatened with exclusion from, or marginalisation in, popular imagined communities ... In almost every case, official nationalism concealed a discrepancy between nation and dynastic realm.[10]

Nineteenth-century European colonialism was a product of this official nationalism, and entailed a colonial equivalent of 'Russification' in the spread of state-languages to colonial administrations: 'Colonial racism was a major element in that conception of 'Empire' which attempted to weld dynastic legitimacy and national community. It did so by generalising a principle of innate, inherited superiority on which its own domestic position was (however shakily) based to the vastness of the overseas possessions.[11]

Two interesting consequences emerge which are important for the discussion of political succession. The new states founded after the Second World War have their own distinctive character, which is nevertheless incomprehensible except in terms of a succession of models based on European historical experience. These new states, however, combine genuine popular nationalism with official nationalism through a precarious bilingualism of their intelligentsia and a linguistically diverse population. The colonial legacy includes languages of state which are also in a sense vernaculars, like West African English, which enabled intellectuals to say to their fellow vernacular speakers, 'we' can be like 'them' in possessing the administrative unit of the previously colonial state.[12]

> Thus the model of official nationalism assumes its relevance above all at the moment when revolutionaries successfully take control of the state and are for the first time in a position to use the power of the state in pursuit of their visions ... Such leaderships come easily to adopt the putative *nationalnost* of the older dynasts and the dynastic state.[13]

Second, in tracing the effects of the inheritance of the European model, it may be particularly important to notice that it is primarily as a state-system rather than as a nation-system that it has been taken up in the post-colonial world. As such, the theoretical prerequisite for modernisation of vernacular linguistic unity, if not its reflection in the modalities of official nationalism, can be considered as weakened.

It might, from a different perspective however, be objected that the post-colonial state is really to be considered as *sui generis*, because it has been 'over-developed' as a result of colonialism, and specifically not by an emergent dominant ethnicity of its own. For the reasons already outlined, this also seems to imply an unnecessarily restricted view of post-colonial development. It arose out of a rather different set of considerations, which should be briefly rehearsed here.

Theorists of underdevelopment such as André Gunder Frank and Samir Amin took to task the assumption of a dualism between the 'modern' and the 'traditional' which, as has been noted already, is deeply rooted in the orthodox analysis of development. Tradition, in the conventional view, was the source of backwardness and the main obstacle to change in the many cases in which the expected transition to modernity was not forthcoming. The critique by theorists of under-development sought to expose the real cause of backwardness by establishing a unity in the relationship between 'centre' and 'periphery' in a capitalist world system. Far from there being a series of patterns or stages of development, there were only patterns of underdevelopment, or a process of incorporation into the world economy through 'extraverted development', or the 'development of underdevelopment', after which little further change was possible. This position has two acknowledged drawbacks. It seems to describe, but hardly to explain, the persistent but by no means unchanging problem of 'dependency'. More seriously, perhaps, it can hardly offer an adequate conception of 'development' itself, since it understands the term only as already known changes which capitalism has undergone, and which the underdeveloped world is held to be unable to follow.[14]

One way forward is to combine ideas from two sources. The first posits the coexistence and interaction of pre-capitalist and capitalist modes of production within the same state at the same point in time, without resorting to dualism, and this leads on to a new interest in the study of class development and the labour process in dependent states. The second, following earlier disenchantment with Nkrumahite and Tanzanian socialism, looks for a more general theory of the capitalist state capable of explaining both developed and backward capitalist states. Although they approach the problem from quite dif-ferent starting points, there is an interesting degree of critical con-vergence between the position of A. D. Smith, who writes: 'Under the influence of the dominant modernisation and Marxist paradigms, most accounts fail to give these essentially political processes enough attention and thereby accord too little weight to an autonomous political sector, which they tend to derive from either basic economic forces or overarching cultural values;[15] and Harry Goulbourne's 'problem of specifying the political'. Goulbourne notes:

> Perhaps the most distinct feature of political life in third-world societies is the tendency for the political and politics to merge, or expressed another way, there is a notable tendency for the political to become preponderant over politics, thus hiding the class struggle, or making it appear muted. This has been variously explained. For Pye, there is an 'avoidance' of politics in these formations because of the monolithic demands of nationalism, the need for planned development, etc, which are used to suppress dissent and discussion, thus denying the existence of legitimate competition. For Alavi, the post-colonial state dispenses with the mediation of politics because the state is 'over-developed' and cannot be controlled by the indigenous capitalist class at the point of political independence. This allows aspects of the state itself (the military and the bureaucracy) to play the dominant part in the state and above social classes. In the view of some development theorists this situation is an instance of the tendency to drift towards authoritarianism.[16]

These arguments tend to redirect attention to the question posed earlier by the idea of a 'post-colonial political succession'. What is it, exactly, that has been involved in this succession? Some broad answers have also been suggested. What is transferred is a specific form of legal order, which is derived from the broader set of traditions of Western state formations, which in turn entail ways of viewing the state as a uniquely legitimate expression of national identity. In two important respects, the post-colonial state may be thought to represent significant changes in the Western tradition. It is at best only tenuously the creation of its own indigenous bourgeoisie, being generally an externally-imposed political unit. Second, there seems to be broad agreement that, in continuing the political programme of national self-determination, the distance between the 'new elites', who may often be better termed the 'political class'[17] and who possess the state language, and the linguistically heterogeneous population may have become much wider than was the case in European history.

The strongest assertion made at the outset was that the process of succession, if successfully carried through, can involve change in the object of succession, in this case the post-colonial state, just as the available object of succession provides the focus for the process of succession, and for the dominant forms of political life in the state. To see how far this perspective may be useful in examining actual political change it is now necessary to turn to a detailed example. The example chosen is one of the larger and more complex post-colonial states, which has experienced a variety of types of economic and political changes, at various times and in various parts of its territory. It is also a state whose politics have so far eluded any analytical consensus or over-simplification of explanation; the Republic of Nigeria.

POLITICAL SUCCESSIONS IN NIGERIA

Nigeria should not be taken as a particularly representative example of the general class of post-colonial states, which is in any case probably rather more heterogeneous than the use of the term would suggest. While there is an extensive literature of social and political analysis on Nigeria, this literature does not have the neatly settled appearance of some area studies. The twists and turns of the analytical frameworks offered reflect the relative complexity of Nigeria's experience in each stage of historical development, whether precolonial, colonial or post-colonial, and the presence within the country of several different 'traditions', none of which has succeeded in becoming dominant, adds to the interest of the case for the study of political succession.

The paradigm which counterposes a relatively undynamic traditional world to a changing modernity already had severe difficulties in comprehending the precolonial history of the relevant part of West Africa, which was subject in the nineteenth century to at least two separate dynamics tending to transform rather than reinforce existing social traditions. As a result, the colonial invasion had to come to terms with, rather than to restructure, the political boundaries which were already in large measure laid down for it by earlier historical movements. This involved a further qualification of the significance of the idea of 'tradition'. In an extreme case, Martin Staniland describes in *The Lions of Dagbon* a radical incoherence between continued pre-colonial social and political conceptions in the colonially divided Kingdom of Dagbon, and the conceptions required by the the state of Ghana.[18] This he traces to the effects of a triple colonial invasion of an otherwise historically insignificant people. Honourable adjustment to such a radical transformation has proved impossible according to this study. Generalisation is always hazardous, but with only minor exceptions the boundaries of colonial Nigeria did not produce divisions among people of this order of significance. The reasons for this are admittedly somewhat fortuitous, in that the demarcation of territories in the Anglo-French agreement of June 1898 which averted the prospect of armed conflict between the colonial powers over the Niger Bend, while it divided the city-states of Borgu, offered Britain almost the entire territory by then precariously claimed by the Sultan of Sokoto, including, very dubiously, major parts of that claimed by Sokoto's historic enemy in Borno.[19]

Nigerian experience has been unusual in two further major respects. Its political unification and eventual independence were achieved by elaborate constitutional devices, involving a federalism which originated from colonial rule but was changed by experience of internal politics after 1945. This federalism, which was later severely tested after the secession of one of its component regions in what properly can be termed a civil war, was sustained not, as was commonly the case, by the abolition of opposition, but by a struggle for power over and within the central institutions and the regional components.

Finally, recovery from the civil war around a new phase of economic development was supported by a dramatic growth in oil exploitation, which was managed by federal military governments with only some further modifications to the established political structures. Oil thus set the seal on a buoyant politics of resource allocation which may now be coming to an end with a decline in oil revenues and a crisis in international liquidity. During the boom years of the 1970s a significant decline took place, with the rise of oil revenues, in the agricultural sector of the economy which, through the development of vegetable oils, timber and cocoa production, had provided the basis of earlier phases of economic growth and social transformation of the parts of colonial Nigeria particularly affected. If it remains a dependent economy Nigeria also presents a degree of complexity of economic development with differential social and political effects, to a greater degree than is usually allowed for by the simpler models of dependency theorists. To see this, it is necessary only to compare the model presented in Samir Amin's *Neocolonialism in West Africa* with the uses made of arguments derived from the political economy of 'dependency' in Gavin Williams' *State and Society in Nigeria.*[20]

To review political succession in Nigeria, in the broad terms now established, involves two main questions, each of which can conveniently be answered within three broad periods of development – pre-colonial, colonial and post-colonial – which in turn will require some subdivision. Within each period it is necessary to identify major changes in the 'object of succession', as well as the principal 'succession events', in order to be able to see how the two are related. One feature is then immediately clear. Although it has been found convenient to refer to the 'colonial succession' as though it were a single event, at least in this case the gaining of formal independence appears as in many ways a relatively minor step in a series of successions to a series of sets of institutions. Second, the question arises, which of various forms of succession can be said to play a dominant role in each period? The main events to be considered are summarised in Table 7.1.

PRE-COLONIAL SUCCESSIONS

To describe pre-colonial successions in the geographical area of modern Nigeria comprehensively would require an extensive history, much of which still remains to be written. Neither is the task of historical interpretation purely a scholarly matter. Readings of pre-colonial history have been almost inextricably involved in the processes of colonial rule and the politics of decolonisation, to the extent that any broad generalisations about 'traditions' and their geographical spread need to be viewed with the greatest caution. The examples to be mentioned here are offered simply to draw attention to the diversity of forms recorded, and in no way to suggest that, by themselves, they either assisted or impeded the development of the modern state.

The colonial invasion of the 1880s encountered two major state-systems whose succession procedures are worthy of note. In the former Hausa states south and west of Lake Chad, one of these resulted from the militant struggle of the nineteenth century to establish an ideal Islamic state, which in this part of West Africa was originated under the leadership of Shaikh Usuman dan Fodio in the early years of the century in Gobir. His decision to announce a *jihad*

(holy war) of the sword against the existing rulers of the Hausa states
was justified in a manifesto, known as the '*Wathigat ahl al-Sudan*',
setting out 27 principles of action, notably the duty to make holy war
on non-Muslim rulers who refuse to pronounce the Shadada, and,
more particularly, to take over the government of a kingdom where
the ruler, a Muslim, abandons Islam for 'heathendom'.[21] He considered, so far as is known correctly, non-Muslim, polytheistic,
beliefs and rituals to be widespread in Hausaland. His forces, a
mixture of Hausa, Fulani and Tuareg, succeeded in overrunning all
the Hausa states by 1809, except for Borno, whose ruler offered both
armed resistance and a detailed written defence of his own Islamic
status, in respect of the practices of unbelievers and assistance to
opponents of the reform movement. The son of Usuman, Mohammed
Bello, succeeded him in 1817 to the Caliphate of Sokoto, which he

Table 7.1   Succession events in Nigeria

Events	Objects of succession	Predominant form
Pre-Colonial		
Various	Various states and non-state systems	Contested dynastic with elaborate rule of eligibility
Colonial		
1900 Consolidation	Protectorates of N. and S. Nigeria	Appointment
1914 Amalgamation	Protectorate of Nigeria	Appointment
1922 'Clifford' Constitution	Protectorate, Executive and Legislative Councils	*Ex-officio* and appointment: 4 elected members
1946 'Richards' Constitution	Protectorate, Executive and Legislative Councils; 3 Provincial Councils	Indirect representation
1951 'Macpherson' Constitution	Nigerian House of Representatives	Direct (elected) and indirect regional representation
1954 'Lyttleton' Constitution	Federation; 3 regions	As above
1959 General Election	Bicameral Federal Parliament; 3 bicameral regional assemblies (self-governing regions until 1.10.60)	Election

Table 7.1 *continued*

Events	Objects of succession	Predominant form
Post-colonial		
1964–5 General Election	Republic of Nigeria (est. 1963); Federal Parliament and 4 regions	Election
Jan. 1966 coup	Unitary state	Military coup
July 1966 coup	Regions and federal institutions	Military
Secession 1967–70	'Biafra'; federation of 12 states	Military
1975 coup	Federation; 12 states	Military
1976 assassination	Federation; 12 states	Military
1979 General Election	Presidency; bicameral assembly; governorships and assemblies of 19 states	Election
1983 General Election	Federation of 19 states	Election
1983 coup	Federation of 19 states	Military
1985 coup	Federation of 19 states	Military

consolidated and extended in later years, to establish new emirates by conquest in Nupe, Ilorin, Misan, Muri and Kontagora by 1859. There was, however, never a time when the reformers were not preoccupied with problems of administration, emigration, internal disputes and the formation of rival reformist states such as the Mahdist state in Adamawa, *c.* 1878–98. They were also plagued with succession disputes involving competition for power among those Fulani clans and other Muslims who had taken part in the *jihad.* Notably, the revolt in Kano over the succession to the office of Emir in the 1890s was too strong for Sokoto to suppress, lacking as it did an adequately equipped standing army.[22]

By contrast, the use of the word 'Yoruba' to refer to the majority peoples of what is now the south-western part of Nigeria is surprisingly recent, dating from the middle of the nineteenth century, when it was introduced by Christian missionaries and linguists. The word originally applied to the Oyo Yoruba, and it is still the case that Yoruba people identify with a particular town or area for most purposes, and a 'Yoruba' identity is important only when dealing with members of other ethnic categories, such as 'Hausa' or 'Nupe', in the context of modern political boundaries.[23] The various Yoruba states of pre-colonial times have a long history of political centralisation, having existed originally as 'ministates' whose main social units were descent groups, often linked by cross-cutting institutions such as age-groups, title associations and secret societies. The political leaders held titles, vested either in a single descent group, or rotating between groups, the main aim being to achieve a balance between competing claims of age, ability and sectional representation.[24] These titles came to be associated with myths of origin, such as those of the arrival of Oduduwa at Ife, which have been collected since the nineteenth century in a form now realised to have been distorted in the light of subsequent political events.

The best example of this process is in Johnson's *History* (1921), in which foundation myths are used to justify the claims of the Alafin of Oyo to primacy over other rulers. 'Old Oyo' was also the centre of a larger kingdom, or 'megastate', which grew in the seventeenth and eighteenth centuries under the indirect influence of the Atlantic slave trade, and in direct rivalry with neighbouring Dahomey. Historical Oyo operated mainly north of the forest belt of the country, using cavalry, and was ruled by a complex political system under the Alafin, whose powers were theoretically absolute, but in practice ritually circumscribed. The palace had a staff of eunuchs and slaves numbering probably several thousand. Outside the palace, the capital was divided into wards administered by a series of chiefs, some of the royal descent group and some not, some of whom made up the Alafin's council. Outside the capital were a series of provinces, controlled with varying degrees of security by further chiefs. Suicide on the death of a titled patron or father was not uncommonly required as part of the processes of succession to the various offices of the state.

The system of 'Old Oyo' collapsed under external pressures, notably from the Islamic north (which conquered the capital and annexed Ilorin in 1835) and from Dahomey to the west. There were in addition internal rivalries between factions concerned respectively with developing trade and with military expansion. While Oyo fell apart in the north, a series of wars developed between Yoruba towns in the south, the prelude to conflicts which engulfed Yorubaland for the rest of the century. Powerful new states such as Ibadan and Abeokuta were founded by refugees and free-booters in the 1820s and 1830s. The political institutions of Oyo were reconstructed in a new capital of the same name further south, although they ceased to have extensive influence. New features of these wars between Yoruba states were the use of firearms by infantry rather than cavalry, and a new type of total warfare in which whole towns were destroyed and their inhabitants enslaved or dispersed. Succession now commonly fell to 'autonomous Yoruba war-leaders, willing to make or break alliances as expediency dictated'. Eades interprets a statement about the Alafin Afonja after 1796 as meaning that the office itself 'had become irrelevant: now he simply wanted to take over the empire'.[25] The successor Yoruba states, including Ibadan which itself enjoyed a short-lived empire between 1847 and 1878 when it faced revolts which dragged on for another 16 years, had to cope with a shift of power away from hereditary rulers to more independent military commanders and balance them against other interests, sometimes including immigrants. This problem persisted into the colonial period, as did the search for solutions.

It appears, therefore, that both in the Sokoto Caliphate and in Yorubaland 'traditional' society involved dramatically changing and contested political forms, in which military might tended to play an increasing role in succession and legitimation, but not to the exclusion of elaborate systems of political justification. The novel military dictatorships of the Niger Delta which mushroomed in connection with the slave trade were rather exceptional products of opportunism, an age-group system which offered a model for militarised 'houses', and of the conditions of the trade itself.[26]

The nineteenth century also saw a steady growth in European influences, through missionary activity, concern for the abolition of the slave trade, and growing 'legitimate' commercial interests. There was, in addition, a direct intervention by British administrators from Badagry in a long-standing dynastic succession dispute in Lagos. The son of the deposed Oba Akitoya, who had offered to stop the local slave trade if reinstated, was installed by force in 1851. To permit firmer control over an expanded coastal trade, Lagos itself was annexed as a colony in 1861, under an appointed governor. After 1862, when the prices of palm oil and kernel suddenly collapsed due to the availability of American petroleum, British firms had the incentive to move inland in search of lower prices by eliminating the middlemen of the Niger Delta and seeking control over navigation on the Niger by virtue of their already-established informal empire on the coast. After the Berlin conference of 1884, Royal Niger

Company agents expanded their territory under the formal protection of the British Crown in over 200 local treaties, including a notable agreement with Sokoto in 1885. Although later claimed as a cession of sovereignty, this appears to have been viewed by Sokoto as no more than a grant of exclusive trading privileges.

Only when rivalry with French interests in the Niger Bend and the Eastern Sudan began to lay stress on 'effective occupation' did the process begin to involve European armed force capable of exposing the fragility and the very disparate nature of many African claims to territorial influence. In particular, most African states lacked fixed boundaries, so that treaties could rapidly be made obsolete by rivalries of which the Europeans could be unaware. Internecine strife was also common among peoples recognising and successfully defending their traditions of independence, like the Bariba states of Borgu who successfully fought off Fulani cavalry in 1820 and 1835 while briefly losing Ilo to Sokoto. In this instance, the kings of Bussa, whom the Niger Company called the 'Sultans of Borgu', apparently signed treaties with both British and French agents in an attempt to manipulate European rivalries to protect their own independence, but by the 1880s in reality enjoyed only ceremonial pre-eminence.[27] Pre-colonial wars, and differing traditions of statehood and sovereignty, thus contributed to the complex diplomacy of colonial partition.

THE COLONIAL ERA

Although European influence in West Africa dates back to the fifteenth century it has become customary to identify the 'high period' of colonialism as beginning after the Berlin Conference of 1884–5, which laid down the rules for the occupation of a part of Africa to be recognised as valid by other European powers. British interests had already begun the process of occupation in a limited way by the annexation of Lagos in 1861, and by systematic attempts at exploration and the development of 'legitimate trade', notably in palm oil, to replace the suppressed Atlantic slave trade.

Frederick Lugard, who was appointed in 1900 as the first High Commissioner of the newly established Protectorate of Northern Nigeria and carried out the subjugation of the Sokoto Caliphate, was originally an official of the Royal Niger Company, whose interests had extended for a circle of about 200 miles around the confluence of the Niger and Benue rivers. The convention between Britain and France of April 1898, which resolved their territoral rivalries in West Africa by giving Britain formal control over almost the entire area claimed by the crumbling empire of Sokoto, left the way clear for the final subjection (if necessary by force) of the emirates, and finally of the capital, which the court historians likened to the sack of Mecca in 930 and the surrender of Baghdad to the Mongols in 1258. The Islamic reaction varied from the notion of '*hijra*' or withdrawal from a territory ruled by non-Muslims, to a military response by Kano and Sokoto which ended with the defeat of 1903, to a variety of Mahdism. A limited Mahdist rebellion in Satiru was crushed in 1906 before it could gain strength. Mahdism persisted, however, into the 1920s, in Kano, where one of the leaders was the son of the leader of the former Mahdist state in Adamawa. There were, on the other hand, those who took a less doctrinaire and hostile view of colonialism, accepted assurances that their religion would not be disturbed, and decided to refrain from outward hostility to the new regime.

Lugard's experience of 'indirect rule' in Northern Nigeria, through accommodation with those emirs who were willing to reach agreements and the replacement, if necessary by force, of those who were not, served as the model for the rest of the country when he took overall responsibility for the colony after 1912. British colonial policy towards Islam was dictated by the need to secure maximum coopera-tion in the task of administering large territories in which European personnel were few and financial resources were meagre. The emirates, in these circumstances, offered a suitable basis of indirect rule through 'native authorities', a system which was modified and 'improved' as time went on. The main early changes concerned the tax system, and the removal from the emir of certain judicial powers, such as the power to impose the death penalty. Under this system, Northern Nigeria became used to a degree of 'protection' of its Islamic institutions, and remained free from the influence of Chris-tian missionaries and educators. Some nevertheless always saw the system as a defeat for the emirs, and others regarded it as a means of restricting development and subjecting Muslims to government by a non-Muslim state.

What preserved existing succession arrangements, subject to good behaviour, and worked well in the former Sokoto Caliphate and in Borno, with their traditions of strong central administration, did not and could not be made to operate effectively elsewhere. Among the Yoruba states, following the failure of indigenous efforts to establish modern administrations out of the kaleidoscopic politics of the late nineteenth century, the application of the Northern Nigerian model of 'native authority' system created problems. Indirect rule served to increase the relative powers of rulers who had not been traditional autocrats, and the new hierarchies of district and village heads, reinforced by the payment of salaries for some offices which were financed out of direct taxation after 1916, often bore little resemblance to the situation existing before the British arrival. In selecting a new Oba, the British were often in a dilemma. 'They wanted to follow traditional procedures, but they also wanted to make sure that a "suitable" candidate was chosen. At times it was impossible to do both which meant supporting a "progressive" but unqualified candidate.'[28] Consequently, some obas retained power only with British support, and the shifts of power produced by British insensitivity to established practices continued to cause trouble until well into the 1930s. The best example of this is provided by the 'New Oyo Empire' presided over by Alafin Ladugbolu and the long-serving British Resident, Captain Ross.[29]

In the south-west of modern Nigeria, the effects of misunderstanding of existing political systems were, if anything, even more pronounced. With the exception of the Western Igbo, who had borrowed a more centralised form of town administration from the neighbouring kingdom of Benin, there were, until the attempt was made to reconstruct native authorities in the 1930s, only four viable political divisions among the majority Igbo people These were the extended family, the 'ummuna' or localised patrilineage, the village and the town or group of villages. Ralph Moor, Consul General of the Niger Coast Protectorate after 1896 and High Commissioner of the Protectorate of Southern Nigeria on its establishment in 1900, attempted to carry out the final conquest of southern Nigeria and the establishment of viable administration on the basis of assumptions which were founded mainly on his recent experience of punitive expeditions by the Royal Niger Company in the Delta. For example, he ascribed to the Aro shrine of Chukwu a much greater political significance than it possessed in reality. Mistakenly regarded as the centre of a 'barbarous' militaristic system akin to Ashanti in the Gold Coast, Aro was the target of a military expedition in 1901–2, but offered no great resistance. Emerging evidence that the Igbo political system was in fact village-based, without chiefs or further centralisation, was interpreted as further evidence of backwardness, or of the 'complete breakdown of native rule under the disintegrating influence of middleman traders and of the Aros.'[30] The consequent establishment of Native Courts in the south-east involved the appointment of 'warrant chiefs' by the British authorities. These became responsible, after 1906, not only for customary courts but also for the lowest level of a British court system administered from Lagos. Problems were compounded by the reluctance of many elders with genuine claims to precedence to offer themselves for appointed office, and the reliance of the system on its educated court clerks, who soon became its *de facto* masters.

A turning point was finally reached as a result of the enquiries which followed extensive riots in Aba, in the east, in 1929, and through re-evaluation of the role of subordinate chiefs in the west. There, by the 1930's, the spread of education and the development of the cocoa industry had resulted in an increase in the number of groups of literates and wealthy businessmen in many of the Yoruba towns, and their influence on local politics started to grow. In some cases, obas were elected from among these groups, and in others they formed the leadership of 'progressive unions' and of opposition to the local oba.[31] For example, after the death of the oba of Ogbomoso in 1940, the local union appealed all the way to the Privy Council its case for a literate successor to be recognised, and finally won in 1944.

Examples of this kind could be multiplied far beyond the scope of this chapter. For present purposes, it is important only to notice that changes in relationships within various local political institutions brought about in the immediate pre-colonial and colonial periods are of much more than marginal relevance to post-colonial politics. This is perhaps most marked among those peoples whose apparent lack of a cohesive tradition of centralisation at the time of the colonial accession led them to be regarded as difficult to deal with since they would acknowledge no head of the whole 'tribe'. Alvin Majid's study of the Idoma, a people of the 'Middle Belt' who identify their origins as migrants from the failing Jukun or Kororofa Empire of East Nigeria after Fulani aggression, demonstrates this point in detail. Their previously strong tradition of chieftaincy appears to have been moribund by the 1930s. Paradoxically, this tradition was always tempered by fear of its autocratic potential. Hence it was regulated by the (*ojira*) assembly, by rituals of office and by rotation and seniority in succession. 'Officialdom, representing the Crown's paramount authority misjudged (or ignored) the depth of that ambivalence.'[32] The search for indigenous leadership in colonial Idoma produced, simultaneously, centralisation throughout, and democracy of a kind, so that the district councillors of the Native Authority under the new law of 1954 became self-consciously 'men in the middle' of conflicting pressures while remaining unwilling to follow their more unruly neighbours in the Tiv Division into open revolt.

Until 1945, the main effort of the colonial state was to extend the Native Administration system throughout the country, although, as has been seen, this could not be done with any great consistency in practice. The Colony and Protectorate of Nigeria, finally unified in 1914 in name, remained divided administratively into two parts, under two Lieutenant Governors. A single executive council existed under the Governor, but only the south was subject to the decisions of a legislative council in which there were a few directly elected members in addition to *ex-officio* and appointed representatives of traditional authorities. In 1946, a belated attempt was made to stem the rising tide of nationalist demands[33] in a constitution which incorporated the north for the first time on the same terms as the south, but in a way which still preserved the division by encouraging the development of separate regionalised nationalisms in the continued absence of any significant central focus for political activity. At a critical period in the development of Nigerian nationalist politics, the 'Richards' Constitution of 1946 introduced advisory regional assemblies into the three administrative regions which had been in existence since 1939, and by which the south was divided into East and West. In a final attempt to sustain the traditions of indirect rule, these regional assemblies were intended only to channel demands to the central Legislative Council in Lagos, which in turn remained advisory in function to the Governor.

By 1951, following vigorous anti-colonial political activity including a General Strike in 1946, a new Governor, Sir John Macpherson, introduced a further, temporary, constitution which acknowledged the by now largely separate foci of nationalist activities by giving each region its own executive and legislative council, but removing the residual directly elected element in the central legislature. This was a crucial step in reinforcing the pattern of nationalist politics, since the main parties were now virtually forced into regional enclaves. A political crisis in the Eastern Region in 1953 served to expose the inadequacies in the system, while severely weakening the party in power in the region, the National Council of Nigeria and the Cameroons (NCNC), which until then was the most established of the southern parties and the one with the strongest claims to be a national force. In addition, southern politicians, especially those of the mainly Yoruba Action Group (AG), were demanding independence by 1956, leaving the northern leadership dragging its feet by comparison, and fearful of the more impressive southern parties.

Following conferences in which, for the first time, Nigerians were dominant in the negotiations, a further constitution was produced in 1954 which tilted the balance finally towards a federal system with regional reserved powers, with decentralised civil service and judiciaries, and with federal budgetary allocation on the principle of derivation. Internal self-government, without a Governor's veto, followed in 1957, and after Federal and Regional elections conducted in 1959, the country became independent on 1 October 1960.[34] The northern-based Northern Peoples' Congress (NPC) won the largest number of seats in the Federal House of Representatives, but could form a governing majority only in coalition with the mainly Eastern Region NCNC, with whom it had cooperated for some time in opposition to the more outspoken and apparently more radical AG, which was strongly entrenched in the Western Region.

This was, then, the critical period of political development in which the idea of a federal constitutional system, reflecting what were widely held to be the three 'dominant' ethnic groups, each accorded 'its own' region, took hold of Nigerian politics and was legitimated by constitutional development. This conception was sufficiently well grounded in (mainly colonial) political experience to make it appear an attractive and quite genuine reflection of the political structure of the country. However, as later changes show, it was the constitutional practices, involving subdivision on ethnic lines the better to be able to maintain a national government, rather than the theory of dominant ethnicities enshrined in these developments, which were to prove more durable after independence. It is worth noticing, for example, that despite the introduction of direct election as part of constitutional developments, women still had no vote in the Northern Region after independence, although the region included non-Muslim divisions which had never been subject historically to Sokoto. It is also important not to be misled by the presence of a profusion of holders of traditional titles among the emergent nationalist leaderships. The main effects of the pre-colonial and colonial periods in Nigeria lay in the modification of indigenous society, through dramatic changes in its material basis and through the political simplifications introduced by the institutions of the colonial state. In some senses it was true that the Nigerian colonial state was 'overdeveloped' in its relationship with society. It occupied a characteristic role in production for export through marketing control and taxation. It was also the case that the great majority of wage-earning workers were state employees in some sense, which gave state employees a dominant role in the emerging trade unions. But it seems more important to notice, in the case of Nigeria at least, how 'traditional' and 'modern' institutions tended to change in a way which brought them together, rather than into conflict, and this aspect of political change is well captured by direct attention to changes in the dominant forms of political succession brought about in the colonial period.

POST-COLONIAL NIGERIA

The constitution under which Nigeria became independent was based on the assumptions that the three regions would act as checks on each other, and that there was a rough parity of strength between north and south. The creation of further regions for 'minorities' was ruled out in favour of larger 'multi-tribal' regions, which were regarded as offering a better safeguard. The period 1960–6 saw the falsification of these assumptions, as each region became a virtual single-party preserve, and the NPC exploited the disarray of the Western Region after 1962 to govern, eventually, with the support only of its own political clients from the west, Chief Akintola's Nigerian National Democratic Party (NNDP). In 1963 Nigeria acquired a republican constitution, with an indirectly-elected president with reduced powers. This followed difficulties with the Privy Council in the aftermath of the Western Region state of emergency and the trial for treason of leading AG politicians. The creation of an additional Mid-West region in 1964 further capitalised on the collapse of the AG, although the immediate beneficiaries of this were the NCNC, still in uneasy federal coalition with the NPC.[35]

A highly controversial census, in which the northern population showed a startling increase compared with earlier assumptions to give the north an overall federal majority, led on to a crisis-ridden federal election in 1964. The election was contested between two alliances of parties. The main southern parties, now united, originally seemed to expect victory by working with minority northern parties, but as polling day approached their fears of irregularities grew and they threatened a boycott if the President refused to postpone the election. After a partial election on 30 December, President Azikiwe tried to use his power to refuse to reappoint the Federal Prime Minister on the grounds that the elections were unsatisfactory, but was obliged to concede defeat. As the postponed Eastern Region election took the expected course in March 1965, it seemed to some observers that a system 'stretched to breaking point' had 'snapped back into much the previous pattern'; that this had been a 'politicians' crisis' only.[36] It was more difficult to maintain this view after the Western Region election on October 1965, in which the NNDP, owing its incumbency to the earlier state of emergency, exploited its position to retain power over a divided AG/NCNC alliance in a way which produced more violence than had ever been seen and a collapse in electoral administration. In this power struggle, which fully exploited all kinds of ethnic and local divisions, obas and other traditional leaders were clearly warned not to oppose the NNDP government. 'When an Oba takes it upon himself to oppose the Government', wrote the *Nigerian Daily Sketch*, 'he has finally shown himself as an enemy of his people'.[37] The Western region erupted into rioting and in places into open rebellion.

Although the army stayed clear of this first crisis of the independent state system, in January 1966 a number of young officers, impatient with what they saw as a failure of the entire constitutional arrangements, acted swiftly to destroy the political system of the first Nigerian republic, and with it the unity of the old Northern region. A short-lived military regime under General Ironsi made the only attempt in Nigerian history to create a unitary state, following a coup in which the Federal Prime Minister, several ministers and the Sardauna of Sokoto himself, Sir Ahmadu Bello, were assassinated. The armed forces, however, had already suffered politicisation of recruitment – on the insistence of the NPC leaders, this had observed strict regional quotas – and a seriously distorted age structure resulting from a rapid 'indigenisation' policy with consequent promotion blocks.

In the 1964 election, the opposition alliance had promised to introduce a policy of recruitment by merit and qualification, irrespective of tribalism. In such a political climate, it was almost inevitable that, given the preponderance of Igbo officers in the coup and in

the military regime, it was interpreted as anti-northern. Ironsi's promotion of a number of Igbo officers against the decision of the
Supreme Military Council (SMC), and above all his abolition of
federalism, produced protests which rapidly degenerated into attacks
on Igbos in the northern cities. As Dudley observes, 'the Ibo were
attacked not because they were the Ibo but because the name Ibo had
become more or less synonymous with exploitation and humiliation.
It was essentially an attack on a mental stereotype.'[38]

The killings which accompanied the 29 July counter-coup began
the mass migration of Igbos and non-Igbos alike from the North back
to the Eastern Region. This coup 'was quite evidently aimed at getting
even with the Ibos ... and to forestall "Ibo domination" '.[39] With
Ironsi dead, Colonel Yakubu Gowon emerged as the new Head of
State, after a period of uncertainty whether the North itself would
leave the federation. Relations deteriorated with the East until in
May 1967 it seceded under the leadership of its military governor,
Colonel Ojukwu. The first fighting between federal and 'Biafran'
troops took place in July 1967, and after some initial rebel successes
in the Mid-West, superior federal resources and international
support finally forced the surrender of the remaining 'Biafran'
territory in January 1970.

A significant early act of the Gowon regime was its restoration of a
federal system of administration based on 12 new states, three of
which originally made up 'Biafra'. The former Northern Region was
divided into six states, only three of which could really be said to
belong unequivocally to the old northern hegemony. In announcing
a separate Benue-Plateau state the military regime recognised a long-
standing claim for separate status, and meeting a similar claim in
Rivers State had the added advantage of circumscribing Igbo
particularism in the seceded areas to the true Igbo heartland.

The SMC's programme of reconstruction, announced in October
1970, envisaged a prolonged period of military rule before a supervised return to civilian rule, which in the event was extended for nine
years instead of the originally announced six. An economic boom as
oil exploitation increased considerably aided recovery from the war,
but did not reduce the problems of government. A census under
military supervision in 1973 rapidly came to resemble a rerun of the
events of 1962–3. Since the military sought to govern through civil
servants, and to engineer support through 'leaders of thought' in a
complex federal system, it is not altogether surprising that it was
necessary increasingly to devote time to achieving consensus

between the SMC and the 12 state military governors, many of whom had put down political roots in nearly seven years of office. Popular unrest was reserved for protests, by 1975, over familiar problems of public service salaries, and the more general effects of inflation and shortages. Strikes occurred in banking and the health services, and delays in the Port of Lagos reached the proportions of an international scandal. On 29 July, exactly nine years after taking power, General Gowon was replaced in a bloodless military succession, while attending the Organisation for African Unity summit meeting in Kampala. Those who held regional office under him were all removed. Many were charged with corruption and one former military governor was executed.

Gowon's successor, Brigadier Murtala Mohammed, was related to the NPC Minister of Defence in the first Republic, but also enjoyed a considerable reputation earned in the Civil War and had been a member of the federal executive since 1974. The new military regime announced a detailed timetable for its own withdrawal from power by October 1979, which was maintained in essentials although Brigadier Mohammed himself was assassinated in an unsuccessful coup attempt in 1976. The next ranking officer, General Obasanjo, another who had made his reputation in the Civil War, succeeded him and maintained the programme and popularity of his predecessor.

The return to civilian rule took place in several carefully supervised stages, the earliest of which involved substantial reforms in local government. These were long overdue since no uniform system had yet been created and the image of 'Native Adminstration' had been hard to shed. It was also decided to 'settle' the question of the creation of further states by early agreement on the number 19, to be achieved by subdivision of existing units. A constitutional drafting committee delivered a series of proposals with a strong emphasis on avoidance of the problems of the past, through constitutional control over state creation beyond the 19 already agreed, and through separate direct election of an executive president and a bicameral federal assembly. This system was replicated at state level by providing for separate election of state governors and assemblies.

Most importantly it was hoped to avoid 'loser forfeits all' party competition by constitutional rules governing the creation of genuinely national parties. In the elected Constituent Assembly which deliberated on the new constitution from October 1977 to June 1978, the significant problems of a reliable census, and of revenue distribution, were not tackled. Instead, there was a substantial debate over the sense in which Nigeria, in the words of the drafting committee at one stage, 'is one and indivisible sovereign Republic, *secular*, democratic and social'.[40] An unsuccessful but highly controversial attempt was made to create a Federal *Shari'a* Court of Appeal, in a debate which raised fundamental political, religious and constitutional problems.[41]

When the ban on parties was finally lifted in September 1978, General Obasanjo employed sporting metaphors, referring to players, spectators, and umpires, in the game which was to begin. The spirit of the early announcements was well captured by *New Nigerian's* columnist who offered 'Comrade Chief Dr. Alhaji Candido's party', standing for democratic dictatorship and capitalistic socialism, with the philosophy 'chop and let chop'. The leading parties which emerged to contest the 1979 sequence of elections, under the supervision of the Federal Electoral Commission, while involving many familiar figures from before 1966, and bearing some resemblance to the national alliances of the 1964–5 elections, were nevertheless highly conscious of the need to strike the right balance of forces to secure a national majority. The task was more uncertain and complicated now that the presidency required not less than one-quarter of the votes cast in each of two-thirds of 19 states, and the elections were conducted in a weekly sequence beginning with the House of Representatives and the Senate, and only ending with the presidential election. Shehu Shagari's winning vote raised immediately a problem of interpretation of the majority requirement, and Chief Awolowo, the runner-up, supported by Azikiwe and Waziri Ibrahim, ultimately appealed to the Supreme Court against the electoral commission's interpretation, that two-thirds of 19 was $12\frac{2}{3}$, and not 13. The constitution therefore came into effect in a political crisis which, it is claimed, was averted more by a wish to see the backs of the military than by widespread acceptance of the ruling.[42] The new electoral map showed significant differences as well as continuities from the past. The chief difference was that all five main parties now had some support in all states; the chief continuity that the remains of the 'old North' supported the National Party of Nigeria (NPN) and the 'old West' the Unity Party of Nigeria (UPN) of former AG leader Chief Awolowo. The Nigerian People's Party (NPP), under the former President Azikiwe, was indentified, by its opponents at least, as an Igbo party after its former chairman and presidential candidate Waziri Ibrahim had detached its northern section to form his own

Great Nigerian People's Party (GNPP). In Kaduna state, the former Northern Elements Progressive Union (NEPU) leader Alhahji Aminu Kano's People's Redemption Party (PRP) held the Governorship, against an Assembly with an NPN majority.[43]

Analyses of the results agree that in eight of the 13 states in which one ethnic group constitutes a majority of the population, the party whose presidential candidate was of that ethnic group won overwhelmingly the support of his group. It was also true, but hardly surprising, that in no election did parties offer candidates who were not indigenous to the state in which they were standing. It was true that 'an outcome of this pattern of voting ... [was] ... to make the legislative assemblies of the states concerned reflect not just the dominant party but also the main ethnic group, thereby undermining the ideal the Constitution sought to achieve – to make political institutions reflect the "federal character', of the nation'.[44]

It was also clear that different constitutional arrangements, and military supervision of party formation, had produced an outcome which was not easy to relate directly to the political patterns of the first Republic. The federal coalition of NPN and NPP added political constraints on President Shagari, in forming his Cabinet, to the constitutional requirement to include at least one Minister from each state, a problem which was overcome only by using his Senate majority to override opposition.

In terms of personnel, the elections of 1979 were regarded as 'the year of the new breeds'.[45] While the presidential candidates all had long political careers, President Shagari having been parliamentary secretary to the Prime Minister of the First Republic, Alhaji Tafawa Balewa, until 1966, and a Federal Commissioner under General Gowon, few of the state governors had held previous major office. The millionaire Vice President Alex Ekwueme, in particular, was seen as a personification of the new style of younger politician.

The prognosis of 'uncertainty in the future of the political parties', due to the election results rather than to the constitution,[46] was more than borne out by the first term of office of President Shagari. The accord between the ruling NPN and NPP soon broke down, and the nine PRP, UPN and GNPP party state governors met regularly as a kind of radical opposition group. Splits also developed in the PRP and GNPP over rivalries between different regional centres, as the Governors proved to wield the key power in their states, despite friction with their legislatures, the judiciary and the federally-controlled police commissioners. The radical governor of Kaduna state (PRP) was successfully impeached, but was replaced by his deputy from the same party, who was better able to deal with a hostile NPN legislation. There was continued strong pressure for more local government units, although it was never found possible to hold the constitutionally required local government elections. The main reason given was the impossibility of compiling adequate registers of voters. There was also strong pressure for the creation of more states. In 1982 the federal legislature passed a bill to subdivide existing states into a total of 40, but this was to depend on local plebiscites which would have to await the outcome of the 1983 federal elections.

There was only a limited change of personnel in the federal government, in response to allegations of misconduct, and two governors survived legislative enquiries into alleged corruption. President Shagari meanwhile cultivated an image of personal rectitude, and supported himself with an ethical committee made up of chiefs and religious leaders to oppose corruption of cultural and moral values.

Anticipation of the 1983 elections effectively dominated the politics of the Second Republic. A sixth political party was registered by the Federal Electoral Commission – Tunji Braithwaite's left-wing Nigeria Advance party (NAP) – but the alliance formed by the main opposition parties, calling itself the People's Progressive Alliance, a title reminiscent of the opposition United Progressive Grand Alliance of 1964–5, could not obtain official recognition and remained a loose grouping of separate parties. The Alliance was in any case subject still to the rivalry between the leaders of the UPN and NPP for pre-eminence in 'southern' politics, which dated back to the years before independence. As the elections drew closer, the governors of three northern states who had been elected for the NPN changed allegiance to the NPP, while Borno's governor decided to run for re-election for the UPN. Had they been successful in gaining re-election, this would have represented an extraordinary shift in the expected regional–political equation, and the example shows, perhaps, the relative fluidity of party allegiances, compared with the support which individual governors thought they enjoyed within their own states. Against this movement to the opposition, the NPN ticket gained the former UPN deputy governor of Ondo State in the west. Another of the less expected features of the 1983 elections was the return to Nigeria of Odumegwu Ojukwu, the former Biafran leader, to stand for the Senate for the NPN. Ojukwu was understood to be trying, together with the former Eastern Region premier Dr Okpara, to induce Igbo voters to accept the government's dominant role and join the side of the winners. In the event, President Shagari's enormously superior resources easily overcame opposition hopes of forcing at least a run-off election for the presidency, and he won a second term, this time with majorities in 11 states, and falling below 25 per cent of the vote only in three.

A bandwagon was confidently predicted between the presidential election which, in 1983 was the first of the sequence of five required by the constitution, and the gubernatorial election which followed it. What was not altogether anticipated was the apparent NPN 'landslide' which followed, as all the Progressive Parties Alliance (PPA) governors except three lost their seats. The NPN now gained a clean sweep of the northern states, with the continued exception of Kano, which still remained loyal to the PRP, now represented by an aide of the late Aminu Kano. The NPN was awarded some quite remarkable wins in the previously solid UPN states of Oyo, Ondo and Bendel. In Ondo, the NPN took the governorship, according to the result first announced, although President Shagari had secured only 20 per cent of the presidential vote in the state only one week earlier. Of the three highly implausible results, only in the case of Ondo was the result overturned in the legal actions which followed the elections, although there was widespread evidence of interference with the results. As the Federal Electoral Commission advised, however, all the aggrieved candidates took their cases to court, while the main opposition leaders publicly protested about what they claimed were the beginnings of a 'democratic one-party state', and of 'native imperialism'.[47]

In spite of evident fears by the opposition that the NPN victory represented a return to the northern domination of the federation of the First Republic struggle for power, the elections seem to have been accepted at the time with resignation and cynicism. It was difficult to escape the conclusion that all parties had engaged to some extent in 'unqualifiable electoral malpractices', even though it was clear that the NPN's superior organisation and powers of patronage had little difficulty in outmanoeuvering a divided opposition, with or without interference with the results.[48] The position of President Shagari within his party was greatly strengthened. He was now able to require the resignation of his entire government, and to include only eight former ministers in a new shorter list of 35 nominees. It was still widely believed that within the NPN a 'Kaduna mafia' prevailed, but it was not clear that Shagari was indeed their preferred representative.

The final acts of political succession to be considered are those which replaced President Shagari with Major General Muhammed Buhari, as the army intervened again on New Year's Eve 1983 to overthrow his government and suspend the civilian constitution after four years of operation, and the displacement of Buhari himself by the present military leadership in August 1985. Evidence later emerged that the 1983 coup was only the latest of several attempts to overthrow Shagari, and that the military leaders had contemplated acting both before and after the August 1983 elections. General Buhari denied that the action was a pre-emptive coup to avoid more radical action by more junior officers, but a remarkable lack of casualties and the flight abroad of several leading NPN figures shortly before it occurred, inevitably raised suspicions about the extent of collusion in the affair. The action taken resembled Murtala Mohammed's coup of July 1975 against General Gowon, in being a 'brigadiers' putsch'. General Buhari himself, a former military governor and Federal Commissioner for Petroleum and Energy after 1976, was seen as a compromise candidate as Head of State between the former Director of Plans at army headquarters, General Babangida, and the commander of the armoured division of Ikeja, Brigadier Abacha, who were both important in the planning of the coup.

The new SMC of 1983 assumed the austerity budget which was initially thought to be the cause of the downfall of Shagari, together with his negotiations with the International Monetary Fund (IMF) for a debt-rescheduling loan made necessary by short-term mis-management prior to the 1983 elections. It was cynically argued that only the military could enforce the necessary financial measures, likely to include a drastic devaluation of the naira, which well-publicised divisions within the civilian parties were preventing.[49] It was also interesting to notice that the SMC, while unexpectedly recruiting a number of previously apolitical academics as civilian advisers, maintained the tradition of strict attention to regional balance in making up its new list of personnel.

However, General Buhari's government rapidly dissipated the initial goodwill which it attracted by appearing insensitive to expressions of public opinion and excessive concern with state security, to which all debate on future political arrangements came finally to be regarded officially as inimical and a distraction from the problems of the economy and of instilling discipline into the society. From January 1984 onwards there were persistent rumours of a possible junior officers' coup and, with probably more foundation, of divisions within the SMC, in which Major General Babangida, Buhari's former supporter and eventual successor, was said to lead a major faction of opposition. The palace coup of 27 August 1985 was conducted quietly, in the absence of General Buhari for an Islamic festival in his home state, and of his Chief of Staff, General Idiagbon, on pilgrimage. All but five of the dissolved SMC members were re-appointed to the new Armed Forces Ruling Council (AFRC), but Major General Babangida, with a reputation for being 'sporting' and 'efficient' rather than politically motivated, immediately attracted a greater personal popularity by a style of government which has enabled him to carry through the most drastic budget reductions any Nigerian government has dared to impose. This has been possible in consequence of a broad 'national debate' which led to popular rejection of the long-negotiated IMF loan, and some astute management of the various lobbies of the multi-ethnic system.

At the time of writing, Major General Babangida has survived at least one well-publicised attempted coup, for his part in which his former classmate from secondary school in Bida in Niger State and AFRC colleague General Vatsa, together with two former military governors, were convicted and executed. Their motivation appears to have been opposition to the more open aspects of Major General Babangida's political approach, coupled with the rejection of the IMF loan and some of its consequences in cuts in military salaries. The new style is reminiscent of General Mohammed's popular period in government. Major General Babangida has followed Mohammed's example in naming a date for the end of the current period of military rule, and has initiated another period of national debate about future political arrangements for the country. It is probably not without significance that in the early contributions to this renewed search for stable and popularly acceptable constutional arrangements, the need to draw inspiration from traditional political institutions is again being stressed and opposition to multi-party democracy is widespread.

In the post-colonial period, therefore, Nigeria has been marked by considerable political changes, the origins and style of which can to a certain extent be traced to the constitutional patterns of the end of the colonial period, but in the course of which new forms and new constitutional practices have emerged that are more clearly of Nigerian origin. Each successive change of state power has produced some reorientation of political practice towards the new institutional forms available, and these in turn have tended to be incorporated into later changes. An underlying feature has been a complex interplay of regional/local interests with the national state, which constitutional and administrative elaboration has attempted to control and reconcile. This history has in one sense intensified various local particularisms, populary referred to as the tribal factor, while providing the means of integrating them into a national framework of identification. One of the main reasons for the prevalence of claims to establish new states within the federation is quite simply the extent of the patronage and resources which are thought to accompany 'opportunity for separate development' and which make this attractive to local political classes, even though it is true that in this respect the constitutional requirement that parties have a 'federal character' may well have served to entrench a new form of political 'tribalism'.[50].

It should not, however, be concluded from this that the country has become less integrated or more difficult to govern as a result. Indeed, the opposite may well be the case. Thus John N. Paden concluded in a detailed study of religion and political community in the troubled city of Kano:

> The state system itself served as the major structural linkage between Kano and the national level. As a result of the alliance of states during the [civil] war there developed a recognition of Nigeria as a multinational nation. State identity became an acceptable surrogate for ethnic or regional identity, so that linguistic and ethnic pluralism could be accommodated through administrative structures.[51]

Paying attention to the main succession events, both in terms of style and personnel, can thus draw attention in a useful way to the main features of Nigerian political change. Paying attention to the *dominant* forms of succession, however, inevitably avoids looking fully at other forms which still exist, and at attempts which fail. It is undoubtedly important not to overlook the potential significance of events such as the Agbekoya rebellion by anti-state small farmers in Oyo in 1968-70, which was hostile to obas and politicians alike, [52] or the numerous deaths resulting from a local-government quarrel between Ife and Modakeke in 1981, or the riots which burned the residence of the PRP governor of Kano state after his threat to dismiss the Emir in the same year. Kano and Yola have also been the scenes of unrest, efficiently crushed by the army (again with thousands of civilian deaths), caused by supporters of Maitatsane Mohammed Marwa, originally from Cameroon, whose followers believe him to have been a prophet of Islam. Their targets have been established mosques and other, richer Muslims. Nigeria can produce popular uprisings against the entire established order, and significant organised action by its limited wage-earning working classes, but so far such expressions have been too localised and particular to pose a serious threat to the state itself and its system of balancing local interests.

CONCLUSIONS

A brief review of political successions in Nigeria since before the advent of colonialism has attempted to show:

1. that the idea of a colonial legacy operating through a simple process of institutional transfer is too simple to serve as an analysis of the complexities of Nigerian development;
2. that constitutional/administrative change has for a long time been the main vehicle for attempted resolution or reconciliation of these political complexities;
3. that each major shift in the method and style of succession has attracted to itself adapted forms of political activity which in their turn have helped to change future political patterns.

Finally, it should perhaps be made clear that this is not to argue for the *necessity* of any particular sequence of events, as revealed by patterns of succession. The establishment of sequences of different types of succession is a hazardous undertaking, except in a strictly historical sense. There is no need to repeat the teleological style of earlier development theory or, for example, of the authors of *Nigeria, Crisis and Beyond,* [53] which covers the period from independence to reconstruction after the civil war but could hardly have anticipated the politics of the oil boom years, or the Shagari government and its downfall. Following A.D. Smith, the point to be made is simply that it is necessary to see the state-system rather than the nation-system as the colonial legacy and then to treat the interaction of various forms of succession and the refinement of the state-system in a particular instance seriously enough to recognise in it a genuine process of political change. Political succession, orderly or not, deals with only one aspect of the general development (or lack of it) in a state, especially one which is 'dependent'. But in 'reconceptualising the political' in such states it is hardly possible to remain content with the view that they are merely 'over-developed'.

Notes

1. Peter Calvert, see Ch. 1 above.
2. F. Burton and P. Carlen, *Official Discourse: On discourse analysis, government publications, ideology and the state* (London: Routledge & Kegan Paul, 1979) Ch. 2. The signature is the paradigm of representation of the subject *in writing*, and hence a leading example of the 'repetition with a difference' of the subject which it represents. Derrida's general argument, for example, in *Marges de la Philosophie* (Paris: Minuit, 1972), is that since every text is a double text, a reading of the 'general text' requires a 'double science' to render apparent its duplicity. See V. Descombes, *Modern French Philosophy* (English edn, Cambridge: Cambridge University Press, 1979) Ch. 5 *passim*. An analogous point could perhaps be made about acts of political succession.
3. This formulation is from P. Anderson, *In the Tracks of Historical Materialism* (London: Verso, 1983) pp. 43ff.
4. A. D. Smith, *State and Nation in the Third World: The Western state and African nationalism* (Brighton: Harvester, 1983) p. 18.
5. R. B. Seidman, *The State, Law and Development* (London: Croom Helm, 1978) p. 46.
6. Cf. Colin Leys and J. P. Nettl, in Colin Leys (ed.), *Politics and Change in Developing Countries* (Cambridge: Cambridge University Press, 1969), esp. p. 15.
7. Smith, *State and Nation*, quoting Walker Connor, p. 11. The general argument above closely follows his Ch. 1, 'The Western model'.
8. B. Anderson, *Imagined Communities: Reflections on the origin and spread of nationalism* (London: New Left Books, 1983) p. 66, his emphases.
9. C. Tilly (ed.), *The Formation of Nation States in Western Europe* (Princeton, NJ: University Press, 1975), esp. pp. 17–46.
10. B. Anderson, pp. 102–3, following H. Seton-Watson, *Nations and States: An inquiry into the origins of nations and the rise of nationalism* (London: Methuen, 1977).
11. Ibid., p. 136.
12. Ibid., pp. 102–28.
13. Ibid., pp. 145–6.
14. Cf. A. Phillips, 'The concept of development', *Review of African Political Economy*, 8 (1977).

15. Smith, *State and Nation*, p. i.
16. Cf. H. Goulbourne (ed.), *Politics and the State in the Third World*, (London: Macmillan, 1979) pp. 26–7, and H. Alavi, 'The state in postcolonial society', reprinted in the same volume, pp. 38–69.
17. Cf. J. O'Connell, 'The political class and economic growth', *Nigerian Journal of Economics and Social Studies*, 8, 1 (1966) pp. 129–40. A. Peace, *Choice Class and Conflict: A study of Southern Nigerian factory workers* (Brighton: Harvester, 1979) pp. 148–9, gives a view of the 'big men' from below.
18. M. Staniland, *The Lions of Dagbon* (Cambridge: Cambridge University Press, 1975), preface. Dagbon was invaded in brief succession by France, Britain and Germany. Since 1907 Yendi has been the royal capital and Tamale the administrative centre.
19. See J. C. Anene, *The International Boundaries of Nigeria 1885–1960* (Harlow: Longman, 1970) pp. 193–228, and C. Hirshfield, *The Diplomacy of Partition: Britain, France and the creation of Nigeria 1890–1898* (The Hague: Martinus Nijhoff, 1979) pp. 185–98 and 215–16.
20. Samir Amin, *Neocolonialism in West Africa* (Harmondsworth: Penguin, 1973), originally *L'Afrique de l'Ouest Bloquée* (Paris: Minuit, 1971). G. Williams, *State and Society in Nigeria* (Idanre, Ondo: Afrografika, 1980).
21. P. B. Clarke, *West Africa and Islam* (London: Edward Arnold, 1982) p. 114.
22. Ibid., pp. 113–19.
23. J. S. Eades, *The Yoruba Today* (Cambridge: Cambridge University Press, 1980) pp. 3–4.
24. H. A. Obayemi, cited in Eades, *Yoruba Today*, Ch. 2. The subsequent reference in the text is to Samuel Johnson's *History of the Yorubas* (Lagos: 1921).
25. Eades, *Yoruba Today*, p. 26.
26. Cf. K. O. Dike, *Trade and Politics in the Niger Delta* (Oxford: Oxford University Press, 1956).
27. Hirshfield, *Diplomacy of Partition*, pp. 108 and 215–6.
28. Eades, *Yoruba Today*, p. 104.
29. J. A. Atanda, cited in Eades, *Yoruba Today*, pp. 103–4.
30. Sir Frederick Lugard, cited in H. A. Gailey, *The Road to Aba: A study of British administrative policy in Eastern Nigeria* (London: University of London Press, 1971) p. 68.
31. Eades, *Yoruba Today*, p. 105. On the effects of British occupation and rule in general, see M. Crowder, *West Africa under Colonial Rule* (London: Hutchinson University Library for Africa, 1968), esp. Part II, Ch. 3, Part III, Chs 3–4, and Part V, *passim*.
32. A. Majid, *Men in the Middle – Leadership and Role Conflict in a Nigerian Society* (Manchester: Manchester University Press, 1976) p. 242.
33. Cf. J. S. Coleman, *Nigeria: Background to nationalism* (Berkeley, Calif.: University of California Press, 1958). See also the biography of Alhaji Adegoke Adelabu (1914–58): K. W. J. Post and G. D. Jenkins, *The Price of Liberty: Personality and politics in colonial Nigeria* (Cambridge: Cambridge University Press, 1973).

34. The main study of the pre-independence elections is K. W. J. Post, *The Nigerian Federal Election of 1959* (Oxford: Oxford University Press, 1963). Constitutional and political developments up to independence and beyond are summarised in K. Ezera, *Constitutional Developments in Nigeria* (Cambridge: Cambridge University Press, 2nd edn, 1964), and O. Arikpo, *The Development of Modern Nigeria* (Harmondsworth: Penguin, 1967).

35. J. A. Brand, 'The Midwest State Movement in Nigeria', *Political Studies*, 13 (1965) pp. 346–65.

36. J. D. Mackintosh, *Nigerian Government and Politics* (London: Allen & Unwin, 1966) p. 60.

37. O. Oyediran, in O. Oyediran (ed.), *Nigerian Government and Politics under Military Rule – 1960–65* (London: Macmillan, 1979) pp. 20–2. See also K. W. J. Post and M. Vickers, *Structure and Conflict in Nigeria 1960–65* (London: Heinemann, 1973), and J. K. Panter-Brick (ed.), *Nigerian Politics and Military Rule: Prelude to the Civil War* (London: Athlone Press, 1970).

38. B. J. Dudley, *Instability and Political Order: Politics and crisis in Nigeria* (Ibadan: University Press, 1973), esp. pp. 118–9.

39. Oyediran, *Nigerian Government*, p. 28.

40. Cited in Clarke, *West Africa* p. 249.

41. *Ibid.*, pp. 250–4. See also B. J. Dudley, *An Introduction to Nigerian Government and Politics* (London: Macmillan Nigeria, 1982) pp. 162–4.

42. O. Oyediran (ed.), *The Nigerian 1979 Elections* (London: Macmillan Nigeria, 1981) Ch. 8 and p. 167.

43. Dudley, *An Introduction* pp. 194–5 and 216–7. See also Oyediran (ed.), *Nigerian Government, passim* and M. Dent, 'Mystery of the missing bandwagon', *West Africa*, 10 Sept. 1979, p. 1633.

44. Ibid., p. 223.

45. *New African*, August 1983, p. 59. See also A. Kirk-Green and D. Rimmer, *Nigeria Since 1970* (London: Hodder & Stoughton, 1981), esp. Part 1.

46. Oyediran, *Nigerian Government*, pp. 169–70.

47. *New African*, October 1983, p. 23.; November 1983, p. 23.

48. *West Africa*, 29 August 1983. See also Wole Soyinka's denunciation of the elections in *Index on Censorship*, 6 (1983).

49. *New African*, March 1984, pp.1 53–9.

50. C. Dennis, 'Capitalist development and women's work: a Nigerian case study', *Review of African Political Economy*, 27/28 (1984) pp. 110–11, gives one example of a state-owned industrial enterprise and its history.

51. J. N. Paden, *Religion and Culture in Kano* (Berkeley, Calif.: University of California Press, 1973). Cf. J. N. Paden, 'Urban pluralism, integration and adaptation of communal identity in Kano, Nigeria', in R. Cohen and J. Middleton (eds), *From Tribe to Nation in Africa: Studies in incorporation processes* (Scranton, Penn.: Chandler, 1970), and A. C. Smock, *Ibo Politics: The role of ethnic unions in Eastern Nigeria* (Cambridge, Mass.: Harvard University Press, 1971), for a somewhat similar argument covering the period up to 1966, and in relation to the NCNC as a party in the East.

52. G. Williams, 'Political consciousness among the Ibadan poor', in Williams, *State and Society*, pp. 110–34. An influential study of Nigerian workers is R. Cohen, *Labour and Politics in Nigeria* (London: Heinemann, 1974).
53. J. Oyinbo, *Nigeria, Crisis and Beyond* (London: Charles Knight, 1971).

8 Domestic Causes of Military Involvement in Political Succession in Argentina

Sue Milbank

Time after time the bugles have sounded and the soldiers have come marching in, promising to clear up the mess the civilians made of things and then lead the country to glory.[1]

It is impossible to consider political succession in Argentina without looking at the role of the armed forces. Of the 33 presidents who have held office since independence, 16 have been military men and 13 of these have served since 1930. The last civilian president to serve a full term in office was Marcelo T. de Alvear (1922–8). Clearly militarism has sources which precede the Radical era, but politicisation of the armed forces was heightened in the years 1916–30, when broader political representation replaced oligarchic government. Military involvement in politics before 1930 was primarily limited to attempting to assist new civilian elements to political power. Even if Potash is correct, that President Justo's (1932–8) confirmation of the military role in politics is more important in setting the pattern for political intervention by the armed forces in the last half-century,[2] it is still clear that the 1930 revolution brought the forces of modern militarism into the political arena to an unprecedented degree (see Table 8.1).

Nevertheless the extensive involvement of the military in Argentine politics does not imply a level of structural discontinuity which would call into question the idea of political succession. If political succession processes are seen as the means of managing legitimacy crises, then both military and civilian methods may achieve this. Constitutional norms are not redefined with military intervention. They may be temporarily set aside as an ideal to which the nation cannot aspire immediately. More often, the political role of the

Table 8.1   Argentina: succession 1810–1940

Date	Succession type	Details
1810	Elite cooptation	Provisional Junta
1811	Elite cooptation	First triumvirate
1812	Elite cooptation	Second triumvirate
1814	Elite cooptation	Directorate with series of Supreme Directors
1826	Elite cooptation	Presidency established by provincial representatives
1827		Provinces reject new Constitution; President resigns
1829	Elite cooptation	Rosas elected Governor of Buenos Aires
1831	Elite cooptation	Litoral Pact
1835	Elite cooptation and electoral	Rosas elected Governor with supreme and absolute power; result confirmed by plebiscite
1852	Military force	Rosas defeated at Battle of Caseros
1854	Elite cooptation	Presidency re-established under Urquiza
1860	Elite cooptation	Derqui
1861		Forces of Buenos Aires defeat Confederation forces
1862	Military force	Provisional National Government (Mitre)
1868	Elite cooptation	Sarmiento
1874	Elite cooptation and military force	Avellaneda
1880	Elite cooptation	Roca
1886	Elite cooptation	Juárez Celman
1890	Vice Presidential	Pelligrini
1892	Elite cooptation	Luis Saenz Peña
1895	Vice Presidential	José E. Uriburu
1898	Elite cooptation	Roca
1904	Elite cooptation	Quintana
1906	Vice Presidential	Alcorta
1910	Elite cooptation	Roque Saenz Peña
1914	Vice Presidential	de la Plaza
1916	Electoral	Yrigoyen
1922	Radical cooptation	de Alvear
1928	Radical cooptation	Yrigoyen
1930	Military coup	José F. Uriburu
1932	Elite cooptation	Justo
1938	Elite cooptation	Ortiz

armed forces is frequently justified in terms of the maintenance of the very constitutional forms it appears to undermine. The symbolism of continuity is much in evidence during interventions; associations with national history and Western Christian values are emphasised.

Such involvement is highly ritualised – the same sort of statements about cleaning up the political arena accompany all military interventions – indeed it must, through its frequency and emphasis on the spirit of the Constitution, be seen as a regular form of political succession, for Argentina at least.

It is by no means clear that military political succession substantially alters the social class backgrounds of incumbents (though of course it changes the incumbents themselves), or the policies or the norms governing political behaviour itself. Argentina is endowed with two contradictory streams of political culture[3] which interact causing alternative forms of political succession to be available. Both elections and military intervention are semi-legitimate means of regime change. Liberal democracy has been adopted as the ideal form of government and Argentina's formal political institutions established in the mid-nineteenth century reflect this. With the collapse of the Spanish Empire, no real alternative to popular sovereignty existed as the basis for governmental authority. However, the liberal democratic model was consolidated at a time when the circle of eligibles for office was extremely limited and the electorate tiny. Cooptation may be seen as the basis of all political succession, since eligibility is always limited, but the coincidence of the establishment of liberal-democratic ideology with the era of consolidation of the Argentine oligarchy as an economic and political elite has coloured the whole political history of the nation since.

An older model of political activity, deriving from the Hispanic culture but reinforced in the national era, remains as a reserve to which recourse may be made if the liberal-democratic mode of succession fails to coopt a set of incumbents which satisfies the various sectors of Argentine society. To achieve this in Argentina's fragmented society is a tall order since benefits to one sector are likely to be seen as detrimental to the others. Thus electoral succession may be set aside in favour of another means which it is hoped will produce a more satisfactory result.

Historical circumstances always lead to a unique evolution of national succession processes and Argentina's experience of the weaving together of two political cultures has led to a distinct pattern of succession (see Table 8.2). Both military and civilian successions involve competition between power contenders and the interaction of rulers and ruled. The form of this interaction is clearly different in the case of military succession, but it is nevertheless essential. Amongst a modernised, mobilised population for whom legitimacy, in ideological terms if not fully at the practical level, is associated with a liberal-democratic model, the military must tread warily. They require support among civilian sectors to take power and to rule. Without the support of key sectors they could not implement their policies. Further, they require at least passive acceptance on the part of much of the population. Repression on a scale sufficient to contain a whole nation against its will would be impossible to maintain in the long term. Military intervention is normally expected as a civilian government, which is only partly legitimate, is increasingly seen to be failing, and accepted because an alternative model of succession exists which may be used 'semi-legitimately' to restore the 'correct' functioning of liberal democracy.

Table 8.2   Argentina: political succession since 1940

Date	Succession type	Details
(1938)		Ortiz
1942	Vice Presidential	Castillo
1943	Military coup	Rawson
1943	Military cooptation	Ramírez
1944	Military cooptation	Farrell
1946	Electoral	Juan D. Perón
1955	Military coup	Lonardi
1955	Military cooptation	Aramburu
1958	Electoral	Frondizi
1962	Military coup and constitutional	Guido
1963	Electoral	Illia
1966	Military coup	Onganía
1970	Military cooptation	Levingston
1971	Military cooptation	Lanusse
1973	Electoral	Cámpora
1973	Peronist cooptation and electoral	Juan D. Perón
1974	Vice Presidential	Isabel Perón
1976	Military coup	Junta
1976	Military cooptation	Videla
1981	Military cooptation	Viola
1981	Military cooptation	Liendo
1981	Military cooptation	Lacoste
1981	Military cooptation	Galtieri
1982	Military cooptation	Saint-Jean
1982	Military cooptation	Bignone
1983	Electoral	Alfonsín

There is no dispute in Argentina about what constitutes the highest office. Indeed the supreme power of the presidency enhances the possibility of military succession. The military or civilian eligibles for that post, although usually from similar socio-economic back-grounds, vary in the manner of the acquisition of their eligibility. Civilian eligibles tend to have held lesser offices and key legislative posts. Military candidates tend to be factional leaders or, most often, commanders-in-chief of the army. (This has not always been so; the colourless and virtually unknown General Levingston, President between 1970 and 1971, was not such a figure, but he was a 'front man' for General Lanusse, who was.) Thus competition amongst military eligibles is likely to be much more confined as their number is smaller by definition. Such competition has certainly occurred as is indicated by simple displacements of one officer by another, for example, Lonardi by Aramburu, Viola and Liendo by Galtieri. Moreover all such displacements have occurred within the army, inter-service rivalry being contained by forming a junta of represen-tatives of the three services which nominates the successor only from among the top ranks of the dominant service. Patronage has a place in both forms of succession and networks of notable families exist among the military elite as they do among civilian eligibles. Similarly cooptation, which is clearly central to military succession, has expanded beyond the traditional selection of political colleagues, reward of key supporters and neutralisation of key opponents in the civilian sector too. The increasing complexities of government and the long-running crisis of economic development have required the cooptation of a new kind of expert into civilian governments. In the present Argentine administration these 'technocrats' have been defined as 'people who can count and have not done their stints in Radical committee rooms'.[4]

A narrow definition of political succession which excludes military intervention is unacceptable to the present author. However, it must be admitted that there is a case for arguing that two streams of succession reflecting the two distinct patterns of cultural influence occur in Argentina. Thus a temporal lag may occur in the process of succession. A regime may be a successor to one which left office many years previously. For example, it would be possible to argue that the fraudulent election of Justo in 1932, made possible by the ousting of Yrigoyen's government by military intervention in 1930, was clearly the restoration, in a more modern context, of the oligarchic parliamentarianism that had given way to Radical government based on universal manhood suffrage in 1916. Thus if continuity of regime is seen as the basis of political succession, then military intervention may be seen as distorting the process but not as destroying it. In a sense, it may be said that the very continuity of some aspects of civilian society contribute to the involvement of the military in Argentine politics, which casts doubt on an argument that discontinuity of regime types negates the idea of political succession.

Explanations of the political involvement of the Argentine armed forces can be clustered into three broad types: those which look within the military institutions for the causes of the actions of the officers, those which seek answers in the domestic social setting and those which look to factors external to Argentina. Obviously, these kinds of explanations are interrelated, and each kind can be in itself only a partial solution. Whilst lack of civilian resistance to military intervention or economic crisis resulting from an international situation may provide a backdrop for action by the military, such action stems directly from within an organisation. Types of explanation are not easily delineated either, for example, external factors (such as foreign military training) may contribute to internal factors (such as fear of subversion). However, despite the difficulties of breaking down factors which promote political intervention, this chapter will primarily be concerned with aspects of Argentine society which are conducive to military intervention in politics.

Janowitz distinguishes between two kinds of militarism. He writes:

> Designed militarism – the type identified with Prussian militarism – involves domination and penetration of civilian institutions by military leaders, acting directly and with premeditation through government and other institutions. Unanticipated militarism develops from a lack of effective traditions for controlling the military establishment, as well as from a failure of civilian leaders to act relevantly and consistently. Under such circumstances, a vacuum is created which not only encourages an extension of the power of military leadership, but actually compels such trends.[5]

Argentina is not devoid of features of 'designed militarism', but her militarism is more frequently of the 'unanticipated' kind. Civilian processes as well as the internal structure and disposition of the armed forces determine military political action.

Evidence of a multiplicity of forces at work can be found in both the 1930 and 1943 revolutions, to take just two important examples. The role of the military in 1930 clearly shows that its actions were motivated by factors external to it as well as within it. The failure of Radical political democracy to offset the effects of the economic crisis and the ineptitude and corruption of politicians are only partial explanations of Uriburu's coup. Likewise, the actions of the GOU (*Grupo de Oficiales Unidos*) in 1943 can only be explained in part by reference to the growth of nationalism during the 'Infamous Decade' (1930–43) and Castillo's (1942–3) attempt to impose his unpopular would-be successor. In both cases long-term structural factors provided the pre-existing situation in which trigger events could pull the military into politics.

These structural factors in Argentine civilian society are again interdependent and not easily separable. However, some attempt at classification must be made, and thus these factors are broadly grouped as:

1. historical forces, such as the legacy of the colonial era, the independence struggle, *caudillismo*, and so on;
2. social forces, including the fragmentary nature of Argentine society, widely held values conducive to (or at least not unconducive to) militarism, socialisation, and so on;
3. economic and developmental factors, whereby the very process of rapid change produces a climate in which intervention becomes more likely;
4. political factors, both institutional and informal.

Spanish authority in Latin America was not conceded gracefully; indeed fears of a possible attempt at reconquest gave the military an important role in the new republics.[6] In addition, the Wars of Independence themselves produced from the outset an association of soldiering and nationhood. The xenophobia of modern Argentina began with the defeat of Spain (1810). But the legacy of the colonial era leading directly to militarism is greater still. As Morse points out, parts of the Spanish colonial heritage are the theme of order, obedience, authority and stability.[7] These values formed the basis of the claims to power of the *caudillos* generally and Rosas (1829–32 and 1835–52) in particular, and continue to provide an alternative basis for political succession. Argentina, like other Latin American nations, inherited absolutism from the autocracy of sixteenth-century Spain.[8] Similarly, fear of separatist movements in sixteenth-century Spain resulted in a legacy of centralisation which has made government an easier prey to force. Some writers have suggested that the colonial era left the new republics with a cultural residue of strong individualist pride which could only be subdued by force and this is reflected in the sectoral structure of modern Argentina.[9]

However, much more important than the positive legacy of colonialism was the negative legacy, that is, the structures and values that might have favoured civilian government, which Spain could not and did not bequeath to her colonies in the Americas. There had been no preparation for independence during the colonial period, which is hardly surprising since independence was not intended by Spain. The central importance of the Spanish Crown as a symbol of authority resulted in a situation in which when independence was won, the whole basis of legitimate authority was lost. There were no strong political institutions commanding the respect of the population as a whole. No public opinion existed to question the policies of those who held power, so ideology was less important than force. Violence became an established pattern used by all elite factions.[10] Andreski writes of this situation:

> When there is neither political consensus nor institutions permitting orderly government, the only possible way of ruling a country is by force. Thus praetorianism was the inevitable consequence of the wars of liberation which destroyed the colonial administration together with its ideological basis, without putting in its place any institutions which could command general assent.[11]

Spain left no tradition of politics, only a legacy of administration.[12] The new republics lacked any experience of functioning democracy and thus when democratic structures were adopted there could be no tradition of understanding and valuing democracy.[13] The absence of any inherited political system gave rise to a personalistic style of politics which would prove conducive to military intervention in three main ways: first, it would promote heroic military figures as potential leaders; second, it would provoke a military response when a personality cult appeared to be undermining national dignity; and third, it would cause mobilisation without real participation on the part of the masses. Also, Spanish colonialism did not leave any group with sufficient political experience and strength to counteract military elements. Supremacy of civil power was part of the British legacy to North America, but no such separation of civil and military power existed under Spain.[14] As a result Argentina (like some other Latin American nations) lacks what S. E. Finer calls 'the principle of civil supremacy'.[15] Finally, Spain left the new Latin American republics without clear senses of their national identities.[16] Argentina's nationalism is at least partly a response to this problem.

The period of apparent political stability in the latter half of the nineteenth century should not be discounted as a source of later militarism either. Certain military elements were active in support of the Radical cause (this activity will be discussed later), but for the most part the armed forces kept out of the factional disputes and personal rivalries amongst the oligarchy as these kept well within agreed rules.[17] Military privileges and wealth came from the elite: for example, grants of newly won pampas land went to military men who had participated in defeating the Indians during Roca's presidency (1880–6), and thus a challenge to oligarchic dominance would have been irrational. Similarly, the military benefited from the beginnings of the process of professionalisation during this period. But, whilst the military remained on the sidelines, a number of weaknesses in the political and social structures were being established. Representative government was consolidated but it was severely limited and more symbolic than real. The essentially defensive nature of oligarchic power was clearly shown by the use of fraud, which set a pattern weakening the popular conception of democracy. Thus the regulation of political succession came to be associated with fraudulent practices and thereby the legitimacy of the process was further undermined. (Later, especially in the years 1930–43, the pattern of electoral fraud was extended until such a high level of political cynicism existed that much of the population could not be stirred to resist militarism by supporting civilian political forces.) Nor was the age devoid of political violence. Both President Mitre (1862–8) and Sarmiento (1868–74) were vicious in their extermination of the *caudillos* and Mitre even attempted to regain the presidency by force.[18]

The position of the oligarchy which was determined in these years contributed to the role of the armed forces in politics later. Argentina had become exceptionally dependent on agricultural exports and thus a powerful elite survived the Radical emergence in 1916 and remained to weaken Radical government.[19] Like other traditional elites, the Argentine oligarchy rested on an insecure base which was threatened by long-term constitutional government.[20] Since the distribution of property tends to be closely associated with the distribution of power, the 1930 revolution was unsurprising in that it restored congruence between economic and political power.[21] The landed upper class recognised that changes were occurring in the international trade situation which threatened their interests and that the Unión Civica Radical (UCR) government was not taking action.[22] The armed forces initially acted as arbiters in the internal conflict between the forces of nationalism and internationalism which was intensified as a result of the economic crisis. By 1932 the intervention of the military could clearly be seen to have been a response to challenges to the hegemony of the ruling class. Just as the oligarchy defensively agreed to extend the franchise in 1912, believing that they could still win elections with an extended electorate,[23] so they were prepared to support action against democracy in 1930 when its results no longer suited them. Thus the revolution was a process of demobilisation. Uriburu and Justo were able to achieve success, according to Goldwert, because of 'the oligarchy's willingness to sacrifice Argentina's fragile tradition of civilian rule by accepting the political leadership of the generals'.[24]

The pragmatic approach of the upper class and their lack of real democratic principles must bear some responsibility for the ensuing crises which provoked, and an atmosphere which did not resist, military involvement in politics. The period of liberal nationalist rule 1932–43 involved the use of the symbolism of democracy to preserve the old order, and 'patriotic fraud' led to middle-class questioning of the whole concept.[25] Also the *vendepatria* quality of the Infamous Decade (especially the Treaty of London, or Roca–Runciman Pact of 1933) antagonised elements of the military and accelerated the growth of nationalism in the army in particular, thus laying the foundations for the 1943 revolution.[26]

Argentina has always been an atomistic society pulled apart by centrifugal forces such as regionalism. It took the iron fist of Rosas to unify the nation, despite his hostility to the Unitarians who opposed the federalism he purported to represent. Some writers even go so far as to argue that the countries of Latin America in general have norms based on conflict rather than consensus, and that crisis is effectively institutionalised.[27] Immigration on a massive scale and rapid urbanisation have further contributed to the fragmented nature of Argentine society. Under such circumstances xenophobic nationalism can be a point of agreement in otherwise divergent societies, and certainly Argentina has a long tradition of nationalism, exemplified in the nineteenth century by Rosas, which emerged with a vengeance when the depression struck. However, it is a negative nationalism built on what it opposes, not on a strong sense of national identity and tolerant pride, and thus it is not a force which unifies, as might be expected.

Fragmentation goes beyond the failure of the three main sectors of society – the landed, industrial and commercial elite, the urban middle class and the urban working class – to cooperate with each other to provide support sufficient to enable civilian governments to rule without recourse to the military. Consensus is rarely achieved within the sectors, which further complicates the situation. The anomic quality of Argentine society and the bitterness of sectional wrangles are pervasive, even penetrating the armed services themselves. Amidst the chaos, the military, or elements of it, come to see themselves as the only force capable of providing some sort of stabilising influence. Theberge and Fontaine recognise the permanence of this trait in writing that: 'The Argentina of the 1970s still resembles in some ways the Argentina of the 1820s – a nation of factions struggling for a larger share of a slower growing national product.'[28]

There are other features of Argentine society which are worth considering as possible sources of the military role in political succession. Perhaps the most important aspect is the tolerance of authoritarianism in civil society. It has frequently been suggested that this stems from the institutions of Hispanic culture which are authoritarian in essence.[29] Certainly civilian elements have powerful weapons that they can use against military domination,[30] but, for example, the period 1976–83 in Argentina was marked by 'the willingness of the general population to put up with abuses that would have spurred democrats elsewhere into noisy rebellion'.[31] A protracted general strike could have forced the military from power sooner, but in the end it was military incompetence more than social reaction that resulted in the civilianisation of Argentine politics.

Argentina suffers from the survival of what Apter terms 'antecedent values',[32] some of which are certainly conducive to a tolerance of militarism. It is a highly individualistic society, and individualism gives rise to admiration of colourful, charismatic (often military) political figures. Elements of the Weberian concept of charismatic authority[33] mark the governments of Yrigoyen (1916–22 and 1928–30) and Perón (1946–55 and 1973–4), for example, and when this type of authority disappears it leaves a political vacuum into which the military may move. The need for charisma has affected the process of political succession and hindered some politicians who might otherwise have contributed to long-term stability. The attempts of Ortiz (1938–42) to restore constitutionalism were thus weakened, and Horowitz cites Frondizi's (1958–62) lack of charisma as a factor for his party's defeat by the Peronists in the 1962 elections, leading to military intervention.[34] Personalism in politics runs counter to constitutionalism and therefore is one further factor which serves to undermine the formal rules of politics. The armed forces are not seen as parasitic by many Argentines, who share their forebears' contempt for manual labour and who do not therefore place great emphasis on a person's productive capacity.[35] Machismo remains strong and thus supports militarism, and also an endemic fatalism which encourages acceptance of whatever occurs.[36]

Many writers have suggested that Argentine economic dependency brought about the 1930 revolution,[37] and that continuing external economic domination has contributed to the pattern established then ever since. However, the effects of the Great Depression had hardly begun to be felt in Argentina when the revolution occurred and therefore 'economic dependence might have emphasised weaknesses within the political system and thus been necessary for the revolution, but it was not in itself a sufficient cause'.[38] But external economic factors can be seen as having an indirect influence in that they helped to generate the development process. Development serves to undermine traditional structures and thus promotes instability. Changes in patterns of production and consumption give rise to changes in the pattern of domination.[39] Economic diversification produces increased role differentiation and thus increased problems of integration which contribute to the fragmentation of an already divided society. In such circumstances the armed forces are seen as a source of stability. Thus rapid socio-economic changes cause crises of participation, legitimacy and distribution, and actions to deal with one crisis may serve to promote the next.[40] Economic development would, however, be less destabilising in its effects if political institutions were more deeply entrenched and more widely respected, if tolerance of political opposition were greater and if the Argentine middle class had been able to establish its hegemony.

Military involvement in politics is closely related to levels of political development, and Argentina has what S. E. Finer terms 'low political culture'.[41] Huntington suggests that Argentina has a high level of 'political modernisation' (meaning mobilisation of new social groups) but is low on 'political development' (or political institutions to cope with these newly mobilised elements). Social and economic advancement has not been matched politically. As political participation (in the sense of mobilisation) exceeds institutionalisation, a politically unstable 'praetorian' society is the result.[42] Similarly, Dahl argues that extension of participation prior to the development of legitimate competitive politics provides a source of instability during the transition period.[43] Extension of formal political participation in 1912 was an attempt to reduce the threat to the then existent structure, but it failed as it mobilised new sectors without fully incorporating them. Voting did not imply representation in government. Positions in government may have passed from the mainstream of the oligarchy to '*políticos*' (such as Yrigoyen) and marginal upper-class elements (such as Alvear) but there remained a massive gulf between those who had political power and those who did not.

Increased participation therefore meant mobilisation without assimilation and this resulted in later attempts to reduce participation by authoritarian means in 1930. The emergence of new groups as a consequence of the processes of urbanisation and industrialisation meant an additional challenge to the traditional structure and the established rules of the political system. Thus the use of what Huntington terms the 'veto coup' occurred in 1955 also.[44] Restrictions on political participation of sectors of the population by the military have frequently been used since to contain the perceived threat of a Peronist restoration.

Militarism is symptomatic of other problems within the political system and perhaps the most important of these is the relative weakness of other institutions which could serve to counteract the political strength of the armed forces. It is not surprising that the military should act politically, just as other social institutions do, but in Argentina effective sources of countervailing political power have not existed. 'Institutional weaknesses stem largely from a lack of trust in impersonal political institutions.'[45] In situtations where institutional legitimacy is the source of authority, agreed procedures determine policy, political succession, conflict resolution and so on. Force is a last resort For the most part the rules of the political game are observed without threat of it. There are a multiplicity of factors working against the establishment of a general belief in popular sovereignty and institutional legitimacy. Some of the most significant, such as the gap between the theory and the reality of politics, incompetence among politicians, and so on, will be discussed later, but it has also been suggested that popular values also contribute to this situation. For example, it is claimed that immigrants came to Argentina from countries lacking democratic political institutions. [46] Whatever the reason, the lack of institutional legitimacy removes the strength of the stigma of illegitimacy from military involvement in politics. It may even, as Imaz has suggested, make the military a source of political legitimation.[47]

The incongruence between formal political structure and political activity and the distrust of the political system by large numbers of people which this produces are legacies of the nineteenth century. They reflect the adoption of an ideology of liberal democracy without the displacement of the then existing model of political activity. There are wide disparities between both governmental apparent intentions and actual performance, and also between law and adherence to it. This situation leads to widespread contempt for government and law. It is an aspect of Argentine politics best exemplified by the lack of application of constitutional theory.

Constitutional theory is not in accord with the usage in Argentina, as is also the case in some other Latin American republics. The 1853 Constitution was the result of external ideological forces rather than being indigenously generated and this is the source of its incapacity to determine domestic political activity. Thus a contradiction between theory and practice was established with the adoption of a Western political model. The Constitution represents an aristocratic concept of government; its liberal-democratic ideological base does not accord with non-pluralistic political reality. As in other Latin American nations, popular sovereignty is the theoretical basis of the Argentine Constitution but this conflicts with other social values, and therefore the Constitution cannot serve as a guideline for the operation of the political system at the practical level. In consequence, it does not provide a clear justification of legitimate authority and thus leaves the freedom to challenge for power by unconstitutional means.

More specifically, the 1853 Constitution leaves much open to wide interpretation. For example, the state of siege suspending individual guarantees was intended as a temporary measure to counteract or to forestall a crisis, but Uriburu (1930–2) maintained a state of siege throughout his administration.[48] Similarly, this power was supposed only to be justifiable in the event of a foreign invasion or domestic upheaval. But the latter justification is not tightly defined and, of 29 declarations of states of siege before 1943, 14 were made by executive decree alone and only one was a response to foreign attack. (This constitutional vagueness established a pattern which was passed down from the federal government to the provincial level. For example, Sarmiento as governor of San Juan declared a provincial state of siege in 1863.) Likewise the Constitution is vague about which individual guarantees may be suspended.[49] and Uriburu suspended them all during his state of siege!

The Constitution makes requirements which allow great flexibility and have fallen into disuse as a result. It requires that the president consult Congress when intervening in the provinces, for example. But if intervention occurs during a Congressional recess, the president is merely required to report on his actions when Congress resumes. This requirement has been largely ignored. Thus the Constitution has become a means by which a government can eliminate political opposition and avoid any necessity to share power. Yrigoyen used intervention repeatedly against Conservative opposition in the provinces. Uriburu followed the same pattern against Radical opposition, intervening in 12 provinces in one week. The Constitution allows intervention to be forcible if necessary; it permits dismissal of officials, suspension of the provincial legislature and the appointment of a new one; it even allows the intervener to disregard law and the Constitution itself.[50]

The liberal political theory behind the Constitution of Argentina emphasises operation of the political system within defined procedural limits, and thus implies compromise amongst politically competing groups and a toleration of opposition and dissent. In Anglo-American political systems both traditions and institutions encourage political compromise and toleration of dissent. Argentine traditions, however, do not have the same effect and indeed run counter to the liberal-democratic theoretical base of the formal political institutions. Iberian culture operates against compromise. As Weatherhead writes: 'In Latin America ..., compromise as a political craft has little prestige and scant effectiveness. Indeed, compromise has clearly derogatory overtones. The verb *transigir*, broadly meaning 'to compromise' implies giving in, in a prejudicial sense'.[51] The inability to make political compromise is part of a wider incapacity to share power with political opponents. A 'zero-sum' approach to political conflict was developed during the period of oligarchic rule in the late nineteenth and early twentieth centuries. This, along with the lack of a national identity that has given Argentina an essentially sectoral structure since the beginning of the national period, has produced a weak and fragmented political system which is conducive to military intervention. Numerous examples of this high level of political intolerance can be found.

Yrigoyen increased political conflict by viewing his victory in 1916 as the first stage in a revolution which would lead to the destruction of the oligarchy. This attitude 'could hardly be expected to convert the conservative politicians of the oligarchy into a loyal opposition'.[52] Instead of reducing antagonism by coopting Conservative elements into his government, Yrigoyen exacerbated the situation by his interventions in Conservative provinces. Likewise cooptation of Antipersonalist Radicals during his second administration could have worked against the declining legitimacy which the UCR was experiencing as a consequence of the split.[53] Radical intolerance of this kind encouraged the growth of political violence in the form of paramilitary groups such as the *Liga Republicana* and the *Liga Patriótica Argentina* opposing the Radical government and the *Klan Radical* supporting it. Similarly, without political compromise and cooptation, the weakening effect on the government of a Senate controlled by Conservatives, Antipersonalist Radicals and Socialists was magnified.[54]

The end of the Radical era did not mean an end to political intransigence. After his initial association with Radical elements against Uriburu, Justo, once in power, had the Radical leaders arrested. (Justo's actions indicate another related problem too, that frequently alliances serve negative purposes; in Argentine history, common ground has often meant a common enemy rather than political consensus.) However, despite such treatment, Radical elements refused to join with the Socialists and Progressive Democrats to form a middle-class political front against the Concordancia (which was itself divided) and militarism. Political realities could not overcome intransigence as the Radicals continued to see themselves as the sole heirs to power. Castillo also refused to entertain any power-sharing, and even provoked a political crisis which paralysed the legislative process by re-introducing electoral fraud to prevent Radical victories in important provinces. In 1941 he dissolved the Socialist and Radical dominated Buenos Aires Municipal Council by presidential decree, and also continued the pattern of using the state of siege to repress criticism.[55] Nor did suppression of dissent disappear with the Infamous Decade; for example, Perón introduced his *desacato* (disrespect) law in 1949. Likewise the technique of building bridges to the political opposition did not increase and Frondizi, lacking popular support, governed by means of dividing the opposition: 'he pitted faction against faction, party against party, resolving individual crises but doing nothing to broaden the political consensus in Argentina'.[56]

The sheer number of political forces at work in Argentina make achieving consensus a difficult task even if the will to do so were present. The commitment of each political force to dominate alone in the long term makes it impossible. Power has been so dispersed amongst civilian groups that no group has been able to contain the other groups or counterbalance military power. Temporary coalitions, united only by what they are opposed to, have not been able to alleviate the chronic civilian political impotence. Various political groups have been 'mutually exclusive forces'[57] weakening each other by their conflicting aims. This situation has two further related effects, both of which indirectly encourage the armed forces to involve themselves in politics. First, the exclusion of the opposition from normal channels drives it outside the formal rules of the political game and invites the military to appear to be responding to a challenge to the constitutional order. Second, the belief in not sharing power has given rise to an emphasis on differences; divisions have been allowed to remain and encouraged to deepen, thus allowing the military to appear to be a force of national unity and stability. Exclusion of opposition has meant that throughout most of the twentieth century, Argentine politics has been dominated by one main party, first the Radicals and then the Peronists. Aspirants have been so involved in in-fighting that the military has been able to present itself as the only effective opposition.[58]

Social fragmentation gives rise to a multiplicity of smaller political parties, mutually hostile and therefore largely impotent. Such antagonisms resulted in parties organising to take power rather than to rule as can be seen in the UCR's lack of a political programme in 1916. (The Unión Cívica Radical del Pueblo's (UCRP's) election victory in 1963 was similarly a consequence of better party organisation, not the presentation of a more popular programme.) Some, such as the Partido Socialista (established 1894–6), were so hide-bound with ideology that they were largely ineffective at the practical level. The Socialist Party was elitist, comprising intellectuals who rarely involved themselves in the labour movement.[59] In addition the political parties were plagued by internal weaknesses, in particular the related problems of personalism and factionalism.

Personalism, deriving from the association of authority with the person of the king in Hispanic culture, contributed to the internal fragmentation of parties, and has at the same time produced leaders who were not well suited for the expanded role of government in the twentieth century. Yrigoyen's highly personalised rule, for example, failed to build up a middle-class political philosophy or establish viable institutions for the continued political involvement of newly mobilised political groups. His individual stubborness, despite criticisms from within the UCR and outside it, prevented him changing his political style and his unpopular political retinue.[60] The conflicts generated by support for or opposition to Perón, and the effects of the man himself, are well-known, pervading Argentina still.

Factionalism has been partly the result of personal rivalries within the parties, and has served to undermine democratic political succession. For example, divisions within the Yrigoyen administration were a source of the success of the 1930 coup.[61] After 1955 internal divisions within the other political parties over their attitude to Peronism prevented the assimilation of the working class and left a large alienated political force, fear of which led to continuing military involvement in politics.[62] Instead of dissolving as it might have done, the Peronist movement remained largely intact outside the formal political structure, developing a new mythology and attracting new youth groups.

The personalism and factionalism of civilian politics, along with corruption, came to be seen by some military elements as a reason for Argentina's failure to fulfil her national destiny. For economic development, these political weaknesses meant government paralysis. Corruption flourished during the Radical era and contributed to military disillusionment with political parties.[63] Corruption within the parties gave the armed forces a moral superiority they might not otherwise have achieved, as they alone remained untainted. The effects were wider still, however, as political socialisation included coming to see politicians and their parties as incompetent and corrupt. Thus the low public status of politics reduced recruitment of party personnel amongst the most able.

As noted previously, the role of elections in the process of political succession was diminished under oligarchic rule in the late nineteenth century. In considering why the legitimacy of elections was reduced so greatly, Dahl compares the situation with eighteenth-century Britain and argues that the extent of fraud and violence in Argentina was much greater. He further suggests that ignoring the law and Constitution, whilst still claiming that governmental legitimacy sprang from them, negated electoral victory as a source of legitimacy. The absence of a transitional period between oligarchic rule and universal manhood suffrage also meant that there was no time during which the legitimacy of elections could be established as a political norm. Oligarchic abuse of elections as a means of political succession established an alternative norm: 'By their own conduct the notables taught the Argentinians that elections need not be binding on the losers or the potential losers.'[64] Thus later electoral rigging such as that which occurred in 1932 and 1937 cannot be seen as aberrant. A pattern had been set whereby the opposition would not lose legitimacy if it by-passed the constitutional means of succession and sought military assistance to gain power. Therefore the *golpe* or coup became an alternative means of political change rather than an inferior and illegitimate means.

The extent of presidential powers have proved a considerable provocation to the military as well. Whilst the 1853 Constitution gives the president massive powers over the armed forces (the president is Commander-in-Chief, controls military distribution and, with Congressional approval, appoints senior personnel), there has frequently been a hostile reaction when these powers have been in the hands of a civilian. Presidentialism was effectively established in the 1880s by Roca who ensured the *unicato* (presidential dominance) by threatening the use of the army to intervene against opposition forces. Presidentialism results in a weakening of civilian institutions for several reasons.

Although Congress is weak itself as a result of the lack of a parliamentary tradition, factionalism and so on, the relative strength of the presidency limits its role still more. The extent of the president's control over political appointments has made the office a prime target for the armed forces. A feature of presidentialism which has caused military antagonism is the way that it personalises the state. For example, from 1946 to 1949 the armed forces were fairly autonomous, but they resented the growing association of Peronism with the state itself after 1949. By 1954 the military was exhibiting a growing disaffection with the personality cult which had developed.[65]

Probably the most important weakness of a presidential system of this kind is that the military come to be seen as the only effective check on executive power. If there are no civilian power bases which can counter presidential power, then military elements are involved in politics by definition; such involvement is structural. On the subject of the 1943 coup, Potash writes:

> In acting to oust the Castillo government, the military was responding to a harsh axiom of Argentine politics: that no constitutional authority is strong enough to prevent a determined president from imposing his will, even if this involves violation of the laws and the constitution itself; and that only the withdrawal of military support can call a halt to such an administration.[66]

The Supreme Court is another formal institution of government which has added its weight to the unconstitutional nature of political succession. Despite 40 years without a revolution, when Uriburu asked the Supreme Court for recognition of his provisional government, within four days it agreed to validate acts of provisional government officials. The Court also granted the new regime the right to exercise the powers given to the executive by the Constitution, though it did emphasise that the government was transitional and could therefore not exercise judicial powers nor legislate, except where absolutely necessary. Likewise when Ramírez (1943–4) assumed power in 1943, he petititoned the Supreme Court for recognition and got it immediately, despite the clearly unconstitutional nature of his regime, which had imposed a state of siege suspending constitutional guarantees and which was interfering with the independence of lower courts. Pierson and Gil write of these actions of the Supreme Court: 'In effect, it had recognised revolution and had legalised certain results thereof, which were in themselves political acts. It had granted to a de facto government the powers of a de jure government, provided that the new regime observed the constitution and the laws'.[67]

Military intervention in politics is not merely a response to weaknesses in the civilian political system. The armed forces are pushed as well as pulled into the political arena. Military government is the military acting on behalf of certain important civilian sectors. Lieuwen writes of Latin America generally: 'The militarism of the postwar period, like that of the 1930s has been principally a reflection of demands made upon the armed forces by antagonistic classes – by the traditional order attempting to maintain the *status quo* and by new forces attempting to alter it.[68]

Without support from certain key economic groups and the bureaucracy, the military could not put their policies into practice. Thus Uriburu's coup received support from nationalist groups, including the paramilitary *Legión Cívica Argentina*, and some provincial political organisations such as the Province of Buenos Aires Conservative Party; also some middle-class elements were willing to trade political democracy for economic nationalism and industrial development.[69] Justo's militarily backed regime was supported by agricultural exporting interests and the UIA (Argentine Industrial Union). Without the support of Radical civilian groups, the nationalist officers of the Government could not have achieved success in 1943.[70] Similarly Onganía's regime (1966–70) rested on its collaboration with foreign investors, domestic financial organisations, domestic industrial and commercial elites and disillusioned members of the middle class.[71] The 1976 coup received a warm welcome too; the Ford Motor Company saw 1976 as the year in which Argentina rediscovered her proper way,[72] and domestically:

> the leaders of the non-military sectors proved all too willing to pay tribute to the new order. Big private firms happily made room on their boards for retired military men, the unions declared a truce, and the political parties, recognising that the struggle was over for the time being, lapsed into a moody silence. Civilian technocrats, moreover, threw their lot in with the military and helped them manage the economy and, of even greater potential importance, the educational system, which was modified to enable the military to indoctrinate the country's youth.[73]

Intellectuals have been the main group opposing militarism, but even their opposition has been less than consistent. For example, the nationalist poet, Leopoldo Lugones, sought a greater role for the armed forces in domestic affairs during Justo's government.[74] Thus a wide spectrum of civilian groups push the military into politics for a multiplicity of reasons.

National independence has come to be seen as synonymous with a powerful military and the prestige of military might is taken as a sign of development. Horowitz, writing in the mid-1960s, suggested that: 'Many of the more well-defined social classes welcome the present military ascendancy as a visible display of national development.'[75]

Strong central government is also favoured by nationalist develop-
mentalist economists such as Raúl Prébisch,[76] who served as an
adviser to President Onganía. The armed forces are good for
business; arms production, for example, is very lucrative, and Argentina
is the seventh largest arms exporter in the world. (There is also a
belief amongst business groups that imported weapons technology
has a beneficial spin-off effect for industry in general.)[77] Fear of the
Left is also a very strong factor for middle-class support of military
intervention and certainly this was the case in 1976.

In addition to civilian support for, and sometimes encouragement
of, political involvement of the armed forces, there has also been
deliberate civilian use of the military for political ends. Political and
economic crises frequently result in civilian calls for military intervention; this particularly occurs when military status is high relative
to that of civilian politicians. Johnson calls this use of the armed
forces 'civil-militarism', and suggests that there are three main
reasons for it. First, the military can be used as a means for ousting a
regime (and are thus an integral part of the process of political
succession). Second, violence remains an important part of the political
culture of Latin America. Third, intra- and inter-service rivalries can
be taken advantage of by politicians.[78] Using the armed forces for
partisan ends is essentially short-sighted, but it is also based on a
contradiction. As Horowitz writes: 'In Latin America the military is
often turned to as a court of ultimate national redemption, even while
at the same time it is recognized that the military has often crushed
democratic and constitutional processes.'[79]

Civilian use of the armed forces is long standing in Argentina.
During the 1890 revolt, for example, Radical elements sought the
support of a secret lodge of junior officers, the *Logia de los 33*.[80] The
Radical involvement of the military in their political conspiracies
and uprisings gave rise to regulations prohibiting such involvement.
As a direct result of the abortive revolt in February 1905, in which
many officers took part, a new military statute was issued emphasising
the apolitical role of army officers.[81] The conspiracies continued
until the Sáenz Peña Law (electoral reform) reduced the grievance
felt by pro-UCR officers, but by then the pattern of conspiracy had
been effectively established. Once in power, Yrigoyen continued to
use the military in his *reparación política* (interventions in the provinces
against Conservative groups). After their overthrow, the Radicals still
sought to use the military, requesting that the armed forces be used to
oversee the honesty of the 1936 elections. The request was refused, but
it did establish a precedent for the use of military personnel for this

purpose in the 1946 (and later) presidential elections. *La Prensa* warned President Ortiz of the dangers inherent in using the armed forces for political purposes no matter how worthy, when in February 1940 he proposed federal intervention in the province of Catamarca against Conservative fraud.[82]

An insensitivity in dealing with the military also marked Yrigoyen's government. Mishandling of the armed forces by politicians in general has been a spur to military political activity. From 1880 to 1916 the Argentine army had undergone professionalisation, and during the Radical era government control of the services was not established as it might have been if military matters had been dealt with more effectively. On assuming power Yrigoyen began rewarding officers who had supported the Radical cause previously and, in so doing, he overlooked those who were senior for promotion purposes. Potash writes: 'The tragedy was that in looking backward and trying to redress the past inequities, Yrigoyen was helping to undermine the none-too-strong tradition of military aloofness from politics and to weaken the sense of unity in the officer corps.'[83]

Upon his return to power in 1928, following the Alvear interlude, Yrigoyen failed to fulfil promises of military equipment made under his predecessor, nepotism returned in appointments, and the president resumed his meddling in assignments, organisation and so on. Yrigoyen was not alone in failing to deal successfully with the military, but the extent of his failure was greater and it occurred at the crucial stage in Argentine history when the newly-professionalised armed forces needed to be brought under effective government control if the principle of civilian supremacy was to be established. The extent of Yrigoyen's personal incompetence in this matter is indicated in Smith's comment that, 'Yrigoyen intervened in military affairs *before* the army intervened decisively in politics, and the officers responded in *reaction* to his interference.'[84]

Despite all the forces operating to encourage military involvement in the process of political succession, it should not be forgotten that there are also forces resisting it. But the partial counterbalancing of military power by civilian institutions causes more frequent changes of regime, and thus the armed forces are frequently involved in politics for relatively short periods. Whilst a single social sector acting alone may not be sufficiently strong to dominate, it may have sufficient power to disrupt government activity.[85] The role of pressure groups is significant in that they are frequently too weak to resist military repression in the short term, but strong enough to react when, in the long term, the repression has to be eased off. The unrest in Córdoba in 1969 which led to the replacement of Onganía is an example of this. Thus Finer describes Argentina as a country in which 'the civilian organisations are strong enough to impede direct military rule but not strong enough to destroy it'.[86]

Although trigger factors may be isolated for any individual coup, military intervention in politics rests on numerous structural weaknesses which reduce the possibilities of political agreement in usage and transference of power. Fragmentation prevents resolution of conflicts through social and political institutions and brings the military into the political arena. The worry for President Alfonsín is habituation; with a history of military revolution, another incident is that much more likely. Intervention by the armed forces establishes a pattern and is itself 'a hindrance to the development of experience in the peaceful transfer of power'.[87]

Notes

1. James Neilson, 'The corporation', *Buenos Aires Herald*, 5 May 1983, p. 10.
2. Robert A. Potash, *The Army and Politics in Argentina 1928–1945: Yrigoyen to Perón* (Stanford, Calif.: Stanford University Press, 1969) p. 283.
3. Víctor M. Sonego, *Las dos Argentinas: Pistas para una lectura crítica de nuestra historia* (Buenos Aires: Ediciones Don Bosco, 1983) p. 15.
4. James Neilson, 'How long will precarious truce last?', *Buenos Aires Herald*, 23 February 1986, p. 3.
5. Morris Janowitz, *The Professional Soldier: A social and political portrait* (Glencoe, Ill.: The Free Press, 1960) pp. 108–9.
6. Peter Calvert, 'Crisis and change: politics and government', in Harold Blakemore (ed.), *Latin America: Essays in continuity and change* (London: British Broadcasting Corporation, 1974) p. 91.
7. David Rock, *Politics in Argentina 1890–1930: The rise and fall of Radicalism* (London: Cambridge University Press, 1975) pp. 98–9; Richard W. Morse, 'Towards a theory of Spanish American government', in Hugh M. Hamill (ed.), *Dictatorship in Spanish America* (New York: Alfred A. Knopf, 1965) pp. 52–68.
8. James D. Theberge and Roger W. Fontaine, *Latin America: Struggle for progress* (Lexington, Mass.: Lexington Books, 1977) p. 127.
9. Jacques Lambert, *Latin America: Social structure and political institutions* (Berkeley, Calif.: University of California Press, 1967) p. 109.
10. John J. Johnson, *The Military and Society in Latin America* (Stanford, Calif.: Stanford University Press, 1964) pp. 36–8.

11. Stanislav Andreski, *Parasitism and Subversion: The case of Latin America* (London: Weidenfeld & Nicolson, 1966) p. 71.
12. Calvert, 'Crisis and change', p. 92.
13. John J. Johnson, 'The Latin American military as a politically competing group in transitional society', in John J. Johnson (ed.), *The Role of the Military in the Underdeveloped Countries* (Princeton, NJ: Princeton University Press, 1962) p. 124.
14. Alexander T. Edelmann, *Latin American Government and Politics: The dynamics of a revolutionary society* (Homewood, Ill.: Dorsey, 1965) p. 190.
15. S. E. Finer, *The Man on Horseback* (Harmondsworth: Penguin, 1975) p. 22.
16. Richard W. Weatherhead, 'Traditions of conflict in Latin America', in Joseph Maier and Richard W. Weatherhead (eds), *Politics of Change in Latin America* (New York: Praeger, 1964) p. 22.
17. Robert J. Alexander, 'The emergence of modern political parties in Latin America', in Maier and Weatherhead, *Politics of Change* p.103.
18. John Gerassi, *The Great Fear in Latin America* (New York: Collier, 1963) p. 54.
19. John J. Johnson, *Political Change in Latin America: The emergence of the middle sectors* (Stanford, Calif.: Stanford University Press, 1958) p. 106.
20. Irving Louis Horowitz, 'The norm of illegitimacy: toward a general theory of Latin-American political development', in Arthur J. Field (ed.), *City and Country in the Third World: Issues in the modernization of Latin America* (Cambridge, Mass.: Schenckman, 1970) p. 31.
21. Rock, *Politics in Argentina*, p. 265.
22. Carlos Alberto Astiz, 'The Argentine armed forces: their role and political involvement', *Western Political Quarterly*, 22 (1969) p. 863.
23. Guillermo A. Makin, "The Military in Argentinian Politics: 1880–1982," in *Millennium, Journal of International Studies* 12, No. 1, Spring 1983, p. 51.
24. Marvin Goldwert, *Democracy, Militarism and Nationalism in Argentina 1930–66: An interpretation* (Austin, Texas: University of Texas Press, 1972) p. xvi.
25. Theberge and Fontaine, *Latin America*, p. 170.
26. Goldwert, *Democracy*, p. 48.
27. Horowitz in Field, *City and Country*, p. 28.
28. Theberge and Fontaine, *Latin America*, p. 129.
29. William S. Stokes, 'Violence as a power factor in Latin American politics', in Robert D. Tomasek (ed.), *Latin American Politics: 24 studies of the contemporary scene* (Garden City, NY: Doubleday, 1966) p. 251.
30. Guillermo O'Donnell, 'Permanent crisis and the failure to create a democratic regime: Argentina, 1955–66', in Juan J. Linz and Alfred Stepan (eds), *The Breakdown of Democratic Regimes: Latin America* (Baltimore, Md: Johns Hopkins University Press, 1978) p. 158.
31. James Neilson, 'The approaching Pact', *Buenos Aires Herald*, 12 May 1983, p. 10.

32. David E. Apter, *The Politics of Modernization* (Chicago, Ill.: University of Chicago Press, 1965) p. 83.
33. Max Weber, *The Theory of Social and Economic Organization* (New York: The Free Press, 1964) p. 358.
34. Irving Louis Horowitz, 'The election in retrospect', in Richard R. Fagen and Wayne A. Cornelius (eds), *Political Power in Latin America: Seven confrontations* (Englewood Cliffs, NJ: Prentice-Hall, 1970) p. 131.
35. Johnson, *Military and Society*, p. 27.
36. John Duncan Powell, 'Military assistance and militarism in Latin America', *Western Political Quarterly*, 28 (1965) p. 388.
37. For example, Arthur P. Whitaker, 'An overview of the period', in Mark Falcoff and Ronald H. Dolkart (eds), *Prologue to Perón: Argentina in depression and war 1930–1943* (Berkeley, Calif.: University of California Press, 1975) p. 2.
38. Peter H. Smith, 'The Breakdown of Democracy in Argentina, 1916–30' in Linz and Stepan, *The Breakdown of Democratic Regimes*, p. 8.
39. Fernando Henrique Cardoso and Enzo Faletto, *Dependency and Development in Latin America* (Berkeley, Calif.: University of California Press, 1979) p. 16.
40. Peter H. Smith, *Argentina and the Failure of Democracy: Conflict among political elites, 1904–1955* (Madison, Wis.: University of Wisconsin Press, 1974) pp. 89–90.
41. Finer, *The Man on Horseback*, p. 99.
42. Samuel P. Huntington, *Political Order in Changing Societies* (New Haven, Conn.: Yale University Press, 1968) pp. 79, 266.
43. Robert A. Dahl, *Polyarchy: Participation and opposition* (New Haven, Conn.: Yale University Press, 1971) pp. 38–9.
44. Huntington, p. 231.
45. Frederick V. D'Antonio and Frederick B. Pike (eds), *Religion, Revolution and Reform: New forces for change in Latin America* (Tenbury Wells, Worcs.: Fowler Wright, 1964) p. 8.
46. General Luís Rodolfo González, speech quoted in K. H. Silvert, *The Conflict Society: Reaction and revolution in Latin America* (New York: American University Field Staff, 1966). pp. 201–2.
47. José Luís de Imaz, *Los que mandan* (Buenos Aires: Editorial Universitaria de Buenos Aires, 1964) p. 118.
48. Arthur P. Whitaker, *Argentina* (Englewood Cliffs, NJ: Prentice-Hall, 1964) p. 88.
49. William W. Pierson and Federico G. Gil, *Governments of Latin America* (New York: McGraw-Hill, 1957) pp. 164–6.
50. Pierson and Gil, *Governments*, pp. 175–6.
51. Weatherhead in Maier and Weatherhead, *Politics of Change*, p. 37.
52. Goldwert, *Democracy*, p. 11.
53. Smith in Linz and Stepan, *The Breakdown of Democratic Regimes*, pp. 21–2.
54. Potash, *Yrigoyen to Perón*, pp. 40–1.
55. Goldwert, *Democracy*, pp. 46, 76–7; Potash, *Yrigoyen to Perón*, pp. 145, 161, 165.

56. Goldwert, *Democracy*, p. 176.
57. Pike's introduction in D'Antonio and Pike, *Religion*, p. 8.
58. Roland H. Dallas, 'The President versus the Generals in Argentina', *The World Today*, 40 (1984) p. 48.
59. Goldwert, *Democracy*, p. 33.
60. Brian Loveman and Thomas M. Davies, 'Modernization, instability and military leadership, 1919–45', in Brian Loveman and Thomas M. Davies (eds), *The Politics of Antipolitics* (Lincoln, Neb.: University of Nebraska Press, 1978) p. 97.
61. Potash, *Yrigoyen to Perón*, pp. 42–3.
62. James W. Rowe, 'Whither the Peronists?', in Tomasek, *Latin American Politics*, p. 434.
63. Frederick M. Nunn, 'An overview of the European military missions in Latin America', in Loveman and Davies, *The Politics of Antipolitics*, p. 44.
64. Dahl, *Polyarchy*, pp. 137, 136.
65. Robert A. Potash, *The Army and Politics in Argentina 1945–62: Perón to Frondizi* (London: The Athlone Press, 1980) pp. 107, 166.
66. Potash, *Yrigoyen to Perón*, p. 202.
67. Pierson and Gil, *Governments*, p. 158.
68. Edwin Lieuwen, *Arms and Politics in Latin America* (New York: Praeger, 1961) p. 123.
69. Potash, *Yrigoyen to Perón*, p. 59; Goldwert, *Democracy*, pp. 37–8.
70. Robert A. Potash, 'The military and Argentine politics', in Loveman and Davies, *The Politcs of Antipolitics*, p. 103.
71. Gary W. Wynia, *The Politics of Latin American Development* (New York: Cambridge University Press, 1978) pp. 228–9.
72. Martin Honeywell and Jenny Pearce, *Falklands/Malvinas: Whose crisis?* (London: Latin American Bureau, 1982) p. 75.
73. Neilson, *Buenos Aires Herald*, 5 May 1983, p. 10.
74. Potash, in Loveman and Davies, *The Politics of Antipolitics*, p. 102.
75. Irving Louis Horowitz, 'The military elites', in Seymour Martin Lipset and Aldo Solari (eds), *Elites in Latin America* (New York: Oxford University Press, 1967) pp. 151–2.
76. Robert E. Scott, 'National integration problems and military regimes in Latin America', in Robert E. Scott (ed.), *Latin American Modernization Problems* (Chicago, Ill.: University of Chicago Press, 1973) pp. 328–9.
77. Simon Barrow, 'Europe, Latin America and the arms trade', in Jenny Pearce (ed.), *The European Challenge: Europe's new role in Latin America* (London: Latin American Bureau, 1982) pp. 195, 181.
78. Johnson, *Military and Society*, pp. 122–3.
79. Horowitz in Lipset and Solari, *Elites*, p. 147.
80. Goldwert, *Democracy*, p. 10.
81. Potash in Loveman and Davies, *The Politics of Antipolitics*, p. 92.
82. Potash, *Yrigoyen to Perón*, pp. 10, 92–3, 112.
83. Ibid., p. 11.

84.   Smith, *Argentina*, p. 95.
85.   Horowitz in Lipset and Solari, *Elites*, pp. 151–2.
86.   S. E. Finer, 'Military and Society in Latin America' in Paul Halmos (ed.), *Latin American Sociological Studies* (Keele, Staffordshire: The University of Keele, 1967). p. 144
87.   Silvert, *The Conflict Society*, p. 24.

Part II
Towards a Theory of
Political Succession

9   Political Succession as Policy Succession: Why so much Stability?

Hannu Nurmi

INTRODUCTION

A couple of years ago the editor of *Public Choice*, Professor Gordon Tullock, invited the readers of the journal to write brief comments on the topic 'Why so much stability?' The underlying motivation for the invitation was an obvious discrepancy between what the spatial models of voting and elections 'predict' and what we observe around us. More specifically, the results achieved by Kramer, McKelvey, Plott and Schofield suggest that in multidimensional policy-spaces the voting equilibria are extremely rare.[1] And yet the real world voting processes seem far from chaotic. Rather, what we see in them is either a relatively orderly change from one policy alternative to another as a non-arbitrary response to preference changes of the voters or no change at all except for the nomenclature of the choices. The purpose of this chapter is to address the above question in the light of social choice theory; in other words, an explanation or a set of explanations will be sought for this apparent stability partly in the very same theory which has been interpreted as implying the instability or chaos.

As the instability results have been widely discussed in the literature, the main results will not be repeated here. The reader is referred to the above works of Kramer, McKelvey, Plott and Schofield along with the literature where the importance of these results is commented upon.[2]

Usually political succession is understood as a succession of political leaders, regimes or administrations, that is, the replacement of a set of people with another set of people. Admittedly it is not always the case that these kinds of replacement would involve a change of policies as well, but in practically all cases the change of personnel is at least intended to signify a change of policies. Consequently in this chapter the problem of political succession will be approached from the angle of policy-succession. One of the justifications for doing this is that people too (leaders and so on) can be characterised by means of sets and variables. Therefore each candidate in an electoral contest or other type of political competition can be viewed as an m-tuple of properties, that is, values of m variables. As the mathematical models of political succession often take as their point of departure just this sort of description it seems natural to adopt it also in the present context. This way of describing is no doubt a simplification – indeed that is one of the main motivations for adopting it – but it is instructive to see how far it carries us towards understanding the complexities of political succession.

One should, however, bear in mind the obvious fact that mathematical models are not statements about reality, that is, they do not say, for instance, that political succession is a process which takes place in an m-dimensional policy-space. The results derived from the models apply to political succession only insofar as the real world processes of political succession are structurally similar to, that is, satisfy the 'givens' of, the mathematical models. To the extent that the real world does not satisfy those givens, we are, of course, not entitled to use our models to draw inferences about reality unless we can resort to *a fortiori* inference, which means that our models deal with a general class of situations while the observed processes take place in special subclasses of this class. The particular cases we shall be dealing with in the following do not involve policy dimensions, but simply choices or candidates. Thus from our point of view there is no difference between policy and political succession.

SINGLE-FACTOR EXPLANATIONS OF STABILITY

Let us start by looking at some features in real world politics that might make the apparent stability intelligible despite the formal validity of the theoretical results referred to above. In this chapter we shall focus on a few specific aspects or factors that could undermine the applicability of the theoretical results.

Large Majorities

The results of Kramer, McKelvey, Plott and Schofield concern the simple majority rule in the case of more than two choices. The obvious query is, therefore, what will happen if more than a simple majority is required in each pairwise comparison? Many present-day legislatures require larger majorities for some issues. For example, in the Finnish parliament, an urgent constitutional amendment requires a five-sixths majority and a new tax law a two-thirds majority. Now intuitively the cycles cannot occur so easily when larger than simple majorities are needed and the individual preferences are both complete and transitive over the alternative set.

This intuition turns out to be true. More specifically, by requiring near unanimity in the determination of the social strict preference between two choices it can be shown that no strict preference cycle can occur. The first authors to point this out were Ferejohn and Grether, who observed that the possibility of the social preference cycles depends both on the size of the required majority and on the number of choices considered.[3] Let n be the number of voters in the voting body and q an integer between 0 and n so that q is the required number of voters needed to determine that an alternative x is socially preferred to another alternative y, that is xPy if and only if (*iff*) $n(x,y) > q$, where P denotes the social strict preference relation and $n(x,y)$ denotes the number of voters strictly preferring x to y. The result of Ferejohn and Grether states that P determined by pairwise comparisons of alternatives with the q-majority rule is acyclic *iff* $q > [n(k-1)/k]$, where k is the number of choices.

Obviously the larger the number of choices k, the nearer to the unanimity rule one needs to guarantee acyclicity, because when $k \longrightarrow \infty$, the expression on the right-hand side approaches n. To exemplify the above condition and its relationship to acyclicity, consider the case where $n = 5, k = 5$ and the preference profile is the following:

PROFILE I

Person 1	Person 2	Person 3	Person 4	Person 5
x	w	v	z	y
y	x	w	v	z
z	y	x	w	v
v	z	y	x	w
w	v	z	y	x

Let now $q = 3$, that is the simple majority. Then we get xPy and yPz and zPv and vPw, but also wPx whereby acyclicity is violated. A similar cycle occurs for $q = 4$ as can easily be observed. The Ferejohn–Grether condition in this example reads $q > 4$. For $q = 5$, we obviously get no cycles in social preference as none of the choices is preferred to any other by all voters. Hence for $q \leqslant 4$ the acyclicity fails, but for $q = 5$ it holds. This illustrates the validity of the condition in a special case. It also illustrates the problems encountered in requiring very large majorities: the rules tend to become rather indecisive. In this example the $q = 5$ rule resulted in the choice of all options.

It is worth observing that the rate at which the condition approaches unanimity in strict preferences is very quick in voting bodies of relatively small size. In the body of five voters if the number of choices is at least five, then the unanimity of all strict preferences is needed to avoid cycles. In general, if the number of choices is as large as the number of voters, then the avoidance of cycles requires the identity of all strict preferences for a social strict preference relation to hold. Obviously if the number of choices is larger than the number of voters, then the same requirement holds *a fortiori*.

The Ferejohn–Grether theorem thus states that the problem of cyclic majorities haunts primarily small voting bodies, such as Cabinets, pondering upon a large number of choices. In political decision-making bodies of 100–700 members, like most contemporary parliaments, the problem is not equally serious. In the Finnish parliament where the number of MPs is 200, the decision rule of 161 would in practice make majority cycles impossible as it is rather uncommon to have more than four or five choices on the agenda. This, in turn, follows from the fact that the number of parties represented is now nine (if the Greens are counted as a party) and has been in the neighbourhood of that figure over recent decades. Of course, if one would like to make sure that even in the case where all parties propose options no majority cycles could occur, the majority threshold would have to be at 178. One should, however, bear in mind that the Ferejohn–Grether condition makes the appearance of majority cycles impossible for larger majorities than the condition states. When smaller majorities are used, the majority cycles do not *necessarily* occur. In the above example where $k = n = 5$, it takes some thinking to construct a preference profile that would lead to a majority cycle. Consequently, we can expect stability from our institutions even outside the theoretical limits.

In Cabinets, on the other hand, the body is typically of the size of 10–20 individuals. Supposing, as a sort of rule of thumb that typically less than four choices are considered, the theoretical lower limit of cycle-exclusion would range from eight in a 10-member body to 16 in a 20-member one. Again for smaller values of q one would not necessarily encounter majority cycles even though their appearance could not be excluded on theoretical grounds. It should be pointed out, however, that in Cabinets the decision method is often not the same as the one used in parliaments. In the Finnish Cabinet, for example, the plurality voting method is used, whereas in the decision-making of the Finnish parliament the amendment method is resorted to. Of course, the notion of a majority cycle is meaningful in the latter context, but not in the former.

The above observations suggest that one reason for the lack of chaos in voting results is the fact that sometimes larger than simple majorities are required in pairwise comparisons. The requirements do not have to be formally instituted to have the same effect, though. It may simply happen that more people than a simple majority have a preference profile that excludes majority cycles. While the theoretical threshold for cycle-exclusion becomes quite high when the number of choices increases, the preference profiles excluding them are rather common in majorities of smaller size than the theoretical limits.

The preceding discussion already points to the importance of taking account of the number of choices in considering the likelihood of cycles. This has also been emphasised by Niemi.[4] Let us now turn to another result that is explicitly based on this number.

The Number of Choices

Each simple voting game – that is, a game in which any coalition of voters is either winning or losing – can be characterised by the set of its winning coalitions. Let this set be D. Now there is typically a considerable overlap between any two coalitions in D, that is, they have several members in common. On the other hand, in voting games where the sole criterion of winning is whether the coalition has a sufficient number of members, one can often find a subset of winning coalitions such that no individual belongs to all of the winning coalitions comprising the subset. That is, one can find $D1$, $D2, \ldots,$ Ds such that $Di \; \varepsilon \; D$, for $i = 1, \ldots, s$ and $\bigcap_{i=1}^{s} Di = \phi$.[5] Consider now, for a fixed q-game, the subset D' of D which has the minimum cardinality and satisfies $\bigcap_{Dj \, \varepsilon \, D'} Dj = \phi$. Denote $\{D'\}$ – the cardinality of D' – by d. Obviously D' need not be unique; there can be several such sets of winning coalitions that satisfy the condition of empty intersection and consist of the same number of winning coalitions. The number d, however, is unique and called the Nakamura number of the voting game in question.

In some simple voting games one may be unable to find such a D' that would satisfy the empty intersection condition. In that case there obviously is a subset of voters belonging to every winning coalition. In other words, the coalition cannot be winning unless these voters are present. Such a set of voters is called a collegium and the corresponding voting game collegial. The Nakamura number of collegial voting games is defined as infinity.

Nakamura proves that if the voters have strict acyclic preferences over the alternative set, then the core of the simple non-collegial voting game is non-empty *iff* the number of choices is strictly less than what has later been called the Nakamura number of the game.[6] By the core of the game we mean those choices x of X that satisfy the condition: x is defeated by no y in X by a simple majority. Consider now a simple q-game Gq where $n/2 < q \leqslant n$ and let $v(Gq)$ denote its Nakamura number. Schofield shows that $v(Gq) = 2 + wq$, where wq is the greatest integer strictly less than $q/(n - q)$. Let now r be any integer.[7] Then $r < 2 + wq$ *iff* $r < 1 + [q/(n - q)]$. In particular if $r = k$, the number of choices, then we have that $k < 2 + wq = v(Gq)$ *iff* $k - 1 < q/(n - q)$. The former inequality holds by Nakamura's theorem *iff* the core of Gq is non-empty. Hence the latter inequality also holds precisely when the core is non-empty. But $k - 1 < q/(n - q)$ *iff* $q > [n(k - 1)]/k$ which is precisely what the Ferejohn–Grether theorem states as the necessary and sufficient condition for the acyclicity of the q-majority rule. Indeed, the latter theorem is actually more informative in the sense that acyclicity guarantees the existence of a non-empty core plus a 'natural' order of all choices, whereas the existence of the core just implies that there are socially best choices.

In the simple majority voting game the Nakamura number is generally 3 because any two winning coalitions have at least one member in common, while one can find three winning coalitions having an empty intersection. An exception to this rule is the game in which $n = 4$ and $q = 3$. The winning coalitions are: $(1, 2, 3), (1, 2, 4),$ $(1, 3, 4), (1, 2, 3, 4), (2, 3, 4)$. No matter which three coalitions we pick, they always have a non-empty intersection. Hence the Nakamura number of this special game is not 3 but 4.

The theorem of Nakamura turns out to be yet another way of showing that the simple majority rule works rather well in cases where no more than two choices are considered. But, of course, this observation was made two centuries ago by the Marquis de Condorcet. May's axiomatisation of the simple majority rule also brings out the nice properties of this rule.[8] One possible explanation for stability would then seem to be that the number of choices is usually very small. But due attention should be paid to the fact that the number of choices must be very small indeed to guarantee stability. A more plausible explanation, therefore, is the combined effect of the small number of choices, large majorities and a rather large number of voters. Let us now turn to some other considerations which – instead of trying to explain stability – question the underlying assumption that the real world political outcomes are, indeed, stable.

THEORETICAL EXPLANATIONS

Voting Procedures and Instability

How can we tell from a voting result that it is a stable or equilibrium result? Consider the Nash equilibrium. It is defined as follows: a preference profile R is a Nash equilibrium if and only if no group of voters can benefit from reporting some other preference order than it does in R. Obviously equilibrium refers now to preference profiles, that is, n-tuples of preference orders. Whether a coalition can or cannot benefit from preference misrepresentation depends both on the preferences of the other voters and the voting procedure which determines for each profile the social choice set, that is the set of winners. The most commonly used procedures do not, however, require that the voters report their preference orders. For example, the widely used amendment procedure is based on pairwise comparisons of choices. Hence, the voters do not necessarily need to have connected and transitive preference relations over the choices for this system to be applicable. Similarly, the plurality voting (PL, for short) and plurality run-off system require very limited information about the individual preference orders: if, indeed, the latter exist.

Let us consider the following example of PL. Let the voting body of size 100 consist of 40 members of party A, 30 members of party B and

30 members of party C. The set of choices is {a, b, c}. Let the preference profile be the following:

PROFILE II

Party A (40 members)	Party B (30 members)	Party C (30 members)
a	b	c
b	c	b
c	a	a

Provided that each votes according to his or her preferences *a* wins with 40 votes. From the distribution of votes one cannot make inferences about whether *a* is an equilibrium outcome in the sense of not being vulnerable to coalitions upsetting it by reporting something other than their true preferences. When the profile is known, one observes that *a* is not an equilibrium outcome as party B can benefit from reporting the preference order *cba*, that is, from voting for *c* because this would, *ceteris paribus*, lead to *c* being chosen. Similarly, party C would benefit from reporting *bca* whereupon *b* would win. Hence, *a* is not an equilibrium outcome.

One could also use the concept of the Condorcet winner in the definition of a stable outcome by saying that whenever the Condorcet winner option is chosen, the outcome is stable.[9] In a sense this is a plausible view as the Condorcet winner is by definition an outcome that defeats all the others by a simple majority in pairwise contests. In the above preference profile there is a Condorcet winner, *viz. b*. Indeed, there is also the mirror image of the Condorcet winner, *viz.* the Condorcet loser, which by definition is the option defeated by all the others in pairwise contests by a simple majority. This should intuitively be the most unstable outcome of all. And yet it is the one chosen by PL, as *a* is the Condorcet loser in the above profile.

Consider now another profile of the same parties:

PROFILE III

Party A (40 members)	Party B (30 members)	Party C (30 members)
a	b	c
b	a	a
c	c	b

Assuming again that the party members vote according to their preferences, the distribution of PL votes will be exactly the same as in Profile II. This time, however, *a* is the Condorcet winner and in that sense the stable outcome. We also notice that *a* is the equilibrium outcome, that is, not susceptible to being upset by any coalition. And yet if just the vote distribution is given, we have no way of distinguishing Profile II from Profile III.

As a matter of fact several most common voting procedures share this feature, that is, they make it very difficult to infer whether the outcome reached is an equilibrium or not. The amendment procedure results in one winning option but typically does not give any clue as to whether the chosen option would defeat all the others or whether it is just one 'lucky' element in a majority cycle.[10] We could thus argue that one of the reasons for observing so much stability around us is that we incorrectly classify unstable outcomes as stable ones just because we cannot tell the latter from the former. In other words, the question 'why so much stability?' may be wrongly posed: there is not necessarily all that much stability around us. It is just that we do not experience instability as somehow intolerable.

How often one could expect to end up with unstable outcomes if a given voting procedure is used? Of course, the answer depends on preference profiles and voting strategies. Some idea of this frequency can be obtained by resorting to computer simulation whereby one generates random preference profiles and determines how often the Condorcet winners are chosen when they exist and when the voting is sincere. Merrill's study reports the Condorcet efficiency of various voting procedures in what are called impartial cultures.[11] These are preference profiles in which each preference order is generated independently of the others. Merrill's results are reproduced in Table 9.1. In the table the number of voters is 25 throughout.

For each cell of the table 10 000 elections were simulated and on the basis of these elections the percentage indicated in the cell was computed. In general there seems to be a tendency of the percentages to decrease when one moves from left to right in each row. An exception is Black's method which by definition always chooses the Condorcet winner when one exists. One might add that were the amendment procedure included in the table, its row would be identical with that of Black's method.

Of the voting procedures in Table 9.1 only two, *viz.* PL and approval voting (AV, for short), can result in the choice of the Condorcet loser, assuming sincere voting.[12] Table 9.2 shows how the relative frequency

Table 9.1   Percentage agreement of electoral outcomes with the Condorcet
winners in Merrill's (1984) study

Procedure	Number of choices					
	2	3	4	5	7	10
Plurality	100.0	84.4	76.6	69.7	61.0	51.7
Borda	100.0	94.1	90.4	88.7	86.2	86.4
Approval	100.0	82.4	77.1	75.3	73.6	70.7
Hare	100.0	96.4	92.1	88.9	83.3	75.8
Plurality run-off	100.0	96.4	89.4	83.7	71.8	60.2
Coombs	100.0	96.1	93.1	90.8	86.1	80.7
Black	100.0	100.0	100.0	100.0	100.0	100.0
% elections with Condorcet winner	100.0	92.0	83.5	76.2	64.7	51.1

of the Condorcet loser choice varies with the number of voters and
choices when PL and AV are used.[13] To obtain data comparable with
Merrill's results 10 000 random elections were simulated for each cell
of the table.

The first observation is that the relative frequency of the Condorcet
loser choice of both AV and PL is very small for all combinations of
voter and option numbers. Second, for a fixed number of voters the
likelihood of the Condorcet loser being chosen diminishes with the
increase in the number of options. Thus, while Merrill's data show
that increasing the number of options tends to deteriorate the perfor-

Table 9.2   The percentage of Condorcet loser choices by AV and PL
under impartial culture assumption

Number of candidates		Number of voters				
		5	10	15	20	25
3	AV	7.1	2.4	6.4	2.8	5.6
	PL	9.9	1.4	7.2	3.3	5.0
4	AV	4.0	1.6	3.4	1.4	2.8
	PL	3.7	3.0	5.2	3.0	4.0
5	AV	2.6	0.7	1.6	1.0	1.4
	PL	5.2	1.5	3.8	2.1	3.2
7	AV	1.3	0.3	1.0	0.5	0.7
	PL	5.8	2.2	3.0	1.6	2.4

mance of all the procedures considered, Table 9.2 suggests that as far as impartial cultures are concerned the increase in the number of options diminishes the likelihood of the most serious type of instability, *viz.* the choice of the Condorcet loser. However, considering a fixed number of voters (25) only does not tell the whole story. Therefore Table 9.2 reports the likelihood of the Condorcet loser choices for voter sets of other sizes as well.

However, impartial cultures are hardly the ones that we encounter in the real world. Hence one cannot make *a fortiori* inferences concerning voting bodies of everyday life on the basis of simulation results obtained under this assumption. All one can do is to determine which factors seem to affect the likelihood of the Condorcet loser choices when the 'cultural' factors are held constant. Table 9.3 shows that the instability in the sense of the choice of the Condorcet loser changes markedly when the impartial culture assumption is replaced with the bipolar culture assumption. The latter means that there are two homogeneous groups of voters of equal size, each comprising 30 per cent of the voting body. In each group the preferences of voters are identical and diametrically opposed to those of the other group. The rest of the body forms an impartial culture.

Table 9.3 The percentage of Condorcet loser choices by AV and PL in elections with a Condorcet loser under the bipolar culture assumption

Number of candidates		Number of voters 5	10	15	20	25
3	AV	15.3	4.32	12.4	7.05	10.6
	PL	33.2	11.5	18.9	11.8	16.0
4	AV	14.6	3.23	9.09	5.47	7.22
	PL	33.1	13.9	17.1	13.0	14.9
5	AV	12.1	2.45	6.15	3.73	5.43
	PL	29.5	14.0	15.8	13.4	14.0
7	AV	9.47	1.31	3.92	2.08	3.04
	PL	23.0	13.7	14.2	13.5	11.2

The effect of this assumption on the likelihood of the Condorcet loser choice is clear. If, on the other hand, the culture is unipolar in the sense that there is only one homogeneous group of voters comprising 30 per cent of the electorate, the likelihood of the Condorcet loser choice by AV or PL decreases to become virtually nil when the size of the voting body increases, as one can see in Table 9.4.

Table 9.4   The percentage of Condorcet loser choices by AV and PL in elections with a Condorcet loser under the unipolar culture assumption

| Number of candidates | Number of voters | | | | |
		5	10	15	20	25
3	AV	3.70	0.92	1.10	0.10	0.18
	PL	8.87	1.46	1.85	0.26	0.47
4	AV	1.85	0.26	0.31	0.01	0.03
	PL	5.00	1.39	0.75	0.08	0.16
5	AV	1.24	0.37	0.08	0.01	0.04
	PL	3.32	1.02	0.30	0.02	0.06
7	AV	0.46	0.02	0.04	0.00	0.01
	PL	1.30	0.25	0.10	0.00	0.01

Even though the above remarks seem to suggest that unstable outcomes are, in the above cultures at least, relatively rare, one should bear in mind that in real world nothing stands in the way of a given preference profile's repeating itself many times in a row. Thus the likelihood calculations are always risky on the basis of simulation data. Yet they seem to suggest something about how 'common' a given type of instability is. But there is another way of looking at the stability-succession problematique. The results that 'predict' instability are typically possibility results, that is, they state that certain types of unstable outcomes can result from a given voting procedure provided that the voters have preference orders over the choices and that they reveal truthfully their preferences. Both of these assumptions can, however, be challenged. Therefore it is worthwhile to see how robust the instability results are *vis-à-vis* changes in these assumptions.

Assumptions Underlying the Instability Results

Do individuals, then, in reality have connected and transitive preference relations over the choices? The answer to this question would intuitively seem to depend on many things, like the number of choices considered, the importance of issues to be decided, and so on. What is perhaps a more important consideration is the fact that there are voting procedures which provide the voters with more incentives to construct connected and transitive preference relations than other procedures. For example, the incentive to produce a preference order is quite obvious when the Borda count is used, while one could well do without such an order when PL is resorted to.

Theoretically the problem is what kind of formal devices to use in describing the opinions of voters. If the latter do not have preference orders over choices, what kind of opinions do they have? In principle, there are two options: either the voters have more detailed or less detailed opinions about the choices than the preference orders. Suppose that we start from the assumption that the voters have more detailed views about the choices than connected and transitive preference relations. Suppose, moreover, that it is generally felt that these views should count in the determination of social choices. The next question, of course, is what precisely is meant by 'more detailed views'. One plausible interpretation is that the voters have von Neumann-Morgenstern utilities over the choices. It is well known that the existence of such utilities is a stronger assumption about individual preferences than connectedness and transitivity of the preference relation. Assuming that such utilities exist, it would seem natural to ask the voters to report them so that the winning choices could be determined by aggregating the reported utilities. There are several methods that could be used in the aggregation. For example: (1) Bentham's method simply sums up for any choice the utilities given to it by the individuals and declares the winner to be the choice with the largest sum score, and (2) Nash's method works otherwise in the same way as Bentham's method but, instead of summing up the individual utilities, multiplies them.[14]

One does not have to go into the details of these and other utility aggregation procedures to observe that they are not more likely to result in stable outcomes than the preference aggregation methods. The use of von Neumann-Morgenstern utilities does not guarantee interpersonal comparability even though the utility scale is, of course, cardinal. Cardinality and interpersonal comparability are conceptually distinct. But from our viewpoint it is more important to notice that the Bentham or Nash winner does not have to be the Condorcet winner, as the following example shows.

PROFILE IV

6 voters	3 voters	4 voters
a (1.0)	b (1.0)	c (1.0)
b (0.6)	c (0.6)	b (0.6)
c (0.5)	a (0.5)	a (0.5)

Here the utility values given to the choices by each individual are indicated in parentheses. Here *b*, the Condorcet winner, is neither the Nash nor the Bentham winner. Indeed, the Bentham and Nash winner *a* is the Condorcet loser, showing that the utility aggregation methods are by no means exempt from the instabilities of the preference aggregation methods. Incidentally, this example also shows that the so-called cumulative voting does not guarantee the choice of the Condorcet winner, but may in fact result in the choice of the Condorcet loser. In cumulative voting voters are each given a fixed amount of value which they are allowed to allocate to the choices as they see fit.[15] Assuming that each voter is given 2.1 units of value and that they allocate their units as shown in the previous example, we observe that the Condorcet loser *a* will be chosen.

So asking the voters to reveal more about their opinions than the preference relations does not seem to help us to avoid the instabilities in social choices insofar as the Condorcet criteria are used as indicators of stability. Perhaps an even more serious threat to stability stems, however, from the fact that utility-based procedures appear to present quite new possibilities for strategic misrepresentation of opinions. Especially in circumstances where one knows enough about the revealed opinions of others to recognise one's favourites among the likely winners as well as their toughest competitors, it obviously pays to give the latter ones the worst and the former ones the best utility scores available.[16]

The fact is, however, that very few of the voting procedures actually resorted to in making social choices use individual utilities of choices as input. Indeed, most of them do not even require the voters to have connected and transitive preference relations over the choices. For example, PL produces social choices as long as the voters are capable of singling out one of the set of options as their favourite. Neither connectedness nor transitivity of the individual preference relation is needed for PL to work. Similarly, the plurality run-off and AV do very well without such preference relations. Could one then avoid the instabilities by assuming that the individual opinions are less detailed than required by the individual preference ordering assumption?

Much, of course, depends on what specifically is meant by opinions that are less detailed than connected and transitive preference relations. Relatively little work has been done in this field. The results achieved by Aizerman and Aleskerov suggest that impossibility theorems akin to that of Arrow cannot altogether be avoided when it is assumed that the voters have individual choice functions over the options.[17] The individual choice functions are set-valued mappings indicating for any subset of choices the (possibly empty) set of best choices in that subset. The individual preference relations underlying these choice functions are not necessarily connected and transitive. To produce theorems Aizerman and Aleskerov need, however, some structural restrictions on both individual and social choice functions. As the transitivity–connectedness assumption has been dropped the results do not pertain to stability in the sense of the Condorcet criteria, but deal with choice set invariances under various transformations of individual choice functions. Nevertheless the results relate to stability, but now in a sense that pertains to the possibilities of agenda or, more generally, institution manipulation. To avoid dictatorial social choice functions while keeping certain innocent-looking assumptions about the individual choice functions, one has to resort to procedures that violate other reasonable properties, like, for instance, heritage, which requires that if an option is among the winners in a 'large' set of options, then it also has to be among the winners in every subset of options to which it belongs.[18] Obviously the violation of heritage is a threat to stability of outcomes because by a suitable change in the option set, the winners could be turned into losers by a skillful manipulator and *vice versa*.

The above remarks concern the assumptions about voter preferences. Another set of assumptions which relates to the stability of social outcomes deals with voter behaviour, that is, how the voters act given that they have fixed preferences. The most straightforward assumption is, of course, that the voters act sincerely in the sense of revealing their true preferences when casting their ballots. Sometimes this assumption is blatantly false, but much of the rationale of 'going to the people' is based on it. The literature dealing with the properties of voting procedures often makes this assumption in order to separate the strategic properties of the voting procedures from the non-strategic ones.[19] A further reason for making the sincere preference revelation assumption is that no obvious theoretical alternative seems to be at hand.

Recently, however, Felsenthal and Maoz have developed the idea of strategic voting along the lines suggested by Farquharson.[20] According to this idea the voters make their choices of voting strategy by eliminating dominated strategies in a sequential fashion. For large voter and option sets the elimination procedure gets very complicated and sometimes indeterminate. Therefore this kind of behaviour is of somewhat questionable descriptive value. It could, however, be viewed as a normative model of rational voting behaviour. Anyway it is instructive to observe that many theoretical properties which characterise some voting procedures when the voting is assumed to be sincere simply vanish from the same procedures when the voting is assumed to be sophisticated in the sense of Farquharson. From the viewpoint of stability it is interesting to note that the satisfaction of the Condorcet criteria by various procedures also depends on the voting behaviour assumptions. For example, the amendment procedure satisfies the Condorcet winner criterion when the voting is assumed to be sincere, but does not necessarily do so when some voters are strategic. Consider the following example.[21]

PROFILE V

2 voters	3 voters	2 voters
a	b	c
b	a	a
c	c	b

Now a, the Condorcet winner, will be chosen regardless of the agenda if the voting is sincere. In particular, if the agenda is: (1) a versus c, and (2) the winner of (1) versus b, then a wins. But if some voters are strategic, then, e.g., the 3-voter group may vote for c in (1) so that in (2) c and not a is confronted with b. Hence b wins. Thus the Condorcet winner a is not chosen.

So the introduction of strategic voting does, indeed, have an effect on the stability of social choices. In the above example the effect was to undermine stability, but there are circumstances in which the opposite occurs, that is, strategic voting may bring about stability in situations where sincere voting would not. Suppose that in the above example PL is used. With sincere voting b will win and not the Condorcet winner a. Obviously the two voters with true preference order *cab* now have an incentive to misrepresent their preferences as *acb* whereupon a, the Condorcet winner, wins.

In conclusion, then, the way in which the voters behave given their true preferences affects the properties of the voting procedures. But as we just observed, the outcomes resulting from strategic voting need not undermine stability. They may in fact make stable outcomes more likely than otherwise. For PL and AV the results of Felsenthal, Maoz and Rapoport suggest that the likelihood of the Condorcet winner being chosen is larger when the voting is sophisticated than when it is sincere.[22] Thus strategic voting could be one explanation of the stability of real world political outcomes.

CONCLUSION

In a recent article Grofman and Uhlaner distinguish several concepts of instability that pertain to social choices.[23] Our discussion has centred around their type 2 instability, that is, the occurrence of a situation where there is no Condorcet winner in the set of choices actually voted upon. We have also discussed other kinds of instabilities that do not directly fall into any of the classes of Grofman and Uhlaner, such as the choice of the Condorcet loser and the possibility of the preference misrepresentation. The above discussion seems to suggest the following 'explanations' of stability in social choices of real world voting bodies.

1. We simply lack the information needed to determine whether the social choice actually made is an equilibrium one. What is even more important is that the voters themselves have no way of knowing whether the voting outcomes are equilibria or not. It would seem that some of our voting procedures – notably the amendment procedure – are especially designed to eliminate the possibility of gaining such knowledge.

2. Results 'predicting' instability are typically based on the assumption that the voters vote sincerely and that they have connected and transitive preferences over the alternatives. Both of these assumptions can be challenged. The latter assumption is particularly problematic as it seems obvious that the voting procedure to be used also determines the type of preference relation that the voters 'need'. Perhaps the voting procedure and the appropriate preference pattern should be assessed together and not separately. Unfortunately not much work has been done along these lines. But obviously if one starts from a different set

of assumptions concerning the preferences of voters, then also the notion of instability has to be redefined. If the sincere voting assumption is replaced with the strategic voting assumption, then many new features of the voting procedures enter the picture. The problem is that we do not have a plausible and general alternative assumption about voting behaviour, given voter preferences. The work on sophisticated PL and AV seems to suggest that stability is more likely when the voting is sophisticated than when it is sincere.

3.   The computer simulations on voting procedures in various 'cultures' show that the choice of the Condorcet loser by AV or PL is relatively rare although logically possible in general. Similarly, Merrill's work on several voting procedures and the Condorcet winner criterion suggests that instability, in the sense of the Condorcet winner being excluded from the social choice set, is not typical although the procedures differ from each other in this respect. The problem with computer simulation is, however, the interpretation of the results.

In sum, part of the explanation of why there is so much stability, is that there is not, but nobody cares because it is next to impossible to find out that the outcomes reached are not stable. Moreover, the results on the basis of which the instability is said to follow are achieved under assumptions that do not always hold in reality. And finally, if the voters knew that the outcomes the procedures lead to are typically unstable, it could still be better from their viewpoint to have some agreed-upon outcomes than to risk the legitimacy of social choices in general. This would mean that unstable outcomes are tolerated because of the general commitment to the procedures being used regardless of the outcomes.[24]

Notes

1. G. H. Kramer, 'On a class of equilibrium conditions for majority rule', *Econometrica*, 41 (1973) pp. 285–97; R. D. McKelvey, 'Intransitivities in multidimensional voting models and some implications for agenda control', *Journal of Economic Theory*, 12 (1976) pp. 472–82; R. D. McKelvey, 'General conditions for global intransitivities in formal voting models', *Econometrica*, 47 (1979) pp. 1085–111; C. R. Plott, 'A notion of equilibrium and its possibility under majority rule', *American Economic Review*, 57 (1967) pp. 787–806; N. Schofield, 'Instability of simple dynamic games', *Review of Economic Studies*, 45 (1978) pp. 575–94. See also W. H. Riker, *Liberalism against Populism: A confrontation between the theory of democracy and the theory of social choice* (San Francisco: W. H. Freeman, 1982).

2. See, for example, Riker, *Liberalism*, and H. Nurmi, 'Majority rule: second thoughts and refutations', *Quality and Quantity*, 14 (1980) pp. 743–65.

3. J. A. Ferejohn and D. M. Grether, 'On a class of rational social decision procedures', *Journal of Economic Theory*, 8 (1974) pp. 471–82.

4. R. G. Niemi, 'Why so much stability?', *Public Choice*, 41 (1983) pp. 261–70.

5. See K. Nakamura, 'The vetoers in a simple game with ordinal preferences', *International Journal of Game Theory*, 8 (1978) pp. 55–61; N. Schofield, 'Classification of voting games on manifolds', *Social Science Working Paper* 488, California Institute of Technology, 1983.

6. Nakamura, 'The Vetoers'.

7. Schofield, 'Classification'.

8. K. O. May, 'A set of independent necessary and sufficient conditions for simple majority decisions', *Econometrica*, 20 (1952) pp. 680–4.

9. Various types of stability are discussed by B. Grofman and C. Uhlaner, 'Metapreferences and the reasons for stability in social choice', *Theory and Decision*, 19 (1985) pp. 31–50.

10. See Riker, *Liberalism*, pp. 69–73 and H. Nurmi, 'On Riker's theory of political succession', *Scandinavian Political Studies*, 6 (1983) pp. 177–94.

11. S. Merrill III, 'A comparison of efficiency of multicandidate electoral systems', *American Journal of Political Science*, 28 (1984) pp. 23–48. For other models, see S. Merrill III, 'A statistical model for Condorcet efficiency based on simulation under spatial model assumption', *Public Choice*, 47 (1985) pp. 389–403.

12. H. Nurmi, 'Voting procedures: a summary analysis', *British Journal of Political Science*, 13 (1983) pp. 181–206.

13. H. Nurmi, 'Mathematical models of elections and their relevance for institutional design', *Electoral Studies*, 5 (1986) pp. 167–81.

14. See Riker, *Liberalism*, Ch. 2.

15. For a discussion on cumulative voting, see S. Merrill III, 'Strategic decisions under one-stage multi-candidate voting systems', *Public Choice*, 26 (1981) pp. 115–34.

16. For comparative analyses of ease of manipulation, see H. Nurmi, 'On the strategic properties of some modern methods of group decision making', *Behavioral Science*, 29 (1984) pp. 248–57; J. R. Chamberlain, 'An investigation into the relative manipulability of four voting systems', *Behavioral Science*, 30 (1985) pp. 195–203.

17. M. A. Aizerman and F. T. Aleskerov, 'Local operators in models of social choice', *Systems and Control Letters* (1983) pp. 1–6; M. A. Aizerman and F. T. Aleskerov, 'Voting operators in the space of choice functions', *Social Science Working Paper* 559, California Institute of Technology, 1985.

18. These assumptions as well as the results are discussed at some length in H. Nurmi *Comparing Voting Systems*, (Dordrecht: D. Reidel, forthcoming). Agenda-manipulation is discussed in Riker, *Liberalism*; Z. M. Lezina, 'Manipulation of option choice (agenda theory)', *Avtomatika i Telemekhanika* (1985) pp. 5–22 (in Russian); and Nurmi, 'On the strategic properties'.

19. See, for example, J. T. Richelson, 'A comparative analysis of social choice functions I, II, III: a summary', *Behavioral Science*, 24 (1979) p. 355; Riker, *Liberalism*; Nurmi, 'Voting procedures'.

20. D. S. Felsenthal and Z. Maoz, 'Monotonicity and consistency reconsidered', Department of Political Science, University of Haifa, mimeo, 1985; R. Farquharson, *Theory of Voting* (New Haven, Conn.: Yale University Press, 1969).

21. Nurmi, 'Mathematical models'.

22. D. S. Felsenthal, Z. Maoz and A. Rapoport, 'The Condorcet efficiency of sophisticated plurality and approval voting', paper prepared for delivery at the 1985 Annual Meeting of the American Political Science Association, 1985. See also R. G. Niemi and A. Q. Frank, 'Sophisticated voting under the plurality procedure', in P. C. Ordeshook and K. A. Shepsle (eds), *Political Equilibrium* (Boston, Mass.: Kluwer-Nijhoff, 1982).

23. Grofman and Uhlaner, 'Metapreferences'.

24. Grofman and Uhlaner, 'Metapreferences', call this explanation of stability the system-stability which is based on the general willingness to accept the voting procedures which are being used.

10 A Structural Analysis of Political Succession

A. M. Potter

INTRODUCTION

This is an analysis of the ritual interpretation of a political succession in which one person follows another (or him- or herself) in a role that is generally taken by the members of the society potently to symbolise the society as politically constituted. The words in parentheses in the previous sentence allow for the case in which someone serving in the role for a limited term is chosen to serve the next. In a political succession there are two elements: individual change (although sometimes only potential) and social continuity. During a political succession as defined above the rituals invoking sentiments in favour of it express human perceptions and feelings about social order in a structure of relations between the elements of the political succession and the rituals which take a universal form.

Top Political Roles

In so-called traditional societies the role succeded to in a political succession might be that of ruler of a segmented society or state. A state is distinguished from a segmented society by its more developed centre of authority and better defined periphery. Typically in traditional societies rulers both reigned and governed: Japanese emperors during the Shogunate made a long-lasting, well-known exception.[1] From the ruler's actual position of providing the sole centre of authority in a segmented society or early state derived the tradition of the ruler's symbolising the society as politically organised in a mature state as well.

In the modern world there is a system of states, European in origin, each 'sovereign' state exercising supreme legal authority in its society, territorially defined. The notion of the continuity of the state is well developed. The gradual displacement of dynastic rule in Europe by constitutional monarchies and republics produced a differentiation between head of state, symbolising the society as politically organised, and head of government. The variations among liberal democracies with these distinct offices, in the real powers of the head of state and the real power of the head of government in relation to the other members of a governing Cabinet, are not of concern here.

After the American Revolution the United States created the archetype of a republican form of government in which the president both inherits the tradition of symbolising the society as politically organised and is the actual political leader. After the Bolshevik Revolution in Russia the Soviet Union created the archetype of the party-state in which the role of leader of the authoritarian party rather than head of state is generally taken by the members of the society potently to symbolise the society as politically organised.

The paragraphs above define the field to which the analysis below applies. To the extent that a society does not have a markedly top person whose role is a powerful symbol of the society as politically organised, the structure of relations between political successions and rituals described here is absent.

An alternative European tradition is of the self-governing community of citizens as the defining element of a political society. It has generally been absorbed into the conception of the modern state without excluding the other tradition, derived from the ruler as defining element, from states where the conditions for it are present. Among present-day European political societies the Swiss Confederation is the purest representative of the communal tradition. The office of President of the Confederation rotates annually among the members of the Federal Council with a minimum of public attention. The ritual expression of perceptions and feelings about the social order is elsewhere.[2] While the structure of relations between political successions and rituals described here, when it occurs, takes a universal form, Switzerland exemplifies that its occurrence is not universal.

Legitimising Rituals

Stereotyped words and actions invoking sentiments in favour of political successions range from the simple and trivial to the elaborate and intense. The most convenient generic term for them is legitimising ritual. Thus, when commenting on the lack of civilities in the struggles in China to succeed Mao, Garside cited, by way of contrast, the 'finely honed ritual'[3] associated with political successions in liberal democracies after the electoral defeat of incumbents, such as an American president attending the inauguration of his successor and a defeated office-holder perhaps 'wishing his successor well and looking forward to spending more time with his grandchildren'.[4]

This usage ignores Evans-Pritchard's stipulation,[5] adhered to by many social anthropologists, that ritual contains 'mystical notions': 'patterns of thought that attribute to phenomena supra-sensible qualities which, or part of which, are not derived from observation or cannot be logically inferred from it, and which they do not possess'.[6] Accordingly, if an American presidential inauguration includes the usual prayer for support from the Judaic-Christian deity, it has a ritual character. If the prayer were to be omitted, the inauguration would become merely 'ceremonious'.[7] While the omission might indicate something significant about a changing role for religion in American society, the function of the inauguration ceremony, in facilitating the success of a political succession by reinforcing the public sense of its legitimacy, would remain the same. It is this attribute which is significant here. In referring to the components of legitimising behaviour during political successions, the words 'rite', 'ritual' and 'ceremony' may be used more or less interchangeably.

The courtesies mentioned by Garside are often said to be 'mere rituals'. Sometimes the implication is that the feelings they conventionally express are not genuinely held. Few believe that a defeated incumbent prefers the company of his grandchildren to office. But this may enhance rather than detract from the efficacy of the courtesies. Preserving them appears as more important than expressing personal feelings.

The more common implication is that 'mere rituals' are of no 'practical' importance: in particular, in relation to political successions, that they are not words or deeds forming part of the successions as events. An American president's taking office is in no way dependent on the attendance of his predecessor at an inauguration ceremony. From this connotation of 'mere rituals' it follows that other rituals are of such practical importance or, to state the converse, that acts forming part of the successions as events may also be rituals.

Many new rulers in many times and places have sought to secure their succession by killing rival claimants. Usually this is the sort of

'Machiavellianism' to be condemned in principle even when followed in practice. However, from the thirteenth to sixteenth centuries the eligibility of all sons of an Ottoman Sultan to succeed him was accompanied by the Law of Fratricide, requiring a new Sultan to kill his brothers. His succession was not ritually as well as practically completed until all the other eligibles were eliminated by civil war or under the Law of Fratricide.[8]

All constitutionally-required elements of a succession as an event are also rituals, for they define the transfers of office which those who believe in the legitimacy of the regime should regard as legitimate. They are a relatively well-defined subset of what Bailey called 'normative rules of proper behaviour' in political contests.[9] These govern the contestants in the interest of preserving the overall order. But the contestants often try to manipulate, and sometimes succeed in changing, them for their own ends. This is so for all kinds of legitimising rituals, including those containing mystical notions.

Figure 1

The rituals associated with the political successions dealt with here fall into the two main categories of human rituals: rituals of transition and rituals of renewal. During a succession the first kind interpret the change of leadership from one person to another so as to increase perception of and affection for the continuity of rule among the members of the society to whom they are addressed. The second kind interpret the continuity of rule as experiencing a purifying rejuvenation during a succession, offering the prospect of beneficial changes in the lives of its individual subjects.

In a development from segmented society to early state in a traditional society, rituals of transition were prominent during political successions. The most vehement means was the temporary suspension of the law and order maintained by a ruler. With the consolidation of the ruler's power in an early state there was less reality in ritual anarchy but more use of human sacrifice in the rituals of state renewal, demonstrating the power of the state over the lives of its subjects in rites purporting to secure greater worldly well-being for the (surviving) members of the (purified) society. During a political succession the ritual sacrifice of the previous ruler's entourage was more common than that of ordinary folk.

For present purposes it is useful to distinguish between a society as politically organised, as in a state, and a political regime, with one political regime differentiated from another by its set of forms of succession, defining the eligibles and procedures, that are recognised as available by its political and military elites. In many cases the set includes military as well as civilian forms of succession. A defining feature of a political revolution or conquest is that the taking of power is not by any of the previously recognised forms of succession or evolution of them. A revolution is an internal, a conquest an external, takeover of the society as politically organised.

In a well-established political regime the ritual emphasis during political successions is normally on rituals of renewal. There are only vestiges of ritual anarchy. With the ending of express religious justification for human sacrifice, only functional equivalents – such as an amnesty for prisoners and milder forms of rotation of office – remain parts of the rituals widely associated with political successions. However, when internal military rule is imposed or external military rule is removed in the cause of rejuvenating a regime, there is still an element of human sacrifice in the rituals of renewal. If a particular succession in a well-established regime departs from the most normal forms, the emphasis in the configuration of rituals shifts from those promising changes in the lives of other individuals to those reaffirming the continuity of rule.

In the following section the interpretation of political successions by rituals of transition and rituals of renewal is explained by reference to the dichotomy between the sacred and the profane in human perception. In the next section, on nature and culture, the use of ritual anarchy and human sacrifice is explained by reference to the dichotomy between nature and culture. In the final section, on change and continuity, the points made in the paragraph immediately preceding are elaborated.

For each section there is a figure illustrating the structure of relations between the elements of a political succession and legitimising rituals. Figure 10.1 (overleaf) presents it as a summary of what follows.

THE SACRED AND THE PROFANE

The society of the people encompassed by a political regime, or of a part of them sufficiently numerous and well-organised to dominate the rest, is not adequately maintained by the 'rational' calculations of individuals pursuing their immediate self-interests in specific

Figure 10.1

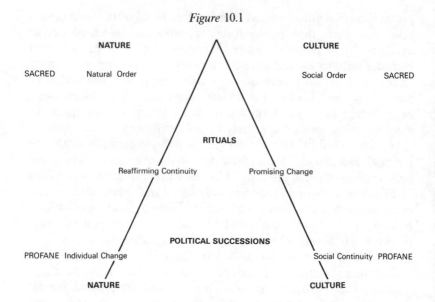

economic and political exchange. Rational in this context means that what the individual gives in a particular exchange is entirely conditioned by what he or she receives for it in the market or by the degree to which the individual is coerced by power. That is what makes exchange specific.

Maintenance of the society depends on generalised exchange or reciprocity, in which what is given in a particular exchange is, at least in part, not conditioned by market forces or the naked exercise of power. Rather, there are elements based on expectations that in appropriate circumstances the giver of something more than what is rationally required in one particular exchange may be the receiver of something more in another. Even so, when the exercise of power, however much legitimised, is involved, exchange is (by definition) never on equal terms.[10]

The expectations of reciprocity are not likely to survive frequent disappointment. But – to apply the general explanation of cultural loyalties[11] to the society encompassed by a political regime – their reasonable fulfilment generates in the individual feelings of identification with others in the society, and with the society as comprising the individual and the others. These feelings are invoked and strengthened by rituals and other uses of conventional symbols.[12]

Throughout most of human existence the most potent symbols have referred to mystical notions and religious ideas. Social order, like the order of the universe with which it has generally been associated or identified, is described in religious terms as eternal and sacred. This is the only way in so-called traditional societies of articulating the perceptions and feelings associated with reciprocity, which requires recognition of obligations that are not confined to the immediacy and expediency of specific exchange. In so-called modern societies the sacred character of social obligations and identities is usually not expressed so explicitly. The emotions are the same. What makes both types of society sacred is that the values associated with the society transcend the immediate self-interests of individuals. In it individuals can strive for the good things of social life also valued by the society as a whole.[13]

Political successions as events take place in the contrasted world of the mortal and the profane. Rituals interpret events of the profane world and infuse them with the sacred. Political successions consist of change and continuity. Change of political leadership from one person to another is an inescapable fact of nature. Human actions may accelerate a change but cannot indefinitely postpone it. The continuity of the political regime in a successful succession is the result of human contrivance. A political regime is a fact of culture. In resolving the opposition between the sacred and the profane in human perception, rituals also resolve that between nature and culture, represented in political succession by change and continuity.

Rituals of Transition

The two main categories into which rituals universal to humankind may be put are rituals of transition and rituals of renewal. Rituals of transition (*rites de passsage*) are concerned with human mortals crossing the boundaries between one social status and another in the profane world: at birth, at the onset of adulthood and other initiations, at marriage and at death. Rituals mark these changes and symbolically produce them by connecting them with the eternal and sacred world. The individual is removed by ritual from the social field in which he or she has been; and, after a ritual 'liminal' period in the timeless world, is incorporated by ritual into his or her new social status.[14]

As Van Gennep pointed out, installation ceremonies fit into this pattern. In political successions they are *rites de passage* symbolically creating the ruler's new status and associating or identifying the new incumbency with the sacred world. The ritual transitional, liminal period in the eternal, sacred world has its counterpart in an interregnum of greatly varying length in the mortal, profane world. 'The Igbo theory of kingship requires an interregnum of not less than seven years after the death of the king. It may extend to twenty.'[15] In the mature state it tends to be as short as physically possible.

The ritual phrase '*le roi est mort, vive le roi*' asserts that in the political succession thus proclaimed the change made inescapable by nature does not disrupt the continuity of the social order maintained by the state of the two rulers, old and new. Symbolically it ends the interregnum even more quickly than may be physically possible, by eliminating it. The accompanying reality of a more developed structure of rule and more rule-determined successions in a maturing state also makes it feasible to organise the formal coronation ceremonies at a leisurely pace.

How the liminal period in the timeless world may both be completed before and extend well beyond the time it takes a political succession as an event to be effected was demonstrated during the succession of Queen Elizabeth II to the throne of the United Kingdom. As advised, she signed herself 'Elizabeth R' from the moment in February 1952 that she, in Kenya, learned of her father's death. But completing the constitutional requirements for an accession took slightly more than two days of profane time. Meanwhile, the two Houses of Parliament, meeting as scheduled after the death of the king, but suspending their sittings until after the Accession Council proclaimed the Queen, studiously avoided identifying the new sovereign. Her coronation was in June 1953.[16]

Rituals of Renewal

Rituals of renewal include: fertility rites in the spring and other ceremonies and festivals connected with the annual cycle of nature; rites of cleansing, forgiveness and expiation, in which the renewal is moral; and tribal feasts and other rites intensifying social identities. associated with rulers and states are ceremonies for renewing attachments to them.

Fitting the ceremonies commemorating rulers and regimes to the annual cycle of other rituals of renewal, often with the rulers as political and religious leaders or the rulers and religious leaders taking part in both, displays the correspondence of social order to the natural world: both are sacred. But the ceremonies of states are likely to be on dates of significance to them rather than related to phases of the natural cycle. The message is that the preservation of social order, however much divinely sanctioned or inspired, is the responsibility of human beings, especially their political regimes: political regimes are part of culture, not nature. Foundation myths, even when they ascribe the founding of the societies to gods, also draw attention to the artificial character of a political regime: it is made. However, interacting with this conception and strengthening the correspondence between rulers and gods is the idea of nature as the product of divine creation: it is made, too.

In traditional societies the accession of a new king is often 'an occasion of repeating symbolically the creative enterprise of kingship, the acts of foundation that established and legitimised it ... The enthronement of the king assures not only the legitimacy of power held, but also the rejuvenation of the kingship.'[17] In the Old Kingdom of Egypt (about 3000 to 2150 BC) ritually 'the beginning of each new rule represented a new creation of the world, a repetition of the original creation. No wonder the coronation day was annually commemorated.[18]

The rituals of political successions symbolically repeat the creative enterprise of rule by using ceremonies from the distant past (imaginary or real), paying homage to founders (mythical or real) or both devices, depending on the history and character of the regimes. The order of ceremony by which Queen Elizabeth was crowned in 1953 was prescribed in a fourteenth-century work 'collating the form of a service which had been used at least as early as the coronation of King Edgar at Bath in AD 973'.[19] The stereotyped references to founding fathers in connection with accessions to the top political leadership in the United States and the Soviet Union are among the many rituals in present day regimes which symbolically renew the acts of their foundation.

Figure 2

Figure 10.2 indicates the functions of the rituals of transition and rituals of renewal associated with political successions. The vertical dimension of this and the other figures displays the dichotomy of the sacred and the profane and the horizontal dimension that of nature and culture, so as appropriately to characterise the entries nearest the four corners. Social order, like the natural order with which it is ritually linked, is sacred. A political succession is a profane event with an element of individual change ultimately, if not immediately, derived from nature and an element of social continuity derived from culture.

Figure 10.2

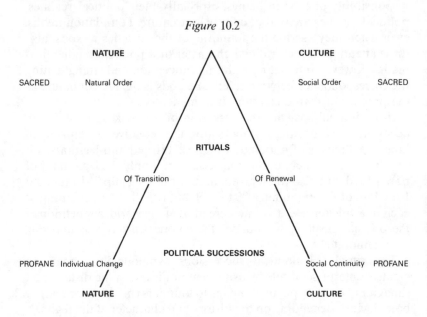

Human societies require their individual members, of each generation, in their continuous natural ageing from birth through maturity to death, to pass through a series of discrete, continuing social roles. Rites of passage make sacred the changes in social status, of which culture is the immediate but nature the ultimate cause, and also the continuing social roles. Installation ceremonies are rituals of transition, performing these functions for political successions. Rituals of renewal interpret the successions as recurrent rejuvenations of the continuing political regimes: the cultural counter-parts of the recurrent rejuvenations of eternal, divinely-created nature. The equivalence is confirmed each year by other rituals of renewal celebrating the original or renewed creation of the social order: the fertility rites of political regimes.

NATURE AND CULTURE

There is an inherent ambiguity in the feelings of the members of a society towards it. For, while social order provides more favourable conditions than its absence for individuals to satisfy their desires, maintaining it also involves putting constraints, enforced by physical and other punishments, on their pursuit of them. In other words, human culture curbs human nature in the interests of the members of the society as a whole at some cost to what they individually perceive to be their immediate interests. Obedience to society's rules comes from a mixture of love and fear.

Rituals associated with political successions express the ambiguous feelings. On the one hand, they reaffirm the benefits that the members of the society derive from the maintenance of order which a successful political succession preserves. On the other hand, they demonstrate the capacity of the political regime to impose constraints and use physical force on individuals. Both sorts of ritual expression have been most vehement when the concentration of ritual on rulers has been greatest: in traditional early states.

In traditional pre-state societies, authority is closely tied to religion with the chiefs or kings usually mediating between the sacred and profane worlds. As the authority of the rulers increases with the development of their states, the ritual elaboration of the rulers' power of mediation and identification with the supernatural increases too. Religion takes on the character of state religion: the social order, now perceived to be maintained by the ruler of the state, is identified with the sacred order of the universe; and the ruler, as the invoker of supernatural forces, is accorded sacred status.[20] However, if the state develops further towards the mature state, there is a shift, from ritual use of the ruler's sacred status and supernatural powers for legitimation, to a legalistic legitimation related to the effectiveness of the governmental apparatus.[21] The state itself increasingly becomes the object of ritual.

During the early-state phase of concentration on sacred rulers, the most dramatic and psychologically-loaded rituals associated with political successions were ritual anarchy, serving to reaffirm the benefits of social order, and human sacrifice. Human sacrifice was purportedly to the gods for the spiritual and material well-being of the society and its members in general or its ruler in particular, and sometimes also for the spiritual well-being of the victims. It demonstrated to men and women the capacity of the state to inflict the ultimate physical deprivation upon them.

Ritual Anarchy

Before ritual anarchy there were civil wars and rituals of rebellion, and before them civil wars and fission. In pre-state, segmented societies (as in most others) the rules of succession for the top position of power define the eligibles but very rarely point automatically to a particular successor.[22] The dependence of the society on the personal qualities of the paramount chief or king is too great for that, which also explains why the eligibles commonly include the brothers as well as sons of the last king so as virtually to ensure the availability of an adult male successor. Normally the last king will have had several wives, each with sons. Sometimes a preference is given to the younger adults among them. Sometimes the rules of succession prefer or prescribe that the last king's successor come from a different part of the royal lineage, perhaps representing a different territorial segment of the society.[23]

In societies that are strongly segmented there is frequent fission, with the inheritance of territories or peoples divided among the leading claimants to their paramountcy, perhaps after some fighting among them. Often there is at least some reintegration later. Societies less strongly segmented are more likely to stay together, with the choice of successor to the paramount chief or king made by those authorised to make it. However, their choices are frequently guided by the outcome of civil wars among the contenders. If and when ideas of the continuity of the social order and kingship begin to develop, the struggles among contenders may be accompanied by rituals of rebellion, which interpret the struggles as exemplifying the conflict and disruption that the absence of the social order and king would permanently release. Gluckman observed that among neighbouring African tribes 'the ceremonies are far more elaborately organised and . . . the rites lay greater stress on the conflicts inherent in the political system in tribes where the cycle of rebellions proceeds without fission'.[24]

When there is not a relapse, the next stage of political development is the early state: like all stages necessarily somewhat arbitrarily defined at the edges. In it ritual anarchy is, in theory, ritual rebellion without the rebellion as well as without fission. The ordinary people suffer a period of lawlessness, sometimes under a 'lord of misrule' (often a lady). The vestiges in some present-day carnivals give little idea of it. For without a definite notion of a continuing state, the king's peace ends with the king's death or burial and is not restored until his successor is chosen or installed. So it was among the Mossi of the Upper Volta: 'The people in the towns immediately looted the markets and stole their neighbour's goods; the prisoners and captives in stocks were released by their guards; the nakomce [nobles, or robber barons] in all territories, districts, and villages subjected the local populations to robbery and pillage.'[25]

In that instance described by Skinner the announcement of the monarch's death had been delayed until 'an army had been raised for keeping order'.[26] Obviously in this context keeping order does not mean maintaining law and order. Rather it means preventing civil wars among the contenders for the succession. But during a period of ritual anarchy things can get out of hand. As a society and its state develop, both ordinary people and the ruling elite increasingly prefer ritual without any anarchy. Data from a cross-section of early states indicate that more than twice as many of them had only mourning rites during an interregnum as had ritual anarchy as well.[27]

Human Sacrifice

The origins of ritual cannibalism (perhaps after live sacrifice) and human sacrifice (perhaps before cannibalism) lie deep in the past of the hominid stock. Peking man, 500 000 years ago, probably prac- tised ritual cannibalism; Neanderthal man certainly did. Until very recently headhunters of Borneo and Melanesia mutilated the base of the skull in exactly the same way as the Neanderthals. There the father of a newborn child killed and ate the brain of a man whose name he knew so that the infant might bear the name.[28] Among the Yoruba of West Africa a new king ate the excised heart of his predecessor so as to acquire his sacred powers.[29]

The Aztecs practised human sacrifice on a grand scale. Almost any religious or state occasion was an excuse for slaughter. The avowed purpose was to nourish the sun and appease the gods. The bodies also nourished the citizenry: as many as 15 000 were eaten in a single year in the Valley of Mexico.[30] The most common victims were prisoners-of-war; next, slaves and criminals; rarely, Aztec citizens in good standing. However, 'a message was conveyed regarding the ultimate power of the state over the life and death of its citizens'.[31]

Generally, in early forms of political societies the practice of human sacrifice becomes more widespread as the power of rulers increases.[32] In early states human sacrifice in rites associated with rulers seems to have been twice as common as ritual anarchy.[33]

Sometimes the only victims were members of a dead king's household buried with him. Usually cannibalism became taboo as supplies of meat improved.

Human sacrifice represents in an extreme form the power of the state to decide the mortal fates of individuals. While ritual anarchy mostly harms ordinary folk, human sacrifice as a ritual associated specifically with political succession tends to centre on the ruler's entourage. It is easy to see why. The ritual of their burial referred to the mystical notion of the victims accompanying the sacred king on his journey to the eternal world. The practice provided the new ruler painlessly (for him) with jobs to give. In the competition among eligibles for a succession positions in the royal household were promised by contenders to supporters; and this form of rotation of office gave the new holders a strong continuing interest in their leader's survival. The practice also made it likely that a contender gaining sufficient support to win would be in the prime of life.

Figure 3

In traditional societies legitimising rituals link the divine forces governing nature as a whole and the human, cultural forces constraining human nature: 'in the case of 'stateless' societies the sacred is of primary importance, while in societies with a highly organised state greater emphasis is placed on the domination exerted over men and things'.[34] Installation ceremonies and ritual new creations of political regimes are specimens of two large classes of rituals for infusing all the socially-valuable activities of the profane world with the sacred. Ritual anarchy and human sacrifice relate specifically to the absence or presence of human authority to exercise physical coercion.

As Figure 10.3 compared with Figure 10.2 indicates, ritual anarchy has the same location in the structure of ritual interpretations of political successions as rituals of transition; and human sacrifice, the same as rituals of renewal. Ritual anarchy marks the change of ruler made inevitable by human mortality, by releasing human nature temporarily from the cultural constraints of rule, so as invoke the desire for continuance of them and the perception of the social order as sacred. Ritual anarchy occupies the 'liminal' period of a social rite of passage as the role of political leadership and the state are increasingly perceived as having identities of their own. The elimination of ritual anarchy. if the state develops further, presages the ritual elimination of the interregnum.

Figure 10.3

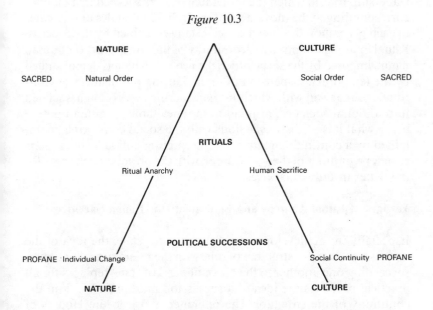

Human sacrifice renews the link between divine and human rule as it demonstrates the god-like power of the latter over the lives of mortals. Rituals of renewal (of which human sacrifice is one instrument) offer the members of the society (who survive the operation) the prospect of welcome changes in their life-chances, in the new cycles cleansed (by the sacrificial blood) of any corruptions attached to the old. Thus both ritual anarchy and human sacrifice indicate why individuals should love the social order, in the course of evoking fear in them: ritual anarchy, fear of the absence of cultural constraints on human nature; human sacrifice, fear of their presence.

CHANGE AND CONTINUITY

During political successions rituals of transition and ritual anarchy deal with the ultimately unavoidable changes of leader in a political regime by ritually reaffirming the continuity of the regime. Rituals of transition endorse the continuity of the kingship or equivalent leadership role, to which the individual leaders succeed in a manner corresponding to the movement of the individual males and females of each generation through the social statuses defined by their society. Ritual anarchy endorses the continuity of the constraints on human nature imposed by the social order, the need for which is demonstrated by the temporary suspension of them. During political successions rituals of renewal, with which human sacrifice was often associated in traditional societies, respond to the inevitable – human nature being what it is – dissatisfactions with the social constraints maintained by a continuing regime, by interpreting political successions as new beginnings of the social order, with the promise of changes for the better in individual lives.

Vestiges of Ritual Anarchy and Equivalents of Human Sacrifice

Especially in the development of the modern state, the idea of the state as a permanent structure of rule, with the rulers, actual or titular, succeeding one another to the office of head of state, replaces for all practical purposes the idea of a succession marking a break in the continuity of the structure. The reference above to the Houses of Parliament meeting during the accession of Queen Elizabeth II draws attention to a late step in this evolution in the United Kingdom: the requirement that Parliament be automatically dissolved by the death of the monarch was eliminated in 1867. The vestiges of ritual anarchy that remain, such as the temporary barring from the City of London of the Officers of Arms come to read the Proclamation of Accession, are mere rituals.[35]

With the disappearance of human sacrifice of ordinary folk from the rituals accompanying successions within political regimes, the device in them that demonstrates most fully the capacity of the state to impose constraints and use physical force on individuals is an amnesty for its prisoners. Where there are political prisoners or detainees, some of them may be released: for his coronation in August 1856 Tsar Alexander II of Russia (who had succeeded his father in February 1855) amnestied the Decembrists.[36] More commonly some ordinary criminals are set free.

In ritual anarchy the forces of human culture yield temporarily to the untamed forces of human nature. The release of prisoners is among the sufferings inflicted on the populace to remind them of the desirability of the social constraints normally maintained by the political regime. An amnesty by a new head of state, like human sacrifice as part of the ritual of a succession, exemplifies the exercise of human social power over individual human beings. It relieves the sufferings of some prisoners so as to signify the potential for beneficial changes in the ritual rejuvenation of the society accompanying the change of political leaders.

Like human sacrifice, amnesty has been part of the ritual of state occasions especially among societies in which there is a strong conception of the role of the ruler or state in imposing order on the society. Among the present-day Western democracies, for example, amnesty is part of the ritual of succession of head of state in continental European rather than English-speaking countries, corresponding to the stronger conception of the state among the former.

In the absence of an express religious justification for human sacrifice, most killings of the previous leader's entourage and lesser political office-holders when new leaders and their supporters succeed, like most killings of an incumbent top leader and rival claimants by contenders for the leadership, are without ritual significance. However, when there is an intensely-felt need to emphasise the cleansing force of the new beginning, there is sometimes an element of human sacrifice in the killings. A temporary military takeover to purge a civilian regime of gross corruption is a likely occasion. The scale of such killings during a change of leadership within a regime is much less than in new beginnings after major revolutions, counter-revolutions and reconquests, when the distinction between political office-holders and ordinary folk is removed by the claim that the victims were all collaborators with the replaced system of rule. During the Second World War, 'as countries were liberated by the advancing Allied armies, the firing squads got to work ... It is said that in France more perished in the "purification" of liberation than in the great terror of 1793.'[37]

Whatever the losers' fate, changes among the holders of prominent offices below that of the top political leader are part of the ritual associated with normal changes at the top. In a regime in which holding the top political office for a term depends on victory by a contender or his or her party in a competitive election, changes among the holders of other prominent political offices (even if only reshuffles) occur when the incumbent of the same party wins another term in office as well as when there is a change of leader or party in power. They symbolise the recurrent rejuvenation of the regime with its promise of better things for the members of the society. Of course, the power to rotate the offices is always of practical importance, too. In a regime in which the head of government is separate from the head of state the power is typically exercised in fact by the former and the rotation of political offices is not part of the political successions dealt with here.

Ritual Emphases in Normal and Other Successions within a Regime

In a well-established political regime the ritual emphasis during political successions taking the most normal forms is on rituals of renewal with their promise of changes. The most normal forms are those recognised as available by the political and military elites of the regime and used at the end of what practice has made expected tenures of the top role. The significant aspect of an expected tenure is whether or not it is for the natural life of the incumbent.

In regimes in which, whatever the formal rules and procedures, practice has created the general expectation that tenure is for natural life, this tenure is a cultural norm no less than an expected tenure which is limited or genuinely subject to periodic renewal. An incumbent with a limited or periodically renewable tenure may fail to finish a term because of illness or death from natural causes or because of death or voluntary or involuntary surrender of office from human causes. An incumbent with the prospect of tenure for his or her natural life may fail to die naturally in office because of assassination or voluntary or involuntary abdication. The failures to complete the expected tenures are failures of culture to tame nature: a limited term may not be finished because of natural illness or death; and both sorts of terms may be cut short for incumbents by human beings breaking the cultural constraints upon their behaviour contained in the norms.

For convenience the most normal political succession in a well-established regime may simply be called normal, in comparison with any other successions which take forms recognised as available by its political and military elites. In a regime that is not well-established there is insufficient normality for differentiating between normal and other successions within it. Excluded from both the normal and the other as defined here are political successions resulting from conquest or revolution. When a succession within a well-established regime is other than normal, the ritual emphasis shifts to reaffirming continuity.

In the United States the expected tenure of presidents is the four-year term for which they have been elected or re-elected. Of the 36 terms betwen 1841 and 1985 nine were not completed: four incumbents died a natural death in office; four were assassinated; and Richard Nixon resigned in August 1974 under threat of impeachment. Sheatsley and Feldman studied the reactions of the American political elites and public to the eight deaths in office. They found that 'waves of anguish in the populace' had been set off not only by the assassinations of presidents and the death from natural causes of a 'heroic figure for much of the public' like President Franklin D. Roosevelt but also by the death of President Warren G. Harding, 'a man of far less heroic stature'.[38] How far, if at all, this finding is to be explained by the unexpected character of the political successions rather than simply by grief at the death of public figures and the temperaments of Americans is obscure. What are most manifest in other than normal successions are the stereotyped words and actions of the political elites reaffirming the continuity of the regime. In contrast to the changes in the president's Cabinet which accompany even the new term for a re-elected incumbent, a vice president succeeding to an unfinished presidential term asks the members of the Cabinet to stay on and they agree. They stay long enough to complete the reaffirmation of continuity. Under Gerald Ford, Nixon's successor, none of the heads of the then eleven Cabinet departments changed in 1974. Eight changed in 1975.

In the early states of Tahiti the hereditary, sacred ruler of a society retired on the birth of a son, so that he could govern as regent during the son's minority free from the taboos restricting the divine king. The transfer of the kingship was accompanied by human sacrifice. Because of the custom of early retiral, death of an incumbent king was unusual. The ritual accompanying such a departure from the normal was witnessed by Spanish missionaries in 1774. The unusually elaborate ceremonies included elements of ritual anarchy absent from normal successions.[39]

In the Soviet Union and most of its East European satellites practice has created the expectation that the tenure of a single top political leader is for life. In Rush's accounts of successions in them there is evidence that the supporting announcements emphasise the prospect of changes in normal, and continuity in other, successions.

The prime message from those who unexpectedly displaced Nikita Khrushchev from the top leadership of the Soviet Union in 1964 was that the positions of others would not be affected.[40]

Figure 4

Figure 10.4 indicates that when successions in a well-established regime are normal there is emphasis on rituals interpreting the continuity of the cultural domination of nature (most evident in normal successions) so as promise changes for the individual members of the society in the new period of rule. Other successions in such a regime arise when nature, including human nature, breaches cultural norms. Then the emphasis is on rituals interpreting a change of leadership (unexpected in these instances) so as to reaffirm social continuity.

Figure 10.4

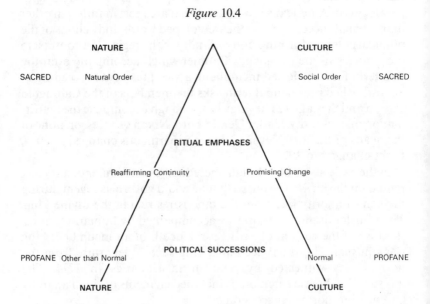

Notes

1. J. M. Roberts, *The Hutchinson History of the World* (London: Hutchinson, 1976).

2. Christopher Hughes, *Switzerland* (London: Ernest Benn, 1975).

3. R. Garside, *Coming Alive! China after Mao* (London: André Deutsch, 1981).

4. Quoted in J. Gardner, *Chinese Politics and the Succession to Mao* (London: Macmillan, 1982) p. 2.

5. E. E. Evans-Pritchard, *Witchcraft, Oracles and Magic among the Azande* (Oxford: Clarendon Press, 1937).

6. Quoted in M. Gluckman, 'Les rites de passage', in M. Gluckman (ed.), *Essays on the Ritual of Social Relations* (Manchester: Manchester University Press, 1962) p. 22.

7. Gluckman, 'Les rites de passage'.

8. Jack Goody, 'Introduction', in Jack Goody (ed.), *Succession to High Office* (Cambridge: Cambridge University Press, 1966).

9. F. G. Bailey, *Strategems and Spoils: A social anthropology of politics* (Oxford: Basil Blackwell, 1969).

10. S. N. Eisenstadt and L. Roniger, *Patrons, Clients and Friends: Interpersonal relations and the structure of trust in society* (Cambridge: Cambridge University Press, 1984).

11. A. L. Stinchcombe, 'Social structure and politics', in F. L. Greenstein and N. W. Polsby (eds), *Handbook of Political Science, III: Macropolitics* (New York: Addison-Wesley, 1975).

12. J. D. Duncan, *Communication and Social Order* (Oxford: Clarendon Press, 1962); A. Cohen, *Two-Dimensional Man: An essay on the anthropology of power and symbolism in complex society* (London: Routledge & Kegan Paul, 1974).

13. M. Fortes and E. E. Evans-Pritchard, 'Introduction', in M. Fortes and E. E. Evans-Pritchard (eds), *African Political Systems* (Oxford: Clarendon Press, 1940); E. Shils and M. Young, 'The meaning of the Coronation', *Sociological Review*, 1 (1953) pp. 63–81.

14. A. Van Gennep, *Rites de Passage* (Paris: Nourry, 1909); Gluckman, 'Les rites de passage'.

15. A. M. Hocart, *Kings and Councillors: An essay in the comparative anatomy of human society* (Chicago, Ill.: Chicago University Press, 1970) p. 136.

16. B. Barker, *When the Queen was Crowned* (London: Routledge & Kegan Paul, 1976).

17. G. Balandier, *Political Anthropology* (London: Allen Lane, 1970) pp. 113 and 114.

18. J. J. Janssen, 'The early state in Ancient Egypt', in H. J. M. Claessen and P. Skalnik, *The Early State* (Paris: Mouton, 1978) p. 222.

19. Barker, *When the Queen was Crowned*, p. 37.

20. R. Cohen, 'State origins: a reappraisal', and P. Skalnik, 'The early state as a process', both in Claessen and Skalnik, *The Early State*.

21. H. J. M. Claessen and P. Skalnik, 'Limits: beginning and end of the early state', in Claessen and Skalnik, *The Early State*.

22. Goody, 'Introduction'.

23. R. Burling, *The Passage of Power: Studies in political succession* (New York: Academic Press, 1974); M. Gluckman, *Order and Rebellion in Tribal Africa* (London: Cohen & West, 1963).

24. Ibid., p. 35.

25. E. P. Skinner, *The Mossi of the Upper Volta: The political development of a Sudanese people* (Stanford, Calif.: Stanford University Press, 1964); quoted in Skalnik, 'Early states in the Voltaic Basin', in Claessen and Skalnik, *The Early State*, p. 485.

26. Skalnik, in Claessen and Skalnik, *The Early State*, p. 485.

27. H. J. M. Claessen, 'The early state: a structural approach', in Claessen and Skalnik, *The Early State*.

28. A. C. Blanc, 'Some evidence for the ideologies of early man', in S. L. Washburn (ed.), *Social Life of Early Man* (London: Methuen, 1962).

29. Goody, 'Introduction'.

30. E. O. Wilson, *On Human Nature* (Cambridge, Mass.: Harvard University Press, 1978).

31. D. V. Kurtz, 'The legitimation of the Aztec state', in Claessen and Skalnik, *The Early State*, p. 184.

32. G. Lenski, *Human Societies: A macrolevel introduction to sociology* (New York: McGraw-Hill, 1970).

33. Claessen, 'The early state'.

34. Balandier, *Political Anthropology*, p. 107.

35. Barker, *When the Queen was Crowned*.

36. C. Sutherland, *The Princess of Siberia: The story of Maria Volkonsky and the Decembrist exiles* (London: Robin Clark, 1985).

37. Roberts, *The Hutchinson History*, p. 988.

38. P. B. Sheatsley and J. J. Feldman, 'A national survey of public reactions and behavior', in B. S. Greenberg and E. B. Parker (eds), *The Kennedy Assassination and the American Public* (Stanford, Calif.: Stanford University Press, 1965) p. 169.

39. Claessen, 'Early state in Tahiti', in Claessen and Skalnik, *The Early State*.

40. M. Rush, *Political Succession in the USSR* (New York: Columbia University Press, 2nd edn, 1968); see also M. Rush, *How Communist States Change their Rulers* (Ithaca, NY: Cornell University Press, 1974) and Chapter 5, above.

11 The Theory of Political Succession

Peter Calvert

The problem of ensuring orderly political succession has been a matter of concern for political thinkers for many hundreds of years. The main concern of the authors of constitutions has been to structure power in such a way that an orderly succession can be established and maintained. It is the conventional wisdom, at a time when the vast majority of newly independent states have already abandoned the structures with which they entered independence, to suggest that such efforts are vain.

The fact is, however, that no authors of a written constitution, however wise and far sighted, can anticipate all the problems which will arise in the future. The United States' Constitution is unique in its longevity, but even by 1861, when it was put to the test by the American Civil War, it had already been substantially modified by political practice. Political parties and electoral procedures, presidential nominating primaries and the Office of Management and Budget, the federal regulatory agencies and the Panama Canal Company, the National Security Council and the CIA, are all unknown to the Constitution of the United States. And the Constitution has had to be modified to take account of the changing circumstances of the transition itself. In 1789 George Washington had to borrow money to travel to his own inauguration, which, as Congress had not yet assembled, took place several weeks late. Today the moment of transition is timed to the second to determine the precise location of responsibility in the event of a nuclear emergency. The President is dead, long live the President; a monarchical problem for an age which some have feared will result in the creation of a new order in which democracy will imperceptibly have ceased to exist.[1]

The apparatus of political change has to cope simultaneously with two problems: the problem of maintaining continuity and the problem of facilitating change.

CONTINUITY

In our examination of political succession we began with the long-established European democracies, and compared and contrasted the experience of some of the newer ones. A striking and significant conclusion from the experience of Europe is that arrangements for political succession can, in favourable circumstances, be very resilient. Despite the two major wars and the turmoil of political ideologies which have swept across Europe in the twentieth century, the major European powers have shown a strong tendency to conserve and restore political succession whenever and however it has been interrupted. France, which since 1940 has undergone occupation, Right-wing reconstruction, war, partisan insurgency, liberation, colonial insurrection, a military pronunciamiento, a Bonapartist regime and a student 'revolt', has often been cited as an outstanding example of political instability. Yet as noted in Chapter 2, despite extensive experience of regime succession, the French have gone on doing the same things in much the same way, and when encouraged to do otherwise, the old habits have tended to reassert themselves. Seen from the perspective of the 1980s it is now the continuity in French politics that impresses the observer, as the Fifth Republic in the age of 'cohabitation' increasingly comes to resemble traditional French parliamentarianism.

Other European countries have no less important lessons to teach us. Ireland, Finland, Czechoslovakia and the Baltic states all had to cope with the problems of nation-building and political change at a time when the ideological turmoil of the post-war world was most unfavourable. Several forms of regime were tried before one achieved consensus. To specify unambiguous procedures for governmental succession was one thing; to have them accepted was another. All were unified only by one factor, in most cases language. All were predominantly agrarian and relatively prosperous compared with the empires from which they had seceded. All emerged into independence at a time when their right to do so legitimately was internationally recognised but when as yet middle-class opinion had got little further than a demand for autonomy. And all confronted the problem of substantial minorities, formerly in the ascendant, and, faced with the challenge of fascism, were to find that their inherent social divisions lent themselves to exploitation in a way that threatened the very foundations of the state itself.

There seems little doubt, as John Coakley shows,[2] that presidential leadership and leader succession was especially significant in consolidating democratic government in Finland and Czechoslovakia. As he also points out, despite a multiplicity of parties and the consequent need for coalition-building, relative stability was in fact achieved in the apparently unpromising circumstances of what he has termed 'complex regime succession', that is, succession which involves the creation or destruction of territorial identities. But those states that later underwent a 'simple regime succession' and adopted authoritarian government did so for very different reasons: in Lithuania the seizure of power coming first and facilitating the spread of fascist ideas, rather than the reverse, in Latvia and Estonia the army acting in conjunction with the civilian leaders to pre-empt a fascist takeover by establishing an emergency dictatorship. In none was the threat of Bolshevism a factor, in the way that it was to be later in Latin America after the Second World War.

In fact, in her detailed study of political succession in Ireland from de Valera to Lemass, Susan Baker, while recognising the 'embeddedness' of traditions, argued strongly for the role of the individual as the agent of change.[3] The Lemass succession followed from his individual role as supporter of de Valera rather than from any personal identification with the rewalist tradition of Fianna Fáil's founder and Constitution. Indeed the post-war realisation of the vulnerability of Ireland's small, isolated economy resulted in the decision to make a positive break with the past.

Belgium's historical legacy, the communal cleavage which bisects it, looks like a recipe for national disaster. The fate of eighteenth-century Poland is part of the historical folk-memory of European politics, revived, as we saw in Chapter 3, by the twentieth-century experiences of the European periphery, and it warns us that a country with a weak unstable government is likely to fall a prey to the larger powers that surround it. Belgium lies in an area traditionally hotly disputed and regarded as of major strategic importance; it was occupied in both World Wars; and since 1945 it has suffered the bitterness of the 'royal question' and considerable communal turbulence which at more than one stage seemed to have fragmented its party structure beyond the capacity to form a stable basis for government. As Wilfried Dewachter has shown, at such times of stress the circulation of elites is accelerated, yet the structure of 'consociational democracy' proved sufficiently durable to be able to accommodate challenges to virtually every aspect of the legitimacy of the state.[4] It survived, it seems, precisely because Belgian government was a wholly practical vehicle for the many interests involved; the epitome of legal/rational political order.

The same is true of the Netherlands. As Arend Lijphart writes: 'The first and foremost rule of the Dutch political game is that politics should not be regarded as a game at all. It is, to borrow von Clausewitz's phrase, "a serious means to a serious end". Or, to put it even more succinctly, it is a business.'[5]

The secret of ensuring stable, orderly succession, discovered by more than one place in Europe in the eighteenth century, lay in the splitting-up of power. But this was not the *separation* of powers advocated by Montesquieu and adopted with indifferent success by revolutionary France. Nor was it the *division* of powers between cantons, länder or states on the one hand and a federal or confederal government on the other. (Federalism too was pioneered in Europe and has been successfully reintroduced into West Germany since the Second World War. But it was across the Atlantic in the United States that it developed into a workable form of government, and it was rejected in France in favour of the unitary state.) What we are talking about here is neither the separation of powers, nor the division of powers, but the *bifurcation* of powers between state and government.

Government directs the destinies of the state, and for many people the terms are synonymous, but not for political scientists. And this is not just because of an academic delight in niceties of expression, but because of important practical differences. The state is the community organised for political purposes; the government is the individual or team of individuals that takes decisions which affect the lives of their fellow citizens. Governments succeed one another; the state endures, and we endure it. Some actions we see as those of the state, some are specific to the government concerned. Governments will, of course, try to represent their own policies as being those of the state, and insofar as they are part of the general consensus they may well in time be accepted as such, but it is one of the attributes of a legitimate government that it can do this with the general acceptance of its citizens.

State power is represented in law by the prerogative powers of the sovereign. In the United Kingdom, unlike the United States, the making and ratification of treaties is an act of the royal prerogative; it is not subject to parliamentary control. The obvious explanation is a historical one; the royal prerogative of the Middle Ages continues, because in a monarchy no one has taken steps to terminate it. But this explanation, characteristic of a large and common category of explanations which are drawn from the experience of a single country, loses virtue in the comparative context when it is observed that the French President, a republican official, also enjoys extensive prerogative powers, even if those powers were in abeyance during much of the Third and all of the Fourth Republics. It is the province of the state to deal with a country's place in the world; the government merely has the temporary ability to manage its affairs and dispose of its resources. In Europe it is relatively easy to believe that it does so to ensure the common welfare of the citizens. But this is not necessarily true, and the fact that a government is illegitimate does not of itself mean that it cannot exercise all the powers of a legitimate one. As the Argentine case shows, even the highest legal authorities may be prepared to endorse the *de facto* rule of an unconstitutional government for fear of what will happen if they do not.

Governmental power, in the European parliamentary state, is embodied in the prime minister and his or her Cabinet, who are collectively responsible to the popularly-elected parliament. In default of a dynastic representative, the state is personified by an elected president, who carries out the largely ceremonial functions of head of state, and represents the country abroad. The ceremonial functions, however, should not and must not be allowed to obscure the real significance of the office, the function of which is to maintain the continuity of the state while facilitating the process of change by which the head of government is replaced.

CHANGE

In default of such an institution, replacing a head of government is a much more hazardous business. It may well be that General Haig, as White House Chief of Staff, performed a notable service to the United States by ensuring that Richard Nixon resigned,[6] but, if so, it was at the cost of whatever political chances he himself might otherwise have had. His efforts to maintain continuity when the President was shot in 1981 were derided[7] and, despite the Twenty-Second and Twenty-Fifth Amendments, the first action of Ronald Reagan on coming out of the anaesthetic following major surgery in 1985 was to say 'Gimme a pen', and resume the powers of the Presidency; which in medical terms he was then and at the least for some time afterwards totally unfit to exercise.[8]

It is one of the curiosities of political power that too obvious a desire to exercise it is seen at one and the same time as a qualification for keeping it and a disqualification for assuming it. The former is clearly irrational, but it has to be recognised to exist. The latter may be a sound instinct; the person who is too eager may rightly be suspected of harbouring authoritarian tendencies. Hence subordinates who would replace an ageing or ailing leader have to move very carefully, signalling their availability only in carefully guarded terms. In the United Kingdom in 1963 Lord Hailsham publicly declared to a stunned Conservative Party Conference, 'My hat is in the ring'. He did not get the job. Part of Pompidou's popularity with the voters was that he was not seen as a career politician; it was his dismissal by de Gaulle that made him available for the top office. By contrast, Gaston Deferre, an outstanding political figure, was unsuccessful in attracting support. The history of democratic government is littered with figures who were fit to govern but unable to attract support and, even more seriously, with those who were able to attract support but not fit to govern.

It is the political party that provides the essential vehicle in Western Europe for achieving power, though the significance of the party to the candidate, and *vice versa*, varies quite markedly even as between Britain, West Germany, France and Ireland. In a single party state it is an even more formidable agency for retaining power, but at the cost of creating a new bifurcation between state and party which sits uneasily with the older one between state and government.

The question of succession in the Soviet Union is intimately bound up with the unique role of the CPSU, and the elaborate and subtle interaction between state and party. It is, however, further complicated by the uncertainty about what constitutes the supreme office. In Marxist theory the very notion of a supreme office was suspect. In 1938 Stalin made it very clear that the nominal head of state, the Chairman of the Presidium of the Supreme Soviet, was intended to be a cypher, and both Kalinin and Shvernik seem to have taken care not to have been of any political significance, the latter being particularly forgettable.[9] Voroshilov, as the cavalry hero of the Civil War, lent the office a certain standing, but when he became incapable of adequately performing its duties the post was used to move Brezhnev out of harm's way. Brezhnev's good fortune was to be first recalled to the Secretariat when Frol Kozlov was struck down by a stroke, and then, when his rival Podgorny was already building up his power base, freed from his formal duties by being replaced by Mikoyan and thus marked out as the 'crown prince': a role which he was to fulfil for only three months.[10]

Malenkov's decision to give up the Party Secretaryship and retain the post of Chairman of the Council of Ministers that Stalin had assumed in the crisis of 1941 has been thought to indicate that he believed that it was with the state and not the party that the real power lay. But the real fear was of the reunion of the two offices, achieved only once more by Khrushchev as the mark of his own personal ascendancy. On his fall they were again separated, and although Brezhnev made it clear abroad that he was to be regarded as the *vozhd* (leader, or more aptly, boss), to the end his colleague Kosygin, a formidable and much underrated figure, retained his independent power base and his control of the machinery of government.[11]

As Stalin had before them, both Khrushchev and Brezhnev built their power on their position as General Secretary of the CPSU, the one post held by every undisputed leader of the Soviet Union since Lenin, though not by Lenin himself, whose authority was purely charismatic.[12] Since Khrushchev was dismissed by the CPSU CC it is clearly not true to say, as is often said, that the Soviet Union has no mechanism for getting rid of failing leaders. But the history of the General Secretaryship of the CPSU since confirms that it is not an easy thing to do and, as Peter Frank has shown, although the convention of the separation between active party and state offices has been maintained, the General Secretary is in a unique position to place his clients in key positions and the longer he holds power the more time he has to secure his power base. Khrushchev's mistake was to move too fast and keep the cadres in constant movement; it was part of Brezhnev's programmatic appeal that he promised stability, and kept his word to the point at which the immoveable rigour of a geriatric leadership defeated the purpose for which it was established.[13]

The Soviet case also reminds us that in political succession changes can and do take place both in personnel and office. The ability of Brezhnev in 1977, at his second attempt, to follow East European practice[14] and himself to resume the formal role of head of state gave him the formal standing that Western powers, despite protocol, had already accorded him as chief of party.[15] This practice was followed by Andropov and Chernenko, but not, despite its apparent logic and convenience, by Gorbachev, who reverted to the practice of using the post as a Soviet House of Lords.

It was made known within a month of his appointment as General Secretary, however, that Gorbachev had been appointed to the third office which, despite its shadowy constitutional position, has for a decade been known to form part of the trinity of Soviet state power. This is the post of Chairman of the Supreme Defence Council.[16] Though formed in the late 1960s, it was not until 1976 that the Council was revealed to exist, at which time its chairmanship was already held by Brezhnev.[17] In May 1983 Marshal Ustinov, then Minister of Defence, revealed that this post was then held by Andropov,[18] and by February 1984 it had already been made known unofficially that Chernenko had been appointed as his successor.[19] The appointment of Gorbachev in his turn confirms not only the importance of the office, but also the relative ease of his succession and the general acceptance of his role as the new leader.[20]

In classical democratic theory, from which the Marxist theory of political succession is derived, the question of who is the leader ought not to matter. Each adult citizen should be as capable of leading as any other. This belief was widely held before the First World War, and was no doubt a healthy reaction to the 'great man' theory of political leadership. Lenin acted as if it were true. But modern Western psychologists have cast serious doubts on the interchangeability of political leaders. For them the individual personality remains one element of the four that make up the complex of leadership the leader, the group, the task and the situation. The survival, though in a much muted form, of the 'personality cult' the Soviet Union makes it all too plain that individual personality still matters. The habit of personifying power in a single individual, consecrated by more than a hundred generations of historically-recorded monarchical succession is hard to break and it is not something that the leaders themselves have worked to break. Leaders want to stay in power, and are accepted for the sake of continuity. Yet if the leader does not change, the group, the task and the situation do, and whereas it may be much easier in principle to change the task than to change the leader, faced with a crisis of confidence the group may well feel that a change in leadership is the *sine qua non* for its own survival.

The Soviet system has well-established constitutional mechanisms for replacing each of the significant offices, but the idea of a fixed term of office, fundamental to the presidential system of the United States, has not taken root. The theory is that all offices are subject to recall: the head of government requires formal re-election on the occasion of the election of a new legislature, and party officials are reappointed at the meeting of each new plenum of the CC. At these times the incumbent can most easily and conveniently be removed, and conversely seek to strengthen his position by demoting or transferring contenders for power. So in practice forced 'resignation' has often disguised the outcome of power struggles within the ruling group. Succession in other East European states has historically been regulated and power struggles muted by the views of Moscow. Where, as in the case of the fall of Gomulka in Poland, indigenous pressure for change became too great to be resisted, the prime consideration then became the choice of a successor acceptable to the Soviet leadership. But in China, which has escaped from the Soviet orbit long before the death of Mao Zedong, a markedly different pattern has emerged, as Eberhard Sandschneider shows. There an element of public confrontation has continued which seems quite alien to the Soviet tradition of secrecy, but which at the same time is in practical consequences very different from the traditions of Western liberal democracy, involving as it has done the possibility of physical attack on, public humiliation and even death of major political actors.

The risk of such consequences is precisely what norms of succession are established to avoid. Any use of force to overthrow a government, whether it be by revolutionaries seeking radical change or the promoters of military coups acting, as they say, to preserve the existing order, opens up an endless horizon of force and reprisal. In China during the period of Cultural Revolution, the deliberate dismantling of all traditional or constitutional restraints resulted in widespread public disorder, ultimately only contained by the army. As Sandschneider shows, it is still too early to say with assurance whether a new synthesis of China's major political traditions has been attained, and the possibilities of peaceful succession in the future still in part rest on the hazards of individual survival, and partly on the medium-term effects of the reform of the structure of party rule

In Nigeria, a former European colony, Alan Brier argues that the origins and style of political changes since independence can be traced to colonial practices at the end of the colonial period. But new forms and new practices have arisen which are more clearly of Nigerian origin, and at each successive simple regime change there has been some reorientation towards the new institutional forms available. But these new forms incorporate very old elements, going back to the chieftainships of pre-colonial times; patronage, an essential part of such forms, fuels the endemic corruption, and the army – which has done much to integrate the earlier regional particularisms – repeatedly intervenes, prompted both by institutional dissatisfaction with civilian government generally and internal competition for power. Brier also reminds us that too much concentration on the dominant forms of succession may lead us to overlook the true significance of those which work only intermittently or – like rural insurgency – voice significant aspirations but fail to achieve their goals.

European traditions have helped shape the political systems of both the Soviet Union and China: the very notion of a political party, so central to each, is a European concept. But the European tradition has been substantially modified even in parts of the world where it has been much more firmly implanted and there is much less consumer resistance to its acceptance. Argentina is the product of the first age of European colonisation; a settlement colony in which the indigenous population was almost wholly eradicated in the Indian wars of General Roca, and a 'quasi-colony' firmly linked by economic ties to the United Kingdom before Lugard had even arrived in Nigeria. Argentines feel themselves to be heirs to European culture, and at times have in the Hispanic tradition behaved as if they were its last defenders.

Yet as Sue Milbank has shown, Argentina today is the product of a divided culture in which what may, for the sake of conciseness, be termed elements of the 'Iberian' and Western 'European' traditions are in constant struggle for ascendancy.[21] In the nineteenth century Argentina went further than any other Latin American country too, in its admiration for, and desire to emulate, the United States. The Constitution of 1853, often suspended but restored even after the fall of Juan Domingo Perón in 1955, follows that of the United States more closely than other Latin American constitutions. Yet its rulers have used some of the provisions in which it follows that model most closely to make of it a charter for a 'bureaucratic-authoritarian' state of quite a different character. With even the ground rules of political conflict themselves in dispute, the two streams of Argentine political culture, today broadly identifiable with the two leading parties, the Radicals and the Peronists, battle it out. And a central part of this contest is the notion of succession; to Perón, to political leadership

and last but not least, to the authority claimed by the leadership of the
armed forces.

For it is the crucial ambiguity in the meaning of the term 'succession' that an individual can at one and the same time be a
successor to more than one predecessor, and to more than one tradition,
and that one may subsume or encapsulate the other. Thus President
Alfonsín today in Argentina is heir simultaneously to his own
leadership of the party of Yrigoyen, to the alternative tradition of the
Perons, and (whether he likes it or not) to the rule of the *de facto*
presidents who owed their position to the will of the armed forces,
and emerged as political leaders because they had reached the top of
the military hierarchy. Similarly in the United States, President
Reagan is successor to both Woodrow Wilson and Calvin Coolidge,
and in Ireland Mr Haughey successor to both Cosgrave and de
Valera. .

PARALLEL, BRANCHED AND CONVERGENT LINES

It seems, therefore, that the problem of interweaving succession in
parallel and branching lines is by no means confined to the Soviet
Union, but is equally significant in other states. Both in stable liberal
democracies and in unstable bureaucratic-authoritarian states we
find parallel lines of succession to the leadership of stable, competitive
political parties. The leaders of such parties compete for power in
such a way that while we can discern a succession within each political
party, we can overlay on that pattern of parallel development a single
overall succession to political power itself. We can call this a
convergent line of succession, given that it is formed by choice from
the succession in two or more parallel lines by the fluctuating success
of each in attracting the support of the electorate. An example of the
way in which this operates in a stable party system with a limited
number of parties is given for the United Kingdom in Table 11.1.

Though there have been examples of exchange of personnel
between parties in Britain, the parties themselves have remained
fairly stable, and this despite the fact that the weakest of the major
parties at any one time has been entirely denied a share of political
power (except in time of national emergency). In West Germany,
where three parties have shared political power since 1949, offices
have been shared, and each party in a coalition gets some say (see
Table 11.2).

Table 11.1   United Kingdom: party leadership since 1940

Date	Conservative		Labour	Liberal
(1935)			Attlee	Sinclair
(1937)	CHAMBERLAIN			
1940	CHURCHILL		*Attlee*	*Sinclair*
1945	CHURCHILL		Attlee	Sinclair
1945	Churchill		ATTLEE	Davies
1950	Churchill		ATTLEE	Davies
1951	CHURCHILL		Attlee	Davies
1955	EDEN		Gaitskell	Davies
1956				Grimond
1957	MACMILLAN			
1959	MACMILLAN		Gaitskell	Grimond
1963			Wilson	
1963	HOME			
1964	Home		WILSON	Grimond
1965	Heath			
1966	Heath		WILSON	
1967				Thorpe
1970	HEATH		Wilson	Thorpe
1974	Heath		WILSON	Thorpe
1974	Heath		WILSON	Thorpe
1975	Thatcher			
1976			CALLAGHAN	
1976				Steel
1979	THATCHER		Callaghan	Steel
			Foot	
1983	THATCHER		Foot	Steel
1984			Kinnock	

Note: Capital letters indicate prime ministers, italicisation indicates those who held Cabinet posts in coalition governments.

In a multi-party system, we find not only parallel but also branching hierarchies being formed, as parties split and new parties are formed. Parties can therefore share loyalties to particular figures of the past, while maintaining very different views as to what those figures stood for. In an extreme case the founding fathers of a state, such as George Washington in the United States or José de San Martin in Argentina, can be claimed by all sides; in fact, succession from George Washington, a Virginian, was used by the states of the Confederacy as a legitimating device in support of their view that it was the North and not themselves that had diverged from the true Constitution of the United States.

Today the United States, however, has a very unusual party struc-

Table 11.2   West Germany: party leadership since 1949

Date	CDU/CSU	SPD	FDP
1949	ADENAUER	Schumacher	*Scheel*
1952	ADENAUER	Brandt	*Scheel*
1959	ADENAUER	Brandt	*Scheel*
1963	ERHARD	Brandt	*Scheel*
1966	KIESINGER	*Brandt*	Scheel
1969	Kiesinger	BRANDT	*Scheel*
1971	Barzel	BRANDT	*Scheel*
1972	Barzel	BRANDT	*Scheel*
1973	Carstens	BRANDT	*Scheel*
1974	Carstens	SCHMIDT	*Genscher*
1976	Kohl	SCHMIDT	*Genscher*
1980	Strauss*	SCHMIDT	*Genscher*
1982	Kohl	SCHMIDT	Genscher
1982	KOHL	Schmidt	*Genscher*
1983	KOHL	Schmidt	*Genscher*
1985	KOHL	Rau*	*Bangemann*
1986	KOHL	Vogel	*Bangemann*

Note: Capitals indicate chancellors, italicisation indicates those who held Cabinet posts in coalition governments. * indicates Chancellor-candidate.

ture, in that the separation of powers has divided it between the various branches in a very uneven fashion. The party in the White House enjoys all the benefits of visibility, patronage and the use of executive leadership for partisan purposes. The defeated presidential candidate is as dead as a Merovingian monarch; his titular leadership of his party is virtually worthless and far from him consecrating an orderly succession, would-be nominees try to distance themselves from him as rapidly as possible.

Now the rush to abandon a defeated candidate is not without examples in other countries: one only has to think of the example of Franz-Josef Strauss after his unsuccessful bid for the chancellorship of West Germany in 1980. Yet Strauss remains a formidable figure in West German politics thanks to his weight in the CDU–CSU team and his position in Bavarian state politics enables him to maintain a substantial team of advisers and publicists which keep him in the public eye. In Ireland, where a would-be prime minister (Taoiseach) has to face the ordeal of being chosen in a public vote by Daíl Eireann, some leaders have been rejected (de Valera, Costello, Lynch, Haughey) but, with a firm local base, have retained their party leadership and later returned to office.[22] In post-Gaullist France, too, politicians show great resilience; a would-be aspirant still needs a local base to climb the mayoral and parliamentary ladder that is the surest route to ultimate political power, and takes into power with him his *Cabinet*; the small group of key advisers he has built up over the years. 'Parachutists' placed in provincial seats by central party organisations have to overcome a substantial tradition of local independence and distrust. By contrast the British political leader is wholly dependent on the structure of the party; only among the minor parties is a local power base a significant asset, and party organisations, despite infrequent protests in individual constituencies, place favoured individuals in supposedly safe seats without much concern for the possible reactions of the electorate; at least it appears so from the frequent surprise with which they greet the defeat in a by-election of one of their choices.

This is all the more peculiar since the mechanism of electoral systems is something that for more than two centuries has attracted the attention of the theorists. As Hannu Nurmi shows, choice of candidates can be assimilated to the now considerable literature on the mechanism of choices between policies.[23] People, like policies, can be treated as sets of variables. What seems to present the most intractable problem is that the possible range of candidates is far wider and, unlike policies, they cannot be combined to form compromise candidates! Hence even more than policies the choice between them should be expected to be extremely unstable, and yet in practice succession from one to another seems to be relatively stable and orderly.

Nurmi demonstrates that, although the problem of cyclicity (inability to arrive at a single stable order of preference) easily arises in small bodies confronted with a large number of choices, in practice where people have stable orders of preference democratic political institutions may be stable well outside their theoretical limits. The simple-majority rule can only be guaranteed to be effective where no more than two options are considered, but even it can give reasonable results where there are few choices, large majorities and a rather large number of voters. Hence it appears that there is not in fact much stability in our processes of choice, but that we do not experience instability of choice as necessarily intolerable. One possible reason is that, contrary to the assumptions behind the notion of the mandate, voters do not necessarily reveal their true preferences even in the secrecy of the polls. Another is that they do not expect too much of the system. In the world of the smoke-filled room sincerity, either in the technical or non-technical sense, is not likely to be operative. And strategic voting which could operate to make choice more stable, even if we do not necessarily like the outcome, can only operate where voters have full information about the outcome of their choice; something that existing electoral systems actually tend to reduce or eliminate.

Nurmi's argument supports the argument of Riker[24] that the key virtue of liberal democracy is that it does ensure the replacement of leaders, and does not seek to extend participation to the choice of policies. Riker claims that, since all known systems of choice can easily be demonstrated to 'fail' on at least one of the criteria, choice can at best be a check on government and not the foundation of decision-making. His argument, taken literally, could be used to support the contention (common in the United Kingdom) that there is no point in changing a demonstrably inadequate form of electoral system unless it can be replaced with a perfect one. But as he himself admits, forcing popular choice into the straightjacket of a two-party system is itself a violation of the principles such a system is expected to serve, and 'simple majority decision cannot be institutionalized without violating fundamental notions of fairness'.[25]

The development of social choice theory may in time solve this problem by providing us with a system of choice that does conform to all criteria of fairness. In the meanwhile many states have gone much further than Britain or the United States in securing proportionality, and few authors attempt to defend plurality systems on the ground that proportionality is occasionally achieved, even if by mistake. Instead they argue that proportional systems are difficult to understand,[26] that elections are not about proportionality, that the important thing is to constitute a strong government, and that whatever system is chosen, minorities must always lose.[27] All these propositions are, of course, themselves very disputable. The electorate of the Irish Republic has twice rejected by referendum moves by their politicians to take proportional representation away from them. The experience of other European states is that proportionality is widely seen as a fundamental factor legitimating liberal democracy, and that moves away from it are closely associated with the authoritarian right; the maintenance of it as an existing system is therefore *prima facie* dubious. Rapidly changing governments are not a sign of weakness – liberal democracy in France, Belgium and the Netherlands has survived much worse threats (war, invasion, occupation) than any recently encountered in Britain – or of technical incapacity: France laid its foundations for its industrial recovery under the Fourth Republic and Italy's industrial production has now passed that of the United Kingdom.

'Strong' governments pass some very silly legislation; conversely coalitions recognise the fugitive nature of public opinion, and adapt to changing circumstances while allowing proper representation of minorities. And coalition politics, by allowing for a much greater degree of continuity and experience in government, makes political succession a continuous process and not a series of erratic changes from one untrained team of politicians to another (the incoming Labour government in Britain in 1964 had, after the surprise defeat of Patrick Gordon-Walker, only one member with previous experience in government, and the incoming prime minister in 1979 had no previous experience in foreign affairs, a subject of which she has needed a more than adequate knowledge and understanding ever since). On this last ground alone, therefore, in an age of technical specialisation in government as in all else, coalition politics may well be accounted a virtue.

The concept of political succession, however, in turn points up a possible lacuna in current social choice theory. There is little doubt that in making their choice of candidates electors are choosing not just one candidate from the field but each candidate against his or her predecessor. This presents some problems even if the outgoing representative is seeking re-election, since incumbency is intuitively recognised as important by party activists, even if its numerical value is uncertain and probably varies very much with circumstances. But even if the incumbent is not seeking re-election, the fact of succession still suggests that the incumbent needs to be incorporated in the matrix of choice if it is to represent accurately the actual processes that go on in the minds of the voters. In other words the incumbent performs for the choice of candidates something of the role which doing nothing performs for the choice of policies; it is the standard against which all the rest are to be judged since electors are not offered the choice of having no representative.[28]

It is at this point that, with Allen Potter, we turn from mathematics to anthropology to explain why leaders are accepted, and the crisis inseparable from political succession averted. For the process of choice does not in practice end the matter. The chosen candidate is presented to the people as the rightful successor, and by manipulation of the context of the presentation the choice rendered generally acceptable. The Soviet leader, who has already emerged from a process of private consultation, is presented as the heir at his predecessor's funeral in a way that symbolises both continuity and change.[29] In the context of electoral politics the process occurs twice; once at nomination, when the candidate is presented as the choice of the party, and again at election, when the choice of the party is received as leader of the government or state with the formal ritual of installation traditional at such times.

Party nomination, whether local or national, is cooptative within parliamentary systems in a way that it may not be within presidential ones. But in presidential systems the option of forming a discrete party or alliance of parties is a possible alternative strategy for those who are unable or unwilling to be coopted and, what is more, it works. In theory candidates can even be drawn from outside the enchanted circle of political notables, but it seems this seldom happens. Hence while the politicians control the process, the apparatus of state is used to convince the electors that the outcome of their efforts is what they wanted.

No theory of political succession, therefore, can be complete without taking account of the mechanism by which before the election candidates are nominated, and after which cognitive dissonance is ameliorated and the outcome of the electoral process rendered psychologically acceptable. Cross-national research on a case-study basis could systematically explore the particular circumstances of political succession in selected states, with a view to determining the full range of cooptative mechanisms employed. Special attention to the way in which the rules of succession are varied, and the interactive process by which the governed secure 'concessions' from the government in the choice of political leaders, would further illuminate the questions of what groups are active in any given case; the extent to which continuity is maintained within the ruling group; and how far a consistent and predictable career pattern is presented to the political aspirant. The role of patronage in determining pre-candidature is undoubted, but a wider range of material would be useful on how it actually works in different political systems. Who, for example, are the 'selectorate'? How far is it open for candidates to propose themselves? Must candidates be presented for the attention of selectors, or do the selectors themselves act to seek candidates?

A reassessment of existing studies of individual governmental structures – the staff, political parties, the bureaucracy, the armed services, provincial government – to determine the role of each in contributing to the pool of political aspirants would seem an essential further step. Where, as in Europe, detailed biographical information on individual political leaders is available, conditions are particularly favourable for making comparative studies of career patterns and illuminating such features as dynastic succession or family relationships. The aim should be to extend the scope of such research cross-nationally, as well as extending it outside the ruling group narrowly defined, to determine how far the features identified as characteristic of that group are common to the society at large. If, as many writers believe, the concept of 'political culture' is of significance in explaining differences between states, an overall assessment of the cultural role attached to political succession in any given state, such as the view of the significance of the problem as seen by opinion leaders and the media, would be of obvious value.

IRREGULAR SUCCESSION

No discussion of political succession would be complete without consideration of the problems presented by irregular political succession. As has already been noted, Western European systems have remained remarkably stable since 1945 in view of the horrendous stresses to which they have been subjected by war, collaboration, insurrection and liberation. Even Britain, most of which was spared actual occupation (the exception being the Channel Islands), has fought a long series of colonial wars and has had to confront a seemingly insoluble insurrection in Northern Ireland. The surprising thing has been the extent to which the problem of Northern Ireland has been treated on a bipartisan basis and allowed to impact as little as possible on British party politics. Neither of the major political parties run candidates in Northern Ireland or allow the inhabitants of the province to take part in them, thus effectively excluding the people from any say in the nomination of their political leadership. And, thus far, attempts to carry violence to the 'mainland' (sic) of Great Britain, though sometimes spectacular, have been infrequent and unsuccessful.

In other parts of the world, however, the use of force to secure political power is seen as 'normal', and any theory of political succession must take account of this. It is, of course, perfectly proper to regard succession as something that takes place only constitutionally, according to agreed rules and procedures. But this is to take rather a limited view of what is in reality a very complex situation. For many modern states, such as Ireland, Portugal[30] or Turkey[31] the myth of revolution is central to the legitimacy of all successor governments. For others, as in Nigeria, military intervention has been accepted as an actual route to power, and in Argentina, given that it has been well established for 150 years, it seems impossible to pretend that it does not exist and potentially misleading not to try to bring it within the scope of a general theory.

Here it has been suggested that succession to military office as a precondition for political leadership may for practical purposes be regarded as equivalent to leadership of a political party. Significantly, as might be expected, just as regular transitions stress novelty and renewal, irregular transitions stress continuity and tradition. Military intervention, as in Nigeria, is nearly always justified as a historic mission to undertake on behalf of the people a distasteful but necessary duty designed to maintain the national integrity in face of corruption, incompetence and malign influences.[32]

The normal outcome of a military transition is to pre-empt change rather than to promote it. Its objective extends little further than to remove the political incumbents and most military governments hold power only for the relatively brief period in which this objective can be achieved. Often the normal constitutional or quasi-constitutional processes are invoked to fill the vacancy. As long as intervention takes place on this level, the principle of constitutional order is maintained and the succession process is reasonably orderly and predictable.

It was a new phenomenon in many ways when, beginning in the Middle East with Nasserism in the 1950s and culminating in Latin America with the military governments of Brazil, Peru, Uruguay, Chile and Argentina after 1964, the armed forces proclaimed a new goal, that of national economic development, for which they would stay in power as long as was 'necessary'. It was – to put it mildly – an unpleasant surprise to many of the inhabitants of such countries to discover that the military governments concerned were prepared to go to great lengths to stay in power, and that the torture and murder of political opponents was regarded by them as an acceptable way of countering what they saw as the threat of externally-prompted revolution. Worse still, it has proved almost impossible to call such military governments to account for their crimes.

The belief that external agencies can bring about a desired political succession in any specified country has its counterpart in the emergence at this same time of the concept of 'destabilisation'.[33] 'Destabilisation' was first used publicly in 1974 by William H. Colby, the incumbent Director of Central Intelligence in the United States, to refer to the process of trying to create political change in another country by the use of indirect pressure, and especially to create such internal problems for a government that it will find itself unable to continue.[34] It has achieved a special notoriety in connection with the events in Chile in September 1973, when the Allende government was overthrown by a revolt of its own armed forces. As in due course evidence emerged of the extent to which the United States had sought to exercise pressure on Chile, it became a convenient word to describe all such acts, falling short of actual military intervention, by which one country's government might seek to weaken the position of another and eventually bring about its downfall.

Destabilisation, therefore, is the obverse of violent political change. To destabilise is to seek to bring about a revolutionary change. Hence use of the term implies three things: that international action can be sufficient to bring about crises in another state, that those crises in turn will bring about political change, and that those changes will result in a favourable political succession. As has been shown elsewhere,[35] it is clear that – at least in the present state of our knowledge – none of these three things can be guaranteed. Measures of destabilisation, in the absence of a detailed understanding of the processes of political succession, are highly unpredictable, and the decision to employ them essentially irresponsible. Taking the example of five Latin American countries known to have been subjected to pressure from the United States, in Cuba and Nicaragua the existing governments were actually strengthened, while in Guatemala and Grenada an unwanted succession resulted, and the situation was only resolved by direct intervention, diplomatic in one case, military in the other. In the case of Chile, it is hard to argue that the United States has not lost more than it gained from its association with a repressive military regime in which no stable constitutional succession appears likely.

Clearly an unfavourable international climate can and does affect the stability of governments. Clearly, too, economic sanctions, collectively applied by the consent of a majority of the world's governments are, as the founders of the League of Nations recognised, much preferable to war as a way of bringing pressure to bear on an individual government which transgresses the norms of the international community. Collective sanctions have therefore been incorporated in international law. But international law as well as the custom of nations rightly opposes the use by individual governments of measures designed to overthrow neighbouring governments. It is all the more important that they should not try to do so when they do not understand the mechanisms of political succession which they are seeking to exploit. Conversely, a greater understanding of the nature and importance of orderly political succession can only strengthen democracy, as it has done with such evident success in its birthplace, Western Europe.

Notes

1. Cf. Amaury de Riencourt, *The Coming Caesars* (New York: Coward-McCann, 1957).
2. John Coakley, 'Political succession on the peripheries of Europe, 1918–1939: nation-building and political change in Ireland, Finland, Czechoslovakia and the Baltic states', paper presented to Workshop on Political Succession, ECPR Joint Sessions of Workshops, Salzburg, April 1984.
3. Susan Baker, 'From economic nationalism to European integration: a study of political succession from Eamon de Valera to Seán Lemass in the Fianna Fáil Party', paper presented to the Workshop on Political Succession, ECPR Joint Sessions of Workshops, Salzburg, April 1984.
4. Wilfred Dewachter, 'The circulation of the elite under macro-social crises. Analysis of the Belgian case since 1919', paper presented to Planning Session on Political Succession, ECPR Joint Sessions of Workshops, Freiburg 1983.
5. Arend Lijphart, *The Politics of Accommodation: Pluralism and democracy in the Netherlands* (Berkeley, Calif.: University of California Press, 2nd edn, revised, 1975) p. 123.
6. Theodore H. White, *Breach of Faith: The fall of Richard Nixon* (New York: Dell, 1975) pp. 21ff.
7. See *inter alia* Alexander M. Haig, Jr, *Caveat: Realism, Reagan and foreign policy* (London: Weidenfeld & Nicolson, 1984).
8. Frank Taylor, 'Black week in the White House', *Sunday Telegraph*, 21 July 1985.
9. Edward Crankshaw, *Russia without Stalin: The emerging pattern* (London: Michael Joseph, 1956) pp. 210–11.
10. John Dornberg, *Brezhnev: The masks of power* (London: André Deutsch, 1974) pp. 158–63, 172–3.
11. Ibid., pp. 23–4, 206–15, 262, 274–5.
12. Martin McCauley, 'Leadership and the succession struggle', in Martin McCauley (ed.), *The Soviet Union after Brezhnev* (London, Heinemann, 1983) pp. 12–13.
13. Archie Brown, 'Political developments: some conclusions and an interpretation', in Archie Brown and Michael Kaser (eds), *The Soviet Union since the Fall of Khrushchev* (London: Macmillan, 2nd edn, 1982) pp. 218–75.

266   *The Theory of Political Succession*

14. Cf. Myron Rush, *How Communist States Change their Rulers* (Ithaca, NY: Cornell University Press, 1974).
15. Archie Brown, 'Political developments 1975–77', in Brown and Kaser, *The Soviet Union*, pp. 308–9.
16. For the structure and composition of the Defence Council see M. Sadykiewicz, 'Soviet military politics', *Survey*, 26 (1982).
17. Robert F. Byrnes (ed.), *After Brezhnev: Sources of Soviet conduct in the 1980s* (London, Indiania University Press 1983) p. 140.
18. E. Abraham and J. Steele, *Andropov in Power From Komsomol to Kremlin* (New York: Doubleday, 1984) 169.
19. Archie Brown, 'The Soviet succession from Andropov to Chernenko', *The World Today*, 40 (1984), pp. 134–141, citing *International Herald Tribune*, 28 February 1984.
20. See also the brief biography and selection of speeches in Mikhail S. Gorbachev, *A Time for Peace* (New York: Richardson & Steirman, 1985).
21. Chapter 8; see also Susan Milbank, 'An Argentinian security perspective', in Caroline Thomas (ed.), *Third World Perceptions of Security* (Cambridge: Cambridge University Press, forthcoming).
22. John Coakley, 'Prime-ministerial succession: the Irish experience', paper presented to the Planning Session on Political Succession, ECPR Joint Sessions of Workshops, Freiburg, March 1983.
23. See Chapter 9.
24. W. H. Riker, *Liberalism against Populism: A confrontation between the theory of democracy and the theory of social choice* (San Francisco, Calif.: W. H. Freeman, 1982), p. 253.
25. Ibid., p. 41.
26. A. J. Milnor, *Elections and Political Stability* (Boston, Mass.: Little, Brown, 1969) p. 90ff.
27. Vernon Bogdanor and David Butler (eds), *Democracy and Elections: Electoral systems and their political consequences* (Cambridge: Cambridge University Press, 1983) pp. 41–3.
28. Duncan Black, *The Theory of Committees and Elections* (Cambridge: Cambridge University Press, 1963) pp. 3–4.
29. See Peter Frank, 'USSR. The Andropov succession', paper presented to Planning Session on Political Succession, ECPR Joint Sessions of Workshops, Freiburg, March 1983.
30. Ken Gladdish, 'Political change in Portugal in the twentieth century; succession in a transitional society', paper presented to Planning Session on Political Succession, ECPR Joint Sessions of Workshops, Freiburg, March 1983.
31. See Chapter 4.
32. See Chapter 7.
33. Peter Calvert, 'Destabilization as applied political succession', paper presented to the Workshop on Political Succession, ECPR Joint Sessions of Workshops, Salzburg 1984.
34. Gary MacEoin, *Chile, the Struggle for Dignity* (London: Coventure, 1975) preface.
35. Peter Calvert, 'Destabilization as applied political succession'.

Bibliography

ABERNATHY, Glenn, HILL, Dilys M. and WILLIAMS, Phil, *The Carter Years: The President and policy-making*, London: Frances Pinter, 1984
ABRAHAM, Eric, and STEELE, Jonathan, *Andropov in Power; From Komsomol to Kremlin*; New York: Doubleday, 1984.
ADENAUER, Konrad, *Memoirs, 1945–53*, trans. Beate Rahm von Oppen, London: Weidenfeld & Nicolson 1966.
AHN, Bjung-joon, 'The Cultural Revolution and China's search for political order', *China Quarterly*, 57 (1974) p. 249ff.
AIZERMAN, M. A. and ALESKEROV, F. T., 'Local operators in models of social choice', *Systems and Control Letters*, 3 (1983) pp. 1–6.
—— and ALESKEROV, F. T., 'Voting operators in the space of choice functions', *Social Science Working Paper* 559, California Institute of Technology, 1985
ALAVI, H., 'The state in postcolonial society', in H. Goulbourne (ed.), *Politics and the State in the Third World*, London: Macmillan, 1979, pp. 38–69.
ALEXANDER, Robert J., 'The emergence of modern political parties in Latin America', in Joseph Maier and Richard W. Weatherhead (eds), *Politics of Change in Latin America*,New York: Praeger, 1964, p.103.
AMIN, Samir, *Neocolonialism in West Africa*, Harmondsworth:Penguin 1973, originally published in French as *L'Afrique de l'Ouest Bloquée* (Paris: Minuit, 1971).
ANDERSON, B., *Imagined Communities: Reflections on the origin and spread of nationalism*, London: New Left Books, 1983.
ANDERSON, Patrick, *The President's Men: White House assistants of Franklin D. Roosevelt, Harry S. Truman, Dwight D. Eisenhower, John F. Kennedy, and Lyndon B. Johnson*, Garden City, NY: Doubleday, 1968.
ANDERSON, Perry, *In the Tracks of Historical Materialism*, London: Verso, 1983.
ANDRESKI, Stanislav, *Parasitism and Subversion: The case of Latin America*, London: Weidenfeld & Nicolson, 1966.
ANDREWS, William G., *Presidential Government in Gaullist France: A study of executive–legislative relations 1958—1974*, Albany, NY: State University of New York Press, 1982.
ANENE, J. C., *The International Boundaries of Nigeria 1885–1960*, Harlow: Longman, 1970.
APTER, David E., *The Politics of Modernization*, Chicago, Ill.: University of Chicago Press, 1965.
ARIKPO, O., *The Development of Modern Nigeria*, Harmondsworth; Penguin, 1967.
ASTIZ, Carlos Alberto, 'The Argentine armed forces: their role and political involvement', *Western Political Quarterly*, 22 (1969) p. 863.
BAILEY, F. G., *Strategems and Spoils: A social anthropology of politics*, Oxford: Basil Blackwell, 1969.

BAKER, Susan, 'From economic nationalism to European integration: a study of political succession from Eamon de Valera to Seán Lemass in the Fianna Fáil Party', paper presented to Workshop on Political Succession, ECPR Joint Sessions of Workshops, Salzburg, April 1984.

BALANDIER, G., *Political Anthropology*, London: Allen Lane, 1970.

BARING, Arnulf, *Machtwechsel: Die Ära Brandt-Scheel*, Stuttgart: Deutsche Verlags-Anstalt, 1982.

BARKER, B., *When the Queen was Crowned*, London: Routledge & Kegan Paul, 1976.

BARNETT, A. Doak, *China After Mao*, Princeton, NJ: Princeton University Press, 1967.

——— 'Round one in China's succession: the shift toward pragmatism', *Current Scene*, 15 (1977), pp. 1–10.

BARROW, Simon, 'Europe, Latin America and the arms trade', in Jenny Pearce (ed.), *The European Challenges: Europe's new role in Latin America*, London: Latin American Bureau, 1982.

BECK, Carl, JARZABEK, William A., and ERNANDEZ, Paul A., 'Political succession in Eastern Europe', *Studies in Comparative Communism*, 9 (Spring/Summer 1976) pp. 35–61.

BELOFF, Nora, *The General Says No: Britain's exclusion from Europe*, Harmondsworth: Penguin, 1963.

BILMANIS, Alfred, *A History of Latvia*, Princeton, NJ: Princeton University Press, 1951.

BLACK, Duncan, *The Theory of Committees and Elections*, Cambridge: Cambridge University Press, 1963.

BLAKEMORE, H. (ed.), *Latin America: Essays in continuity and change*, London: British Broadcasting Corporation, 1974.

BLANC, A. C., 'Some evidence for the ideologies of early man', in S. L. Washburn (ed.), *Social Life of Early Man*, London: Methuen, 1962.

BOGDANOR, Vernon, and BUTLER, David (eds), *Democracy and Elections: Electoral systems and their political consequences*, Cambridge: Cambridge University Press, 1983.

Bol'shaya Sovetskaya Entsiklopediya.

BOTHOREL, Jean, *Historic du septennat giscardien I: Le Pharaon, 19 mai 1974–22 mars 1978*, Paris: Bernard Grasset, 1983.

BRAND, J. A., 'The Midwest State Movement in Nigeria', *Political Studies* 13 (1965) pp. 346–65.

BRANDT, Willy, *A Peace Policy for Europe*, trans. Joel Carmichael, London: Weidenfeld & Nicolson, 1969.

BROGAN, D. W., *The Development of Modern France 1870–1939*, London: Hamish Hamilton, 1940.

BROGAN, D. W. and VERNEY, Douglas V., *Political Patterns in Today's World*, London: Hamish Hamilton, 1963.

BROWN, Archie, 'The Soviet succession from Andropov to Chernenko', *The World Today*, 40 (1984), pp. 134–41

——— and Kaser, Michael (eds), *The Soviet Union since the Fall of Krushchev*, London: Macmillan, 2nd edn, 1982.

BURKETT, Tony, *Parties and Elections in West Germany: The search for stability*, London: C. Hurst, 1975.

BURLING, R., *The Passage of Power: Studies in political succession*, New York: Academic Press, 1974.

BURTON, F. and CARLEN, P., *Official Discourse: on discourse analysis, government publications, ideology and the state*, London: Routledge & Kegan Paul, 1979.

BYRNES, Robert F. (ed.), *After Brezhnev: Sources of Soviet conduct in the 1980s*, London: Indiana University Press 1983.

CALVERT, Peter, 'Crisis and change: politics and government', in Harold Blakemore (ed.), *Latin America: Essays in continuity and change*, London: British Broadcasting Corporation, 1974, p.91.

—— 'Destabilization as applied political succession', paper presented to Workshop on Political Succession, ECPR joint sessions of Workshops, Salzburg, April 1984.

—— *Politics, Power and Revolution: An introduction to comparative politics* Brighton: Wheatsheaf, 1983.

CAMPBELL, Peter, *French Electoral Systems and Elections since 1789*, Hamden, Conn.: Archon, 1965.

CARDOSO, Fernando Henrique and FALETTO, Enzo, *Dependency and Development in Latin America*, Berkeley, Calif.: University of California Press, 1979.

CARR, Jonathan, *Helmut Schmidt, Helmsman of Germany*, London: Weidenfeld & Nicolson, 1985.

CARTER, James Earl Jr (Jimmy), *Keeping Faith: Memoirs of a President*, New York: Bantam Books, 1982.

CHALMERS, Douglas A., *The Social Democratic Party of Germany: from working-class movement to modern political party*, New Haven, Conn.: Yale University Press, 1964.

CHAMBERLAIN, J. R., An investigation into the relative manipulability of four voting systems', *Behavioral Science*, 30 (1985) pp. 195–203.

CHANG Chen-pang, 'The succession problem in Communist China', *Issues and Studies*, 9 (1983) p. 10ff.

CLAESSEN, H. J. M., 'Early state in Tahiti', in H.J.M. Claessen and P. Skalnik, *The Early State*, Paris: Mouton, 1978, pp. 441–67.

—— The early state: a structural approach', in H.J.M. Claessen and P. Skalnik, *The Early State*, Paris: Mouton, 1978, pp. 533–96.

—— and SKALNIK, P., 'Limits: beginnings and end of the early state', in H.J.M. Claesson and P. Skalnik, *The Early State*, Paris: Mouton, 1978, pp. 619–35.

—— and SKALNIK, P., *The Early State*, Paris: Mouton, 1978.

CLARKE, P. B., *West Africa and Islam*, London: Edward Arnold, 1982.

COAKLEY, John, 'Political succession on the peripheries of Europe, 1918–1939: Nation-building and political change in Ireland, Finland, Czechoslovakia and the Baltic states', paper presented to Workshop on Political Succession, ECPR joint sessions of Workshops, Salzburg, April 1984.

—— 'Prime-ministerial succession; the Irish experience', paper presented to Planning Session on Political Succession, ECPR Joint Sessions of Workshops, Freiburg, March 1983; revised version published as 'Selecting a prime minister – the Irish experience' in *Parliamentary Affairs*, 37 (1984) pp. 403–17.

COHEN, A., *Two Dimensional Man: An essay on the anthropology and symbolism in complex society*, London: Routledge & Kegan Paul, 1974.

COHEN, R., *Labour and Politics in Nigeria*, London: Heinemann, 1974.

―――― 'State origins: a reappraisal', in H. J. M. Claessen and P.Skalnik, *The Early State*, Paris: Mouton, 1978, pp. 31–75.

―――― and MIDDLETON, J. (eds), *From Tribe to Nation in Africa: Studies in incorporation processes*, Scranton, Penn.: Chandler, 1970

COLEMAN, James S., *Nigeria: Background to nationalism*, Berkeley, Calif.: University of California Press, 1958.

CRANKSHAW, Edward, *Russia Without Stalin: The emerging pattern*, London: Michael Joseph, 1956.

CRONIN, Thomas E., 'An imperiled presidency?', in Vincent Davis (ed.), *The Post-Imperial Presidency*, New York: Praeger, 1980, pp. 137–51.

CROWDER, M., *West Africa under Colonial Rule*, London: Hutchinson University Library for Africa, 1968.

CUNLIFFE, Marcus, *American Presidents and the Presidency*, London: Fontana/Collins, 1972.

DAHL, Robert A., *Polyarchy: Participation and opposition*, New Haven, Conn.: Yale University Press, 1971.

DAHRENDORF, Ralf and VOGT, Martin (eds), *Theodor Heuss, Politiker und Publizist*, Tübingen: Rainer Wunderlich, 1984.

DALLAS, Roland H., 'The President versus the Generals in Argentina', *The World Today*, 40 (1984) p. 48.

D'ANTONIO, Frederick V. and PIKE, Frederick B. (eds), *Religion, Revolution and Reform: New forces for change in Latin America*, Tenbury Wells, Worcs.: Fowler Wright, 1964.

DAVIS, Vincent (ed.), *The Post-Imperial Presidency*, New York: Praeger, 1980.

DENNIS, C., 'Capitalist development and women's work: a Nigerian case study', *Review of African Political Economy*, 27/28 (1984) pp. 110–11.

DENT, M., 'Mystery of the missing bandwagon', *West Africa*, 10 September 1979, p. 1633.

DERRIDA, *Marges de la Philosophie*, Paris: Minuit, 1972.

DESCOMBES, V., *Modern French Philosophy*, English edn, Cambridge: Cambridge University Press, 1979.

DEUTSCHER, Luke, *Stalin: a political biography*, Harmondsworth: Penguin Books, 1966.

DEWACHTER, Wilfried, 'The circulation of the elite under Macro-social crises. Analysis of the Belgian case since 1919, paper presented to Planning Session on Political Succession, ECPR Joint Sessions of Workshops, Freiburg, March 1983.

DIKE, K. O., *Trade and Politics in the Niger Delta*, Oxford: Oxford University Press, 1956.

Di PALMA, Giuseppe, *Surviving Without Governing: the Italian parties in parliament*, Berkeley, Calif.: University of California Press, 1977.

DITTMER, Lowell, 'Bases in power in Chinese politics: a theory and and analysis of the fall of the "Gang of Four" ', *World Politics*, 31 (1978–9) pp. 26–60.

———, 'Power and personality in China: Mao Tse-tung, Liu Shao-ch'i, and the politics of charismatic succession', *Studies in Comparative Communism*, 7 (1974) pp. 21–49.

DODD, C. H., *Politics and Government in Turkey*, Manchester: Manchester University Press, and Berkeley, Calif.: University of California Press, 1969.

DOGAN, Matteri, 'Le sélection des ministres en Italie: Dix règles non-écrits', *International Political Science Review*, 2 (1981) pp. 189–209.

DOMES, Jürgen, *China nach der Kulturrevolution: Politik zwischen zwei Parteitagen*, München: Fenk, 1975.

———, *Government and Politics in the People's Republic of China: A time of transition*, Boulder, Colo.: Westview, 1985.

———, *Politische Soziologie der VR China*, Wiesbaden: Akademische Verlagsgesellschaft, 1980.

DORNBERG, John, *Brezhnev: the masks of power*, London: André Deutsch, 1974.

DRAGNICH, Alex M. and RASMUSSEN, Jorgen, *Major European Governments*, Homewood, Ill.: Dorsey, 6th edn, 1982.

DREW, Elizabeth, *Portrait of an Election: the 1980 presidential campaign*, London: Routledge & Kegan Paul, 1981.

DUDLEY, B. J., *Instability and Political Order: Politics and crisis in Nigeria*, Ibadan: Ibadan University Press, 1973.

———, *An Introduction to Nigerian Government and Politics*, London: Macmillan Nigeria, 1982.

DUNCAN, J. D., *Communication and Social Order*, Oxford: Clarendon Press, 1962.

EADES, J. S., *The Yoruba Today*, Cambridge: Cambridge University Press, 1980.

EDELMANN, Alexander T., *Latin American Government and Politics: The dynamics of a revolutionary society*, Homewood, Ill.: Dorsey, 1965.

EHRMANN, Henry W., *Politics in France*, Boston, Mass.: Little, Brown, 2nd edn, 1971.

EISENSTADT, S. N. and RONIGER, L., *Patrons, Clients and Friends: Interpersonal relations and the structure of trust in society*, Cambridge: Cambridge University Press, 1984.

EVANS-PRITCHARD, E. E., *Witchcraft, Oracles and Magic among the Azande*, Oxford: Clarendon Press, 1937.

EZERA, K., *Constitutional developments in Nigeria*, Cambridge: Cambridge University Press, 2nd edn, 1964.

EZERGAILIS, Andrew, *The 1917 Revolution in Latvia*, Boulder, Colo.: East European Quarterly, 1974.

FAGEN, Richard R. and CORNELIUS, Wayne A. (eds.), *Political Power in Latin America: seven confrontations*, Englewood Cliffs, NJ: Prentice-Hall, 1970.

FALCOFF, Mark, and DOLKART, Ronald H. (eds), *Prologue to Perón: Argentina in depression and war 1930–1943*, Berkeley Calif.: University of California Press, 1975.

FARNETI, Paolo, *The Italian Party System (1945–1980)*, ed. S. E. Finer and Alfio Mastropaolo, forward Hans Daalder, London: Frances Pinter, 1985.

FARQUHARSON, R., *Theory of Voting*, New Haven, Conn.: Yale University Press, 1969.

FELSENTHAL, D. S. and MAOZ, Z., 'Monotonicity and consistency reconsidered', Department of Political Science, University of Haifa, mimeo, 1985.

———, MAOZ, Z. and RAPOPORT, A., 'The Condorcet efficiency of sophisticated plurality and approval voting', paper prepared for delivery at the 1985 Annual Meeting of APSA.

FEREJOHN, J. A., and GRETHER, D. M., 'On a class of rational social decision procedures', *Journal of Economic Theory*, 8 (1974) pp. 471–82.

FIELD, Arthur J. (ed.), *City and Country in the Third World: Issues in the modernization of Latin America*, Cambridge, Mass.: Schenckman, 1970.

FINER, S. E. (ed.), *Five Constitutions*, Brighton: Harvester, 1979.

———, *The Man on Horseback*, Harmondsworth: Penguin, 1975.

———, 'Military and Society in Latin America', in Paul Halmos (ed.), *Latin American Sociological Studies*, Keele, Staffordshire: University of Keele, 1967, p. 144.

FORTES, M. and EVANS-PRITCHARD, E. E., Introduction', in M. Fortes and E. E. Evans-Pritchard (eds), *African Political Systems*, Oxford: Clarendon Press, 1940.

FRANCE, Anatole, *Penguin Island*, trans. A. W. Evans, London: John Lane, The Bodley Head, 1927.

FRANK, Peter, 'USSR. The Andropov succession', paper presented to Planning Session on Political Succession, ECPR Joint Sessions of Workshops, Freiburg, March 1983.

FREARS, J. R., *Political Parties and Elections in the French Fifth Republic*, London: C. Hurst, 1977.

FREY, F., *The Turkish Political Elite*, Cambridge, Mass.: MIT Press, 1965.

GAILEY, H. A., *The Road to Aba: A study of British administrative policy in Eastern Nigeria*, London: University of London Press, 1971.

GARDNER, J., *Chinese Politics and the Succession to Mao*, London: Macmillan, 1982.

GARSIDE, R., *Coming Alive! China after Mao*, London: André Deutsch, 1981.

GERASSI, John, *The Great Fear in Latin America*, New York: Collier, 1963.

GLADDISH, Ken, 'Political change in Portugal in the twentieth century; succession in a transitional society', paper presented to Planning Session on Political Succession, ECPR Joint Sessions of Workshops, Freiburg, March 1983.

GLUCKMAN, M. (ed.). *Essays on the Ritual of Social Relations*, Manchester: Manchester University Press, 1962

———, 'Les Rites de Passage', in M. Gluckman (ed.), *Essays on the Ritual of Social Relations*, Manchester: Manchester University Press, 1962.

———, *Order and rebellion in Tribal Africa*, London: Cohen & West, 1963.

GOLDWERT, Marvin, *Democracy, Militarism and Nationalism in Argentina 1930–1966: An interpretation*, Austin, Texas: University of Texas Press, 1972.

GONZÁLEZ CASANOVA, Pablo, *Democracia en México*, Mexico: Ediciones Era, 2nd edn, 1967.

GOODMAN, David S. G., 'China: the politics of succession', *The World Today*, April 1977, p. 134.

GOODY, J., 'Introduction', in J. Goody (ed.), *Succession to High Office*, Cambridge: Cambridge University Press, 1966.

GORBACHEV, Mikhail S., *A Time for Peace*, New York, Richardson & Steirman, 1985.

GOULBOURNE, H. (ed.), *Politics and the State in the Third World*, London: Macmillan, 1979.

GRAHAM, Malbone W., *New Governments of Eastern Europe*, New York: Henry Holt, 1927.

GREENBERG, B. S. and PARKER, E. B., (eds), *The Kennedy Assassination and the American Public*, Stanford, Calif.: Stanford University Press, 1965.

GREENSTEIN, Fred L. and POLSBY, Nelson W. (eds), *Handbook of Political Science*, III: *Macropolitics*, New York: Addison-Wesley, 1975.

GRINDLE, Merrilee S., *Bureaucrats, Politicians and Peasants in Mexico*, Berkeley, Calif.: University of California Press, 1977.

GROFMAN, B. and UHLANER, C., 'Metapreferences and the reasons for stability in social choice', *Theory and Decision*, 19 (1985) pp. 31–50.

HAIG, Alexander M. Jr, *Caveat: Realism, Reagan and foreign policy*, London: Weidenfeld & Nicolson, 1984.

HAINES, Joe, *The Politics of Power*, London: Jonathan Cape, 1977.

HALMOS, Paul (ed.) *Latin American Sociological Studies*, Keele, Staffordshire: University of Keele, 1967

HAMILL, Hugh M. (ed.), *Dictatorship in Spanish America*, New York: Alfred A. Knopf, 1965.

HARDING, Harry, 'Competing models of the Chinese Communist policy process: towards a sorting and evaluation', *Issues and Studies*, 20 (1984) pp. 13–36.

HARRISON, James P., *The Long March to Power: A history of the Chinese Communist Party, 1921–1972*, London: Macmillan, 1972.

HAYWARD, Jack, *The One and Indivisible French Republic*, New York: Norton, 1973.

HEIDENHEIMER, Arnold J., *Adenauer and the CDU: The rise of the leader and the integration of the party*, The Hague: Martinus Nijhoff, 1960.

HEPER, Metin, 'Recent trends in Turkish politics: end of a monocentrist polity?', *International Journal of Turkish Studies*, 1 (1979–80) pp. 102–13.

HESS, Stephen, *Organizing the Presidency*, Washington, DC: The Brookings Institution, 1976.

HINE, David 'The Italian Socialist Party under Craxi: surviving but not reviving', in Peter Lange and Sidney Tarrow (eds.), *Italy in Transition: Conflict and consensus*, Frank Cass, 1980, pp. 133–48.

———, 'Social democracy in Italy', in W. E. Paterson and A. H. Thomas (eds). *Social Democratic Parties in Western Europe*, London: Croom Helm, 1977, pp. 67–85.

HINTON, Harold, 'The succession problem in Communist China', *Current Scene*, 1 (1961).

HIRSHFIELD, C., *The Diplomacy of Partition: Britain, France and the creation of Nigeria 1890–1898*, The Hague: Martinus Nijhoff, 1979.

HOCART, A. M., *Kings and Councillors: An essay in the comparative anatomy of human society*, Chicago: Chicago University Press, 1970.

HOFFMANN, Stanley H., 'Succession and stability in France', in Arend Lijphart (ed.) *Politics in Europe: Comparisons and interpretations*, Englewood Cliffs, NJ: Prentice-Hall, 1969, pp. 150–64.

HONEYWELL, Martin and PEARCE, Jenny, *Falklands/Malvinas: Whose crisis?* London: Latin American Bureau, 1982.

HOROWITZ, Irving Louis, 'The election in retrospect', in Richard R. Fagen and Wayne A. Cornelius (ed), *Political Power in Latin America: Seven confrontations*, Englewood Cliffs, NJ: Prentice-Hall, 1970, p. 131.

———, 'The military elites', in Seymour Martin Lipset and Aldo Solari (eds), *Elites in Latin America*, New York: Oxford University Press, 1967, p. 151–2.

———, 'The norm of illegitimacy: toward a general theory of Latin American political development', in Arthur J. Field (ed.), *City and Country in the Third World: Issues in the modernization of Latin America*, Cambridge, Mass.: Schenckman, 1970, p. 131.

HUGHES, C., *Switzerland*, London: Ernest Benn, 1975.

HUNTINGTON, Samuel P., *Political Order in Changing Societies*, New Haven, Conn.: Yale University Press, 1968.

IMAZ, José Luís de, *Los que mandan*, Buenos Aires: Editorial Universitaria de Buenos Aires, 1964.

JACKSON, J. H., *Estonia*, London: Allen & Unwin, 2nd edn, 1948.

JAKOBS, Peter Michael, 'Kritik an Lin Piao und Konfuzius', dissertation Saarbrücken, 1978, publ. Köln: 1983.

JANOWITZ, Morris, *The Professional Soldier: A social and political portrait*, Glencoe, Ill.: The Free Press, 1960.

JANSSEN, J. J., 'The early state in Ancient Egypt', In H. J. M. Claessen and P. Skalnik, *The Early State*, Paris: Mouton, 1978.

JOFFE, Ellis, 'The Chinese Army after the Cultural Revolution: the effects of intervention', *China Quarterly*, 55 (1973) pp. 427–49.

JOHNSON, John J., *The Military and Society in Latin America*, Stanford, Calif.: Stanford University Press, 1964.

———, *Political Change in Latin America: The emergence of the middle sectors*, Stanford, Calif.: Stanford University Press, 1958.

———, (ed.), *The Role of the Military in Underdeveloped Countries*, Princeton, NJ: Princeton University Press, 1962.

JOHNSON, Samuel, *History of the Yorubas*, Lagos, 1921.

JUTIKKALA, E., *A History of Finland*, London: Thames & Hudson, 1962.

KATZ, Robert, *Days of Wrath: The public agony of Aldo Moro,* London: Granada, 1980.

KESSEL, John H., 'The structures of the Reagan White House', *American Journal of Political Science*, 28 (1984) pp. 231–58.

KIRBY, D. G., *Finland in the Twentieth Century: A history and an interpretation*, London: C. Hurst, 1979.

KIRK-GREEN, A. and RIMMER, D., *Nigeria since 1970*, London: Hodder & Stoughton, 1981.

KORBONSKI, Andrzej, 'Leadership succession and political change in Eastern Europe', *Studies in Comparative Communism*, 9 (Spring/Summer 1976) pp. 18–19.

KRAMER, G. H., 'On a class of equilibrium conditions for majority rule', *Econometrica*, 41 (1973) pp. 285–97.

KURTZ, D. V., 'The legitimation of the Aztec state', in H. J. M. Claessen and P. Skalnik, *The Early State*, Paris: Mouton, 1978, p. 184.

LAMBERT, Jacques, *Latin America: Social structure and political institutions*, Berkeley, Calif.: University of California Press, 1967.

LANGE, Peter, 'Crisis and consent, change and compromise: dilemmas of Italian communism in the 1970s', in Peter Lange and Sidney Tarrow (eds), *Italy in Transition: Conflict and consensus,* London: Frank Cass, 1980, pp. 110–32.

LANGE, Peter and TARROW, Sidney (eds), *Italy in Transition: Conflict and Consensus*, London: Frank Cass, 1980.

LEES, John D., *The Political System of the United States*, London: Faber, 1969.

LENSKI, G., *Human Societies: A macrolevel introduction to sociology*, New York: McGraw-Hill, 1970.

LEYS, Colin (ed.), *Politics and Change in Developing Countries*, Cambridge: Cambridge University Press, 1969.

LEZINA, Z. M., 'Manipulation of option choice (agenda theory)', *Avtomatika i Telemekhanika* (1985) pp. 5–22 (in Russian).

LI, Tien-min, *Liu Shao-ch'i: Mao's first heir-apparent*, Taipei: 1975.

LIEBERTHAL, Kenneth, *Research Guide to Central Party and Government Meetings in China, 1949–1975*, White Plains, NY: 1976.

LIEUWEN, Edwin, *Arms and Politics in Latin America*, New York: Praeger, 1961.

LIJPHART, Arend (ed.), *Politics in Europe: Comparisons and interpretations*, Englewood Cliffs, NJ: Prentice-Hall, 1969.

———, *The Politics of Accommodation: Pluralism and democracy in the Netherlands*, Berkeley, Calif.: University of California Press, 2nd edn, revised, 1975.

LINZ, Juan J. and STEPAN, Alfred, *The Breakdown of Democratic Regimes: Latin America*, Baltimore, Md: Johns Hopkins University Press, 1978.

LIPSET, Seymour Martin, and SOLARI, Aldo (eds.), *Elites in Latin America*, New York: Oxford University Press, 1967.

LIU, Alan P. L., 'The "Gang of Four" and the Chinese People's Liberation Army', *Asian Survey*, 19 (1979) pp. 817–37.

LLOYD, (James) Selwyn (Brooke) (Lord Selwyn-Lloyd), *Suez 1956: A personal account*, London: Hodder & Stoughton/Coronet, 1980.

LOVEMAN, Brian and DAVIES, Thomas M., 'Modernization, instability and military leadership, 1919–45', in Brian Loveman and Thomas M. Davies (eds), *The Politics of Antipolitics: The military in Latin America*, Lincoln, Neb.: University of Nebraska Press, 1978, p. 97.

——— and DAVIES, Thomas M. (eds), *The Politics of Antipolitics: The military in Latin America*, Lincoln, Neb.: University of Nebraska Press, 1978.

LYONS, F. S. L., *Ireland since the Famine*, London: Collins/Fontana, rev. edn, 1973.

LYONS, Martyn, *France under the Directory*, Cambridge: Cambridge University Press, 1975.

MACARTNEY, C. A. *The Habsburg Empire, 1790–1918*, London: Weidenfeld & Nicolson, 1969.

McCAULEY, Martin (ed.), *The Soviet Union after Brezhnev*, London: Heinemann, 1983.

MacEOIN, G., *Chile, the Struggle for Dignity*, London: Coventure, 1975.

MACHIN, Howard (ed), *National Communism in Western Europe: A third way for socialism?*, London: Methuen, 1973.

MACKINTOSH, John P., *Nigerian Government and Politics*, London: Allen & Unwin, 1966.

MACK SMITH, Denis, *Mussolini*, London: Weidenfeld & Nicolson, 1982.

McKELVEY, R. D., 'General conditions for global intransitivities in formal voting models', *Econometrica*, 47 (1979) pp. 1085–111.

———, 'Intransitivities in multidimensional voting models and some implications for agenda control', *Journal of Economic Theory*, 12 (1976) pp. 472–82.

MacRAE, Duncan, *Parliament, Parties, and Society in France 1946–1958*, New York: St Martin's Press, 1967.

MAIER, Joseph and WEATHERHEAD, Richard W. (eds), *Politics of Change in Latin America*, New York: Praeger, 1964.

MAJID, A., *Men in the Middle – Leadership and Role Conflict in a Nigerian Society*, Manchester: Manchester University Press, 1976.

MAKIN, Guillermo A., 'The Military in Argentinian Politics, 1880–1982', in *Millennium: Journal of International Studies*, 12, No. 1, Spring, 1983, p. 51. p. 51.

MAMATEY, Victor S. and LUZA, Radomir (eds), *A History of the Czechoslovak Republic 1918–1948*, Princeton, NJ: Princeton University Press, 1973.

MAO Zedong, 'On the correct handling of contradictions among the people', Peking: Foreign Lanugages Press, 1957.

MAY, K. O., 'A set of independent necessary and sufficient conditions for simple majority decisions', *Econometrica*, 20 (1952) pp. 680–4.

MEISEL, James H., *The Fall of Republic: Military revolt in France*, Ann Arbor, Mich.: University of Michigan Press, 1962.

MERRILL, S., III, 'A comparison of efficiency of multicandidate electoral systems', *American Journal of Political Science*, 28 (1984) pp. 23–48.

———, 'A statistical model for Condorcet efficiency based on simulation under spatial model assumption', *Public Choice*, 47 (1985) pp. 389–403.

———, 'Strategic decisions under one-stage multi-candidate voting systems', *Public Choice*, 26 (1981) pp. 115–34.

MILBANK, Susan, 'An Argentinian security perspective', in Caroline Thomas (ed.), *Third World Perceptions of Security*, Cambridge: Cambridge University Press, forthcoming.

MILLS, William de B., 'Generational change in China', *Problems of Communism*, November/December 1983, pp. 16–35.

MILNOR, A. J., *Elections and Political Stability*, Boston, Mass.: Little, Brown, 1969.

MORSE, Richard W., 'Towards a theory of Spanish American government', in Hugh M. Hamill (ed.), *Dictatorship in Spanish America*, New York: Alfred A. Knopf, 1965, pp. 52–68.

NAKAMURA, K., 'The vetoers in a simple game with ordinal preferences', *International Journal of Game Theory*, 8 (1978) pp. 55–61.

NEILSON, James, 'The approaching pact', *Buenos Aires Herald*, 12 May 1983.

———, 'The corporation', *Buenos Aires Herald*, 5 May 1983.

——, 'How long will precarious truce last?', *Buenos Aires Herald*, 23 February 1986.

NEUSTADT, Richard E., *Presidential Power*, New York: New American Library, 1964.

NEWTON, Gerald, *The Netherlands: An historical and cultural survey 1795–1977*, London: Ernest Benn, 1978.

NIEMI, R. G., 'Why so much stability?', *Public Choice*, 41 (1983) pp. 261–70.

—— and FRANK, Z. Q., 'Sophisticated voting under the plurality procedure', in P. C. Ordeshook and K. A. Shepsle (eds), *Political Equilibrium*, Boston, Mass.: Kluwer-Nijhoff, 1982.

NUNN, Frederick M., 'An overview of the European military missions in Latin America', in Brian Loveman and Thomas M. Davies (eds), *The Politics of Antipolitics: The military in Latin America*, Lincoln, Neb.: University of Nebraska Press, 1978, p. 44.

NURMI, Hannu, *Comparing voting systems*, (Dordrecht: D. Reidel, forthcoming).

——, 'Majority rule: second thoughts and refutations', *Quality and Quantity*, 14 (1980) pp. 743–65.

——, 'Mathematical models of elections and their relevance for institutional design', *Electoral Studies*, 5 (1986) pp. 167–81.

——, 'On Riker's theory of political succession', *Scandinavian Political Studies*, 6 (1983) pp. 177–94.

——, 'On the strategic properties of some modern methods of group decision making', *Behavioral Science*, 29 (1984) pp. 248–257.

——, 'Voting procedures: a summary analysis', *British Journal of Political Science*, 13 (1983) pp. 181–206.

O'CONNELL, J., 'The political class and economic growth', *Nigerian Journal of Economics and Social Studies*, 8, 1 (1966) pp. 129–40.

O'DONNELL, Guillermo, 'Permanent crisis and the failure to create a democratic regime: Argentina, 1955–66', in Juan J. Linz and Alfred Stepan (eds), *The Breakdown of Democratic Regimes: Latin America*, Baltimore, Md: Johns Hopkins University Press, 1978, p. 158.

ORDESHOOK, P. C. and SHEPSLE, K. A. (eds), *Political Equilibrium*, Boston, Mass.: Kluwer-Nijhoff, 1982.

OYEDIRAN, O., *The Nigerian 1979 Elections*, London: Macmillan Nigeria, 1981.

——, (ed.), *Nigerian Government and Politics under Military Rule – 1960–65*, London: Macmillan, 1979.

OYINBO, J., *Nigeria, Crisis and Beyond*, London: Charles Knight, 1971.

PADEN, J. N., *Religion and Culture in Kano*, Berkeley, Calif: University of California Press, 1973.

——, 'Urban pluralism, integration and adaptation of communal identity in Kano, Nigeria', in R. Cohen and J. Middleton (eds), *From Tribe to Nation in Africa: Studies in incorporation processes*, Scranton, Penn.: Chandler, 1970.

PAGE, Stanley W., *The Formation of the Baltic States: A study of the effects of great power politics upon the emergence of Lithuania, Latvia and Estonia*, Cambridge, Mass.: Harvard University Press, 1959.

PALMER, R. R., *Twelve Who Ruled: The Year of Terror in the French Revolution*, Princeton, NJ: Princeton University Press, 1941.

PANTER-BRICK, J. K. (ed.), *Nigerian Politics and Military Rule: Prelude to the Civil War*, London: Athlone Press, 1970.

PASQUINO, Gianfranco, 'Italian Christian Democracy: a party for all seasons?', in Peter Lange and Sidney Tarrow (eds), *Italy in Transition: Conflict and consensus*, London: Frank Cass, 1980, pp. 88–109.

PATERSON, W. E and THOMAS, A. H. (eds.), *Social Democratic Parties in Western Europe*, London: Croom Helm, 1977.

PEACE, A., *Choice, Class and Conflict: A study of Southern Nigerian factory workers*, Brighton: Harvester, 1979.

PEARCE, Jenny (ed.) *The European Challenge: Europe's new role in Latin America*, London: Latin America Bureau, 1982.

PETHYBRIDGE, R. W., *A History of Postwar Russia*, London: Allen & Unwin, 1966.

PHILIPS, A., 'The concept of development', *Review of African Political Economy*, 8 (1977).

PIERSON, William W. and GIL, Federico G., *Governments of Latin America*, New York: McGraw-Hill, 1957.

PLOTT, C. R., 'A notion of equilibrium and its possibility under majority rule', *American Economic Review*, 57 (1967) pp. 787–806.

POST, K. W. J., *The Nigerian Federal Election of 1959*, Oxford: Oxford University Press, 1963.

——, and JENKINS, G. D., *The Price of Liberty: Personality and politics in colonial Nigeria*, Cambridge: Cambridge University Press, 1973.

——, and VICKERS, M., *Structure and Conflict in Nigeria 1960–65*, London: Heinemann, 1973.

POTASH, Robert A., *The Army and Politics in Argentina 1928–1945: Yrigoyen to Perón*, Stanford, Calif.: Stanford University Press, 1969.

——, *The army and Politics in Argentina 1945–62: Perón to Frondizi*, London: The Athlone Press, 1980.

——, 'The military and Argentine politics', in Brian Loveman and Thomas M. Davies (eds), *The Politics of Antipolitics: The military in Latin America*, Lincoln, Neb.: University of Nebraska Press, 1978, p. 103.

POWELL, John Duncan, 'Military assistance and militarism in Latin America', *Western Political Quarterly*, 28 (1965) p. 388.

PRIDHAM, Geoffrey, *Christian Democracy in Western Germany: The CDU/CSU in government and opposition, 1945–1976*, London: Croom Helm, 1977.

PRITTIE, Terrence, *Konrad Adenauer, 1876–1967*, London: Tom Stacey, 1972.

PYE, Lucian W., 'Generational politics in a gerontocracy: the Chinese succession problem', Current Scene, 14 (1976), pp. 1–9.

RADKEY, O. H., *The Election to the Russian Constituent Assembly of 1917*, Cambridge, Mass.: Harvard University Press, 1950.

RAUCH, Georg von, *The Baltic States: The years of independence: Estonia, Latvia, Lithuania 1917–1940*, London: C. Hurst, 1970.

RICHELSON, J. T., 'A comparative analysis of social choice functions I, II, III: a summary', *Behavioral Science*, 24 (1979) p. 355.

RIENCOURT, Amaury de, *The Coming Caesars*, New York: Coward-McCann, 1957.

RIGBY, T. H. (ed.), *The Stalin Dictatorship: Khrushchev's 'Secret Speech' and other documents*, Sydney: Sydney University Press, 1968.

RIKER, W. H., *Liberalism against Populism: A confrontation between the theory of democracy and the theory of social choice*, San Francisco, Calif.: W. H. Freeman, 1982.

ROBERTS, J. M., *The Hutchinson History of the World*, London: Hutchinson, 1976.

ROBINSON, Thomas W., 'Political succession in China', *World Politics*, 27 (1976) p. 1–38.

ROCK, David, *Politics in Argentina 1890–1930: The rise and fall of Radicalism*, London: Cambridge Unversity Press, 1975.

ROSSITER, Clinton, *The American Presidency*, New York: Time, 1960.

ROWE, James W., 'Whither the Peronists?' in Robert D. Tomasek (ed.), *Latin American Politics: 24 studies of the contemporary scene*, Garden City, NY: Doubleday, 1966.

RUSH, Myron, *How Communist States Change their Rulers*, Ithaca, NY: Cornell University Press, 1974.

———, *Political Succession in the USSR*, New York: Columbia University Press, 2nd edn, 1968.

SADYKIEWICZ, M., 'Soviet military politics', *Survey*, 26 (1982).

SALINGER, Pierre, *With Kennedy*, Garden City, NY: Doubleday, 1966.

SARTORI, Giovanni, *Parties and Party Systems: A framework for analysis*, Cambridge: Cambridge University Press, 1976.

SCHMIDT, Helmut, *The Balance of Power: Germany's peace policy and the super powers*, trans. Edward Thomas, London: William Kimber, 1971.

SCHOFIELD, N., 'Classification of voting games on manifolds', *Social Science Working Paper* 488, California Institute of Technology, 1983.

———, 'Instability of simple dynamic games', *Review of Economic Studies*, 45 (1978) pp. 575–94.

SCOTT, Robert E., 'National integration problems and military regimes in Latin America', in Robert E. Scott (ed.), *Latin American Modernization Problems*, Chicago, Ill.: University of Illinois Press, 1973, pp. 328–9.

SEALE, Patrick and McCONVILLE, Maureen, *French Revolution 1968*, London: Heinemann with Penguin, 1968.

SEIDMAN, R. B., *The State, Law and Development*, London: Croom Helm, 1978.

SENN, Alfred Erich, *The Emergence of Modern Lithuania*, New York: Columbia University Press, 1959.

SETON-WATSON, Hugh, *Nations and States: An inquiry into the origins of nations and the rise of nationalism*, London: Methuen, 1977.

SHEATSLEY, P. B. and FELDMAN, J. J., 'A national survey of public reactions and behavior', in B. S. Greenberg and E. B. Parker (eds), *The Kennedy Assassination and the American Public*, Stanford, Calif.: Stanford University Press, 1965, p. 169.

SHILS, E. and YOUNG, M., 'The meaning of the Coronation', *Sociological Review*, 1 (1953) pp. 63–81.

SHIRER, William L., *The Collapse of the Third Republic: An inquiry into the fall of France in 1940*, London: Heinemann and Secker & Warburg, 1970.
———, *The Rise and Fall of the Third Reich: A history of Nazi Germany*, London: Pan, 1968.
SIEGFRIED, André, *De la IIIe à la IVe République*, Paris: Bernard Grasset, 1956.
SILVERT, Kalman H., *The Conflict Society: Reaction and revolution in Latin America*, New York: American Universities Field Staff, 1966.
SKALNIK, P., 'The early state as a process', in H. J. M. Claessen and P. Skalnik, *The Early State*, Paris: Mouton, 1978, pp. 597–618.
———, 'Early states in the Voltaic Basin', in H. J. M. Claessen and P. Skalnik, *The Early State*, Paris: Mouton, 1978, p. 485.
SKINNER, E. P., *The Mossi of the Upper Volta: The political development of a Sudanese people*, Stanford, Calif.: Stanford University Press, 1964.
SMITH, A. D., *State and Nation in the Third World: The Western state and African nationalism*, Brighton: Harvester, 1983.
SMITH, Gordon, *Politics in Western Europe: A comparative analysis*, London: Heinemann, 1972.
SMITH, Peter H., *Argentina and the Failure of Democracy: Conflict among political elites, 1904–1955*, Madison, Wis.: University of Wisconsin Press, 1974.
SMITH, Peter H., 'The breakdown of democracy in Argentina, 1961–30', in Juan J. Linz and Alfred Stepan (eds), *The Breakdown of Democratic Regimes: Latin America*, Baltimore, Md: Johns Hopkins University Press, 1978, p. 8.
SMOCK, A. C., *Ibo Politics: The role of ethnic unions in Eastern Nigeria*, Cambridge, Mass., Harvard University Press, 1971.
SONEGO, Victor M., *Las dos Argentinas: Pistas para una lectura crítica de nuestra historia*, Buenos Aires: Ediciones Don Bosco, 1983.
STANILAND, M., *The Lions of Dagbon*, Cambridge: Cambridge University Press, 1975.
STEINBERG, Alfred, *Sam Johnson's Boy: A close-up of the President from Texas*, New York: Macmillan; London: Collier-Macmillan, 1968.
STINCHCOMBE, A. L., 'Social structure and politics', in Fred L. Greenstein and Nelson W. Polsby (eds), *Handbook of Political Science, III: Macropolitics*, New York: Addison-Wesley, 1975.
STOKES, William S., 'Violence as a power factor in Latin American politics', in Robert D. Tomasek (ed.), *Latin American Politics: 24 studies of the contemporary scene*, Garden City, NY: Doubleday, 1966, p. 251.
STUCKI, Walter, *La Fin du Régime de Vichy*, Neuchatel: Editions de la Baconnière, 1947.
SUTHERLAND, C., *The Princess of Siberia: The story of Maria Volkonsky and the Decembrist exiles*, London: Robin Clark, 1985.
SYDENHAM, M. J., *The First French Republic 1792–1804*, London: Batsford, 1974.
SZYLIOWICZ, Joseph S., 'Elite recruitment in Turkey: the role of the *Mülkiye*', *World Politics*, 23 (April 1971), pp. 371–95.

TARROW, Sidney, 'Historic compromise or bourgeois majority? Euro-communism in Italy, 1976–9,' in Howard Machin (ed.), *National Communism in Western Europe: A third way for socialism?* London: Methuen, 1983, pp. 124–53.

TATU, Michel, 'Andropov in power: the succession reconsidered', *Radio Liberty Research Bulletin* RL 405/83.

TAYLOR, F., 'Black week in the White House', *Sunday Telegraph*, 21 July 1985.

THEBERGE, James D. and FONTAINE, Roger W., *Latin America: Struggle for Progress*, Lexington, Mass.: Lexington Books, 1977.

THOMAS, Caroline (ed.), *Third World Perceptions of Security*, Cambridge: Cambridge University Press, forthcoming.

TEIWES, Frederick C., *Politics and Purges in China: Rectification and the decline of party norms, 1950–1965*, New York: 1979.

TILLY, Charles (ed.), *The Formation of Nation States in Western Europe*, Princeton, NJ: Princeton University Press, 1975.

TOMASEK, Robert D. (ed.), *Latin American Politics: 24 studies of the contemporary scene*, Garden City, NY: Doubleday, 1966.

USSR, Communist Party, *XXIII s"ezd KPSS* (Minutes of the XXIII Congress of the CPSU, 1966).

——, *XXIV s"ezd KPSS* (1971).

——, *XXV s"ezd KPSS* (1976).

——, Supreme Soviet, *Deputaty Verkhnovnogo Soveta SSSR*.

URWIN, D. W., *Western Europe since 1945: A short political history*, London: Longham, 3rd edn, 1981.

VAN GENNEP, A., *Rites de Passage*, Paris: Nourry, 1909.

WANG, Ting, 'The succession problem', *Problems of Communism*, May–June 1973, pp. 13–24.

WASHBURN, S. L. (ed.), *Social Life of Early Man*, London: Methuen, 1962.

WAYNE, Stephen J., *The Road to the White House: The politics of presidential elections*, London, Macmillan, 1980.

WEATHERHEAD, Richard W., 'Traditions of conflict in Latin America', in Joseph Maier and Richard W. Weatherhead (eds), *Politics of Change in Latin America*, New York: Praeger, 1964, p. 22.

WEBER, Max, *The Theory of Social and Economic Organization*, New York: The Free Press, 1964.

WEIL, Gordon L., *The Benelux Nations: The politics of small-country democracies*, New York: Holt, Rinehart & Winston, 1970.

WERTH, Alexander, *De Gaulle, a Political Biography*, Harmondsworth: Penguin, 1965.

WHITAKER, Arthur P., *Argentina*, Englewood Cliffs, NJ: Prentice-Hall, 1964.

WHITAKER, Arthur P., 'An overview of the period', in Mark Falcoff and Ronald H. Dolkart (eds), *Prologue to Perón: Argentina in depression and war 1930–1943*, Berkeley, Calif.: University of California Press, 1975, p. 2.

WHITE, Theodore H., *Breach of Faith: The fall of Richard Nixon*, New York: Dell, 1975.

WHITSON, William W., and HUANG Chen-shia, *The Chinese High Command: A history of Communist military politics, 1927–1971*, New York: Praeger,1973.

Who's Who in Communist China, vols I and II, Hong Kong: Union Research Institute, 1969 and 1970.

WILLIAMS, G., *State and Society in Nigeria*, Idanre, Ondo: Afrografika, 1980.

WILLIAMS, Philip M., *Crisis and Compromise: Politics in the Fourth Republic*, London: Longman, 1964.

——, *Wars, Plots and Scandals in Post-War France*, Cambridge: Cambridge University Press, 1970.

WILSON, E. O., *On Human Nature*, Cambridge, Mass.: Harvard University Press, 1978.

WILSON, Harold, *The Governance of Britain*, London: Weidenfeld & Nicolson and Michael Joseph, 1976.

WISKEMANN, Elizabeth, *Italy since 1945*, London: Macmillan, 1971.

WOOLF, S. J. (ed.), *The Rebirth of Italy 1943–50*, London: Longman, 1972.

WRIGHT, Gordon, *Raymond Poincaré and the French Presidency*, New York: Octagon, 1967.

——, *The Reshaping of French Democracy*, London: Methuen, 1950.

WYNIA, Gary W., *The Politics of Latin American Development*, New York: Cambridge University Press, 1978.

Newspapers Cited

Beijing Review
Far Eastern Economic Review
Guardian
Index on Censorship
International Herald Tribune
Liberation Army Daily
New African
Observer
People's Daily
Pravda
Red Flag
Sunday Telegraph
The Times
West Africa
Zhonggong Yanjiu

Index